Learning Microsoft Cognitive Services

Second Edition

Leverage Machine Learning APIs to build smart applications

Leif Larsen

BIRMINGHAM - MUMBAI

Learning Microsoft Cognitive Services

Second Edition

First published: March 2017

Second edition: October 2017

Production reference: 1181017

Published by Packt Publishing Ltd.
Livery Place
35 Livery Street
Birmingham
B3 2PB, UK.
ISBN 978-1-78862-302-5

www.packtpub.com

Credits

Author
Leif Larsen

Reviewer
Abhishek Kumar

Commissioning Editor
Richa Tripathi

Acquisition Editor
Chaitanya Nair

Content Development Editor
Rohit Kumar Singh

Technical Editor
Pavan Ramchandani

Copy Editor
Sameen Siddiqui

Project Coordinator
Vaidehi Sawant

Proofreader
Safis Editing

Indexer
Rekha Nair

Graphics
Abhinash Sahu

Production Coordinator
Aparna Bhagat

About the Author

Leif Larsen is a software engineer based in Norway. After earning a degree in computer engineering, he went on to work with the design and configuration of industrial control systems, for the most part, in the oil and gas industry. Over the last few years, he has worked as a developer, developing and maintaining geographical information systems, working with .NET technology. In his spare time, he develops mobile apps and explores new technologies to keep up with a high-paced tech world.

You can find out more about him by checking his blog (`http://blog.leiflarsen.org/`) and following him on Twitter (`@leif_larsen`) and LinkedIn (`lhlarsen`).

Writing a book requires a lot of work from a team of people. I would like to give a huge thanks to the team at Packt Publishing, who have helped make this book a reality. Specifically, I would like to thank Rohit Kumar Singh and Pavan Ramchandani, for excellent guidance and feedback for each chapter, and Denim Pinto and Chaitanya Nair, for proposing the book and guiding me through the start. I also need to direct a thanks to Abhishek Kumar for providing good technical feedback.

Also, I would like to say thanks to my friends and colleagues who have been supportive and patient when I have not been able to give them as much time as they deserve.

Thanks to my mom and my dad for always supporting me.

Thanks to my sister, Susanne, and my friend Steffen for providing me with ideas from the start, and images where needed.

I need to thank John Sonmez and his great work, without which, I probably would not have got the chance to write this book.

Last, and most importantly, I would like to thank my friend, Miriam, for supporting me through this process, for pushing me to work when I was stuck, and being there when I needed time off. I could not have done this without her.

About the Reviewer

Abhishek Kumar works as a consultant with Datacom, New Zealand, with more than 9 years of experience in the field of designing, building, and implementing Microsoft Solution. He is a coauthor of the book *Robust Cloud Integration with Azure, Packt Publishing*.

Abhishek is a Microsoft Azure MVP and has worked with multiple clients worldwide on modern integration strategies and solutions. He started his career in India with Tata Consultancy Services before taking up multiple roles as consultant at Cognizant Technology Services and Robert Bosch GmbH.

He has published several articles on modern integration strategy over the Web and Microsoft TechNet wiki. His areas of interest include technologies such as Logic Apps, API Apps, Azure Functions, Cognitive Services, PowerBI, and Microsoft BizTalk Server.

His Twitter username is @Abhishekcskumar.

I would like to thank the people close to my heart, my mom, dad, and elder bothers, Suyasham and Anket, for the their continuous support in all phases of life.

I would also like to take this opportunity to thank Datacom and my manager, Brett Atkins, to for their guidance and support throughout our write-up journey.

www.PacktPub.com

For support files and downloads related to your book, please visit www.PacktPub.com.

Did you know that Packt offers eBook versions of every book published, with PDF and ePub files available? You can upgrade to the eBook version at www.PacktPub.com and as a print book customer, you are entitled to a discount on the eBook copy. Get in touch with us at service@packtpub.com for more details.

At www.PacktPub.com, you can also read a collection of free technical articles, sign up for a range of free newsletters and receive exclusive discounts and offers on Packt books and eBooks.

https://www.packtpub.com/mapt

Get the most in-demand software skills with Mapt. Mapt gives you full access to all Packt books and video courses, as well as industry-leading tools to help you plan your personal development and advance your career.

Why subscribe?

- Fully searchable across every book published by Packt
- Copy and paste, print, and bookmark content
- On demand and accessible via a web browser

Customer Feedback

Thanks for purchasing this Packt book. At Packt, quality is at the heart of our editorial process. To help us improve, please leave us an honest review on this book's Amazon page at https://www.amazon.com/dp/1788623029.

If you'd like to join our team of regular reviewers, you can e-mail us at customerreviews@packtpub.com. We award our regular reviewers with free eBooks and videos in exchange for their valuable feedback. Help us be relentless in improving our products!

Table of Contents

Preface

Artificial intelligence and machine learning are complex topics, and adding such features to applications has historically required a lot of processing power, not to mention tremendous amounts of learning. The introduction of Microsoft Cognitive Service gives developers the possibility to add these features with ease. It allows us to make smarter and more human-like applications.

This book aims to teach you how to utilize the APIs from Microsoft Cognitive Services. You will learn what each API has to offer and how you can add it to your application. We will see what the different API calls expect in terms of input data and what you can expect in return. Most of the APIs in this book are covered with both theory and practical examples.

This book has been written to help you get started. It focuses on showing how to use Microsoft Cognitive Service, keeping current best practices in mind. It is not intended to show advanced use cases, but to give you a starting point to start playing with the APIs yourself.

What this book covers

Chapter 1, *Getting Started with Microsoft Cognitive Services*, introduces Microsoft Cognitive Services by describing what it offers and providing some basic examples.

Chapter 2, *Analyzing Images to Recognize a Face*, covers most of the image APIs, introducing face recognition and identification, image analysis, optical character recognition, and more.

Chapter 3, *Analyzing Videos*, introduces emotion analysis and a variety of video operations.

Chapter 4, *Letting Applications Understand Commands*, goes deep into setting up Language Understanding Intelligent Service (LUIS) to allow your application to understand the end users' intents.

Chapter 5, *Speaking with Your Application*, dives into different speech APIs, covering text-to-speech and speech-to-text conversions, speaker recognition and identification, and recognizing custom speaking styles and environments.

Chapter 6, *Understanding Text*, covers a different way to analyze text, utilizing powerful linguistic analysis tools, web language models and much more.

Chapter 7, *Extending Knowledge Based on Context*, introduces entity linking based on the context. In addition, it moves more into e-commerce, where it covers the Recommendation API.

Chapter 8, *Querying Structured Data in a Natural Way*, deals with the exploration of academic papers and journals. Through this chapter, we look into how to use the Academic API and set up a similar service ourselves.

Chapter 9, *Adding Specialized Search*, takes a deep dive into the different search APIs from Bing. This includes news, web, image, and video search as well as auto suggestions.

Chapter 10, *Connecting the Pieces*, ties several APIs together and concludes the book by looking at some natural steps from here.

Appendix A, *LUIS Entities and Additional Information on Linguistic Analysis*, presents a complete list of all pre-built LUIS entities, part-of-speech tags, and phrase types.

Appendix B, *License Information*, presents relevant license information for all third-party libraries used in the example code.

What you need for this book

To follow the examples in this book you will need Visual Studio 2015 Community Edition or later. You will also need a working Internet connection and a subscription to Microsoft Azure; a trial subscriptions is OK too.

To get the full experience of the examples, you should have access to a web camera and have speakers and a microphone connected to the computer; however, neither is mandatory.

Who this book is for

This book is for .NET developers with some programming experience. It is assumed that you know how to do basic programming tasks as well as how to navigate in Visual Studio. No prior knowledge of artificial intelligence or machine learning is required to follow this book.

It is beneficial, but not required, to understand how web requests work.

Conventions

In this book, you will find a number of text styles that distinguish between different kinds of information. Here are some examples of these styles and an explanation of their meaning.

Code words in text, database table names, folder names, filenames, file extensions, pathnames, dummy URLs, user input, and Twitter handles are shown as follows: "With the top emotion score selected, we go through a `switch` statement, to find the correct emotion."

A block of code is set as follows:

```
public BitmapImage ImageSource
{
    get { return _imageSource; }
    set
    {
        _imageSource = value;
        RaisePropertyChangedEvent("ImageSource");
    }
}
```

When we wish to draw your attention to a particular part of a code block, the relevant lines or items are set in bold:

```
private BitmapImage _imageSource;
public BitmapImage ImageSource
{
    set
    {
        _imageSource = value;
        RaisePropertyChangedEvent("ImageSource");
    }
}
```

New terms and **important words** are shown in bold. Words that you see on the screen, for example, in menus or dialog boxes, appear in the text like this: "In order to download new modules, we will go to **Files** | **Settings** | **Project Name** | **Project Interpreter**."

 Warnings or important notes appear like this.

Tips and tricks appear like this.

Reader feedback

Feedback from our readers is always welcome. Let us know what you think about this book-what you liked or disliked. Reader feedback is important for us as it helps us develop titles that you will really get the most out of. To send us general feedback, simply e-mail feedback@packtpub.com, and mention the book's title in the subject of your message. If there is a topic that you have expertise in and you are interested in either writing or contributing to a book, see our author guide at www.packtpub.com/authors.

Customer support

Now that you are the proud owner of a Packt book, we have a number of things to help you to get the most from your purchase.

Downloading the example code

You can download the example code files for this book from your account at http://www.packtpub.com. If you purchased this book elsewhere, you can visit http://www.packtpub.com/support and register to have the files e-mailed directly to you.

You can download the code files by following these steps:

1. Log in or register to our website using your e-mail address and password.
2. Hover the mouse pointer on the **SUPPORT** tab at the top.
3. Click on **Code Downloads & Errata**.
4. Enter the name of the book in the **Search** box.
5. Select the book for which you're looking to download the code files.
6. Choose from the drop-down menu where you purchased this book from.
7. Click on **Code Download**.

Once the file is downloaded, please make sure that you unzip or extract the folder using the latest version of:

- WinRAR / 7-Zip for Windows
- Zipeg / iZip / UnRarX for Mac
- 7-Zip / PeaZip for Linux

The code bundle for the book is also hosted on GitHub at `https://github.com/PacktPublishing/Learning-Microsoft-Cognitive-Services-Second-Edition`. We also have other code bundles from our rich catalog of books and videos available at `https://github.com/PacktPublishing/`. Check them out!

Downloading the color images of this book

We also provide you with a PDF file that has color images of the screenshots/diagrams used in this book. The color images will help you better understand the changes in the output. You can download this file from `https://www.packtpub.com/sites/default/files/downloads/LearningMicrosoftCognitiveServicesSecondEdition_ColorImages.pdf`.

Errata

Although we have taken every care to ensure the accuracy of our content, mistakes do happen. If you find a mistake in one of our books-maybe a mistake in the text or the code-we would be grateful if you could report this to us. By doing so, you can save other readers from frustration and help us improve subsequent versions of this book. If you find any errata, please report them by visiting `http://www.packtpub.com/submit-errata`, selecting your book, clicking on the **Errata Submission Form** link, and entering the details of your errata. Once your errata are verified, your submission will be accepted and the errata will be uploaded to our website or added to any list of existing errata under the Errata section of that title.

To view the previously submitted errata, go to `https://www.packtpub.com/books/content/support` and enter the name of the book in the search field. The required information will appear under the **Errata** section.

Piracy

Piracy of copyrighted material on the Internet is an ongoing problem across all media. At Packt, we take the protection of our copyright and licenses very seriously. If you come across any illegal copies of our works in any form on the Internet, please provide us with the location address or website name immediately so that we can pursue a remedy.

Please contact us at copyright@packtpub.com with a link to the suspected pirated material.

We appreciate your help in protecting our authors and our ability to bring you valuable content.

Questions

If you have a problem with any aspect of this book, you can contact us at questions@packtpub.com, and we will do our best to address the problem.

1
Getting Started with Microsoft Cognitive Services

You have just started on the road to learning about Microsoft Cognitive Services. This chapter will serve as a gentle introduction to the services. The end goal is to understand a bit more about what these cognitive APIs can do for you. By the end of this chapter, we will have created an easy-to-use project template. You will have learned how to detect faces in images and have the number of faces spoken back to you.

Throughout this chapter, we will cover the following topics:

- Learning about some applications already using Microsoft Cognitive Services
- Creating a template project
- Detecting faces in images using Face API
- Discovering what Microsoft Cognitive Services can offer
- Doing text-to-speech conversion using Bing Speech API

Cognitive Services in action for fun and life-changing purposes

The best way to introduce Microsoft Cognitive Services is to see how it can be used in action. Microsoft, and others, has created a lot of example applications to show off its capabilities. Several may be seen as silly, such as the How-Old.net (`http://how-old.net/`) image analysis and the *what if I were that person* application. These applications have generated quite some buzz, and they show off some of the APIs in a good way.

The one demonstration that is truly inspiring, though, is the one featuring a visually impaired person. Talking computers inspired him to create an application to allow blind and visually impaired people to understand what is going on around them. The application has been built upon Microsoft Cognitive Services. It gives a good idea of how the APIs can be used to change the world, for the better. Before moving on, head over to `https://www.youtube.com/watch?v=R2mC-NUAmMk` and take a peek into the world of Microsoft Cognitive Services.

Setting up boilerplate code

Before we start diving into the action, we will go through some setup. More to the point, we will set up some boilerplate code which we will utilize throughout this book.

To get started, you will need to install a version of Visual Studio, preferably Visual Studio 2015 or higher. The Community Edition will work fine for this purpose. You do not need anything more than what the default installation offers.

 You can find Visual Studio 2017 at `https://www.microsoft.com/en-us/download/details.aspx?id=48146`.

Throughout this book, we will utilize the different APIs to build a smart-house application. The application will be created to see how one can imagine a futuristic house to be. If you have seen the Iron Man movies, you can think of the application as resembling Jarvis, in some ways.

In addition, we will be doing smaller sample applications using the cognitive APIs. Doing so will allow us to cover each API, even those that did not make it to the final application.

What's common with all the applications that we will build is that they will be **Windows Presentation Foundation** (**WPF**) applications. This is fairly well known and allows us to build applications using the **Model View ViewModel** (**MVVM**) pattern. One of the advantages of taking this road is that we will be able to see the API usage quite clearly. It also separates code so that you can bring the API logic to other applications with ease.

The following steps describe the process of creating a new WPF project:

1. Open Visual Studio and select **File | New | Project**.
2. In the dialog, select the **WPF Application** option from **Templates | Visual C#**, as shown in the following screenshot:

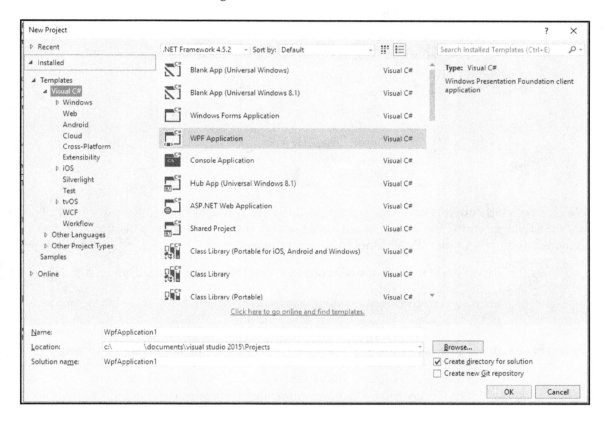

3. Delete the `MainWindow.xaml` file and create files and folders matching the following image:

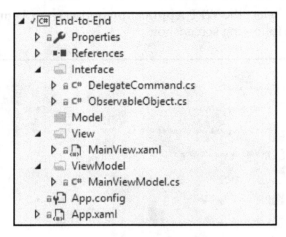

We will not go through the MVVM pattern in detail, as this is out of scope of this book. The key takeaway from the image is that we have separated the View from what becomes the logic. We then rely on the ViewModel to connect the pieces.

 If you want to learn more about MVVM, I recommend reading an article from CodeProject at
`http://www.codeproject.com/Articles/100175/Model-View-ViewModel-MVVM-Explained`.

To be able to run this, we do, however, need to cover some of the details in the project:

1. Open the `App.xaml` file and make sure `StartupUri` is set to the correct `View`, as shown in the following code (class name and namespace may vary based on the name of your application):

```
<Application x:Class="Chapter1.App"
      xmlns="http://schemas.microsoft.com/
winfx/2006/xaml/presentation"
      xmlns:x = "http://schemas.microsoft.com/winfx/2006/xaml"
      xmlns:local="clr-namespace:Chapter1"
      StartupUri="View/MainView.xaml">
```

2. Open the `MainViewModel.cs` file and make it inherit from the `ObservableObject` class.

3. Open the `MainView.xaml` file and add the `MainViewModel` file as datacontext to it, as shown in the following code (namespace and class names may vary based on the name of your application):

```
<Window x:Class="Chapter1.View.MainView"
       xmlns="http://schemas.microsoft.com/
winfx/2006/xaml/presentation"
       xmlns:x="http://schemas.microsoft.com/winfx/2006/xaml"
       xmlns:d="http://schemas.microsoft.com/
expression/blend/2008"
xmlns:mc="http://schemas.openxmlformats.org/markup-compatibility/2006"
       xmlns:local="clr-namespace:Chapter1.View"
       xmlns:viewmodel="clr-namespace:Chapter1.ViewModel"
mc:Ignorable="d"
       Title="Chapter 1" Height="300" Width="300">
       <Window.DataContext>
           <viewmodel:MainViewModel />
       </Window.DataContext>
```

Following this, we need to fill in the content of the `ObservableObject.cs` file. We start off by having it inherit from the `INotifyPropertyChanged` class as follows:

```
public class ObservableObject : INotifyPropertyChanged
```

This is a rather small class, which should contain the following:

```
public event PropertyChangedEventHandlerPropertyChanged;
protected void RaisePropertyChangedEvent(string propertyName)
{
    PropertyChanged?.Invoke(this, new
PropertyChangedEventArgs(propertyName));
}
```

We declare a property changed event and create a function to raise the event. This will allow the **User Interface** (**UI**) to update its values when a given property has changed.

We also need to be able to execute actions when buttons are pressed. This can be achieved when we put some content into the `DelegateCommand.cs` file. Start by making the class inherit the `ICommand` class, and declare the following two variables:

```
public class DelegateCommand : ICommand
{
    private readonly Predicate<object> _canExecute;
    private readonly Action<object> _execute;
```

The two variables we have created will be set in the constructor. As you will notice, you are not required to add the _canExecute parameter, and you will see why in a bit:

```
public DelegateCommand(Action<object> execute,
Predicate<object> canExecute = null)
    {
        _execute = execute;
        _canExecute = canExecute;
    }
```

To complete the class, we add two public functions and one public event as follows:

```
public bool CanExecute(object parameter)
{
    if (_canExecute == null) return true;
    return _canExecute(parameter);
}

public void Execute(object parameter)
{
    _execute(parameter);
}
public event EventHandlerCanExecuteChanged
{
    add
    {
        CommandManager.RequerySuggested += value;
    }
    remove
    {
        CommandManager.RequerySuggested -= value;
    }
}
}
```

The functions declared will return the corresponding predicate, or action, declared in the constructor. This will be something we declare in our ViewModels, which, in turn, will be something that executes an action or tells the application that it can or cannot execute an action. If a button is in a state where it is disabled (the CanExecute function returns false) and the state of the CanExecute function changes, the event declared will let the button know.

With that in place, you should be able to compile and run the application, so go on and try that. You will notice that the application does not actually do anything or present any data yet, but we have an excellent starting point.

Before we do anything else with the code, we are going to export the project as a template. This is so that we do not have to redo all these steps for each small sample project we create:

1. Replace namespace names with substitute parameters:

    1. In all the `.cs` files, replace the namespace name with `$safeprojectname$`.

    2. In all the `.xaml` files, replace the project name with `$safeprojectname$` where applicable (typically class name and namespace declarations).

2. Navigate to **File** | **Export Template**. This will open the **Export Template** wizard, as shown in the following screenshot:

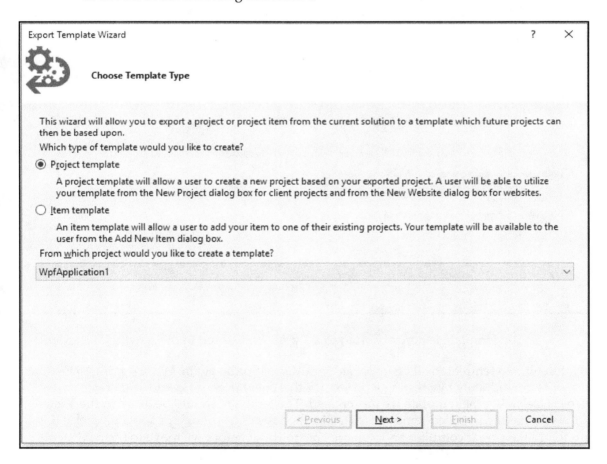

3. Click on the **Project Template** button. Select the project we just created and click on the **Next** button.

4. Just leave the icon and preview image empty. Enter a recognizable name and description. Click on the **Finish** button:

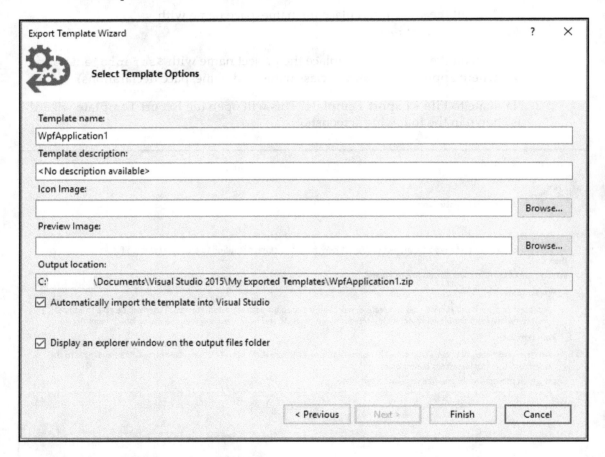

5. The template is now exported to a zip file and stored in the specified location.

By default, the template will be imported into Visual Studio again. We are going to test that it works immediately by creating a project for this chapter. So go ahead and create a new project, selecting the template we just created. The template should be listed in the **Visual C#** section of the installed templates list. Call the project Chapter1 or something else if you prefer. Make sure it compiles and you are able to run it before we move to the next step.

Detecting faces with the Face API

With the newly created project, we will now try our first API, the Face API. We will not be doing a whole lot, but we will see how simple it is to detect faces in images.

The steps we need to cover to do this are as follows:

1. Register for a Face API preview subscription at Microsoft Azure.
2. Add the necessary **NuGet** packages to our project.
3. Add some UI to the application.
4. Detect faces on command.

Head over to `https://portal.azure.com` to start the process of registering for a free subscription to the Face API. You will be taken to a login page. Log on with your Microsoft account, or if you do not have one, register for one.

Once logged in, you will need to add a new resource by clicking on **+ New** on the right-hand side menu. Search for **Face API** and select the first entry:

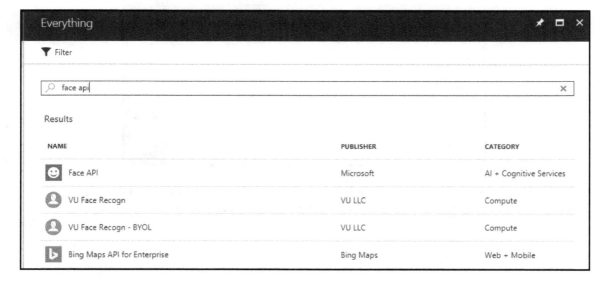

Enter a name and select the subscription, location, and pricing tier. At the time of writing, there are two pricing options, one free and one paid:

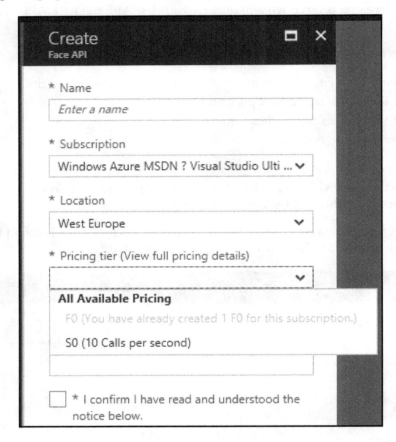

Once created, you can go into the newly created resource. You will need one of the two available API keys. These can be found in the **Keys** option of the resource menu:

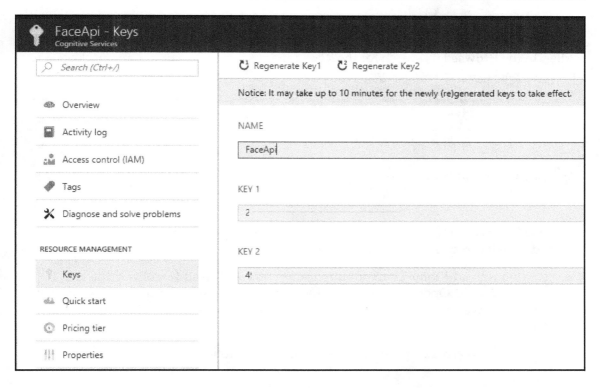

This is where we will be creating all of our API resources throughout this book. You can choose to create everything now or when we come to the respective chapters.

Some of the APIs that we will cover have their own NuGet packages created. Whenever this is the case, we will utilize those packages to do the operations we want to do. Common for all APIs is that they are REST APIs, which means that in practice you can use them with whichever language you want. For those APIs that do not have their own NuGet package, we call the APIs directly through HTTP.

For the Face API we are using now, a NuGet package does exist, so we need to add that to our project. Head over to the **NuGet Package Manager** option for the project we created earlier. In the **Browse** tab, search for the `Microsoft.ProjectOxford.Face` package and install the package from Microsoft:

As you will notice, another package will also be installed. This is the `Newtonsoft.Json` package, which is required by the Face API.

The next step is to add some UI to our application. We will be adding this in the `MainView.xaml` file. Open this file where the template code we created earlier should be. This means that we have a datacontext and can make bindings for our elements, which we will define now.

First we add a grid and define some rows for the grid as follows:

```
<Grid>
    <Grid.RowDefinitions>
        <RowDefinition Height="*" />
        <RowDefinition Height="20" />
        <RowDefinition Height="30" />
    </Grid.RowDefinitions>
</Grid.RowDefinitions>
```

Three rows are defined. The first is a row where we will have an image. The second is a line for the status message, and the last is where we will place some buttons.

Next we add our image element as follows:

```
<Image x:Name="FaceImage" Stretch="Uniform" Source=
    "{Binding ImageSource}" Grid.Row="0" />
```

We have given it a unique name. By setting the `Stretch` parameter to `Uniform`, we ensure that the image keeps its aspect ratio. Further on, we place this element in the first row. Last, we bind the image source to a `BitmapImage` in the ViewModel, which we will look at in a bit.

The next row will contain a text block with some status text. The `Text` property will be bound to a string property in the ViewModel as follows:

```
<TextBlockx:Name="StatusTextBlock" Text=
    "{Binding StatusText}" Grid.Row="1" />
```

The last row will contain one button to browse for an image and one button to be able to detect faces. The `command` properties of both buttons will be bound to the `DelegateCommand` properties in the ViewModel as follows:

```
<Button x:Name = "BrowseButton"
        Content = "Browse" Height="20" Width="140"
        HorizontalAlignment = "Left"
        Command="{Binding BrowseButtonCommand}"
        Margin="5, 0, 0, 5"Grid.Row="2" />

<Button x:Name="DetectFaceButton"
        Content="Detect face" Height="20" Width="140"
        HorizontalAlignment="Right"
        Command="{Binding DetectFaceCommand}"
        Margin="0, 0, 5, 5"Grid.Row="2"/>
```

With the View in place, make sure the code compiles and run it. This should present you with the following UI:

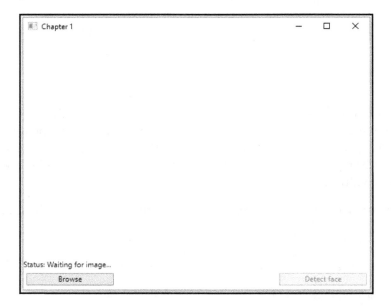

The last part is to create the binding properties in our ViewModel and make the buttons execute something. Open the `MainViewModel.cs` file. The class should already inherit from the `ObservableObject` class. First we define two variables as follows:

```
private string _filePath;
private IFaceServiceClient _faceServiceClient;
```

The string variable will hold the path to our image, while the `IFaceServiceClient` variable is to interface the Face API. Next, we define two properties as follows:

```
private BitmapImage _imageSource;
public BitmapImage ImageSource
{
    get { return _imageSource; }
    set
    {
        _imageSource = value;
        RaisePropertyChangedEvent("ImageSource");
    }
}

private string _statusText;
public string StatusText
{
    get { return _statusText; }
    set
    {
        _statusText = value;
        RaisePropertyChangedEvent("StatusText");
    }
}
```

What we have here is a property for the `BitmapImage`, mapped to the `Image` element in the View. We also have a `string` property for the status text, mapped to the text block element in the View. As you also may notice, when either of the properties is set, we call the `RaisePropertyChangedEvent` event. This will ensure that the UI updates when either property has new values.

Next we define our two `DelegateCommand` objects, and do some initialization through the constructor:

```
public ICommand BrowseButtonCommand { get; private set; }
public ICommand DetectFaceCommand { get; private set; }

public MainViewModel()
{
    StatusText = "Status: Waiting for image...";
```

```
        _faceServiceClient = new FaceServiceClient("YOUR_API_KEY_HERE",
"ROOT_URI);

        BrowseButtonCommand = new DelegateCommand(Browse);
        DetectFaceCommand = new DelegateCommand(DetectFace, CanDetectFace);
    }
```

The properties for the commands are both `public` to get but `private` to set. This means we can only set them from within the ViewModel. In our constructor, we start off by setting the status text. Next we create an object of the Face API, which needs to be created with the API key we got earlier. In addition, it needs to specify the root URI, pointing at the location of the service. It can, for instance, be `https://westeurope.api.cognitive.microsoft.com/face/v1.0` if the service is located in west Europe. If the service is located in the west US, you would replace `westeurope` with `westus`. The root URI can be found in the following place in the Azure Portal:

At last, we create the `DelegateCommand` constructor for our command properties. Notice how the browse command does not specify a predicate. This means it will always be possible to click on the corresponding button. To make this compile, we need to create the functions specified in the `DelegateCommand` constructors: the `Browse`, `DetectFace`, and `CanDetectFace` functions.

We start the `Browse` function by creating an `OpenFileDialog` object. This dialog is assigned a filter for JPEG images, and, in turn, it is opened. When the dialog is closed, we check the result. If the dialog was cancelled, we simply stop further execution:

```
    private void Browse(object obj)
    {
        var openDialog = new Microsoft.Win32.OpenFileDialog();

        openDialog.Filter = "JPEG Image(*.jpg)|*.jpg";
        bool? result = openDialog.ShowDialog();

        if (!(bool)result) return;
```

With the dialog closed, we grab the filename of the file selected and create a new URI from it:

```
_filePath = openDialog.FileName;
Uri fileUri = new Uri(_filePath);
```

With the newly created URI, we want to create a new `BitmapImage`. We specify it to use no cache, and we set the URI source of the URI we created:

```
BitmapImage image = new BitmapImage(fileUri);

image.CacheOption = BitmapCacheOption.None;
image.UriSource = fileUri;
```

The last step we take is to assign the bitmap image to our `BitmapImage` property, so the image is shown in the UI. We also update the status text to let the user know the image has been loaded:

```
ImageSource = image;
StatusText = "Status: Image loaded...";
}
```

The `CanDetectFace` function checks whether or not the `DetectFacesButton` button should be enabled. In this case, it checks if our image property actually has a URI. If it does by extension that means we have an image and we should be able to detect faces:

```
private boolCanDetectFace(object obj)
{
    return !string.IsNullOrEmpty(ImageSource?.UriSource.ToString());
}
```

Our `DetectFace` method calls an `async` method to upload and detect faces. The return value contains an array of the `FaceRectangles` variable. This array contains the rectangle area for all face positions in the given image. We will look into the function that we are going to call in a bit.

After the call has finished executing, we print a line with the number of faces to the debug console window as follows:

```
private async void DetectFace(object obj)
{
    FaceRectangle[] faceRects = await UploadAndDetectFacesAsync();

    string textToSpeak = "No faces detected";

    if (faceRects.Length == 1)
        textToSpeak = "1 face detected";
```

```
    else if (faceRects.Length> 1)
        textToSpeak = $"{faceRects.Length} faces detected";

    Debug.WriteLine(textToSpeak);
}
```

In the `UploadAndDetectFacesAsync` function, we create a `Stream` from the image. This stream will be used as input for the actual call to the Face API service:

```
private async Task<FaceRectangle[]>UploadAndDetectFacesAsync()
{
    StatusText = "Status: Detecting faces...";

    try
    {
        using (Stream imageFileStream = File.OpenRead(_filePath))
```

The following line is the actual call to the detection endpoint for the Face API:

```
    Face[] faces = await
_faceServiceClient.DetectAsync(imageFileStream, true, true, new
List<FaceAttributeType>() { FaceAttributeType.Age });
```

The first parameter is the file stream we created in the previous step. The rest of the parameters are all optional. The second parameter should be true if you want to get a face ID. The next parameter specifies whether you want to receive face landmarks or not. The last parameter takes a list of facial attributes you may want to receive. In our case, we want the age parameter to be returned, so we need to specify that.

The return type of this function call is an array of faces, with all the parameters you have specified:

```
        List<double> ages = faces.Select(face
=>face.FaceAttributes.Age).ToList();
        FaceRectangle[] faceRects = faces.Select(face
=>face.FaceRectangle).ToArray();

        StatusText = "Status: Finished detecting faces...";

        foreach(var age in ages) {
            Console.WriteLine(age);
        }
        return faceRects;
    }
}
```

The first line iterates over all faces and retrieves the approximate age of all faces. This is later printed to the debug console window, in the `foreach` loop.

The second line iterates over all faces and retrieves the face rectangle, with the rectangular location of all faces. This is the data we return to the calling function.

Add a `catch` clause to finish the method. Where an exception is thrown in our API call, we catch that. You want to show the error message and return an empty `FaceRectangle` array.

With that code in place, you should now be able to run the full example. The end result will look like the following screenshot:

The resulting debug console window will print the following text:

```
1 face detected
23,7
```

An overview of what we are dealing with

Now that you have seen a basic example of how to detect faces, it is time to learn a bit about what else Cognitive Services can do for you. When using Cognitive Services, you have 21 different APIs to hand. These are, in turn, separated into five top-level domains according to what they do. They are vision, speech, language, knowledge, and search. Let's learn more about them in the following sections.

Vision

APIs under the **Vision** flags allows your apps to understand images and video content. It allows you to retrieve information about faces, feelings, and other visual content. You can stabilize videos and recognize celebrities. You can read text in images and generate thumbnails from videos and images.

There are four APIs contained in the Vision area, which we will look at now.

Computer Vision

Using the **Computer Vision** API, you can retrieve actionable information from images. This means that you can identify content (such as image format, image size, colors, faces, and more). You can detect whether or not an image is adult/racy. This API can recognize text in images and extract it to machine-readable words. It can detect celebrities from a variety of areas. Lastly it can generate storage-efficient thumbnails with smart cropping functionality.

We will look into Computer Vision in Chapter 2, *Analyzing Images to Recognize a Face*.

Emotion

The **Emotion** API allows you to recognize emotions, both in images and in videos. This can allow for more personalized experiences in applications. Emotions detected are cross-cultural emotions: anger, contempt, disgust, fear, happiness, neutral, sadness, and surprise.

We will cover Emotion API over two chapters: Chapter 2, *Analyzing Images to Recognize a Face*, for image-based emotions, and Chapter 3, *Analyzing Videos*, for video-based emotions.

Face

We have already seen a very basic example of what the **Face** API can do. The rest of the API revolves around this detecting, identifying, organizing, and tagging faces in photos. Apart from face detection, you can see how likely it is that two faces belong to the same person. You can identify faces and also find similar-looking faces.

We will dive further into Face API in Chapter 2, *Analyzing Images to Recognize a Face*.

Video

The **Video** API is about the analyzing, editing, and processing of videos in your app. If you have a video that is shaky, the API allows you to stabilize it. You can detect and track faces in videos. If a video contains a stationary background, you can detect motion. The API lets you generate thumbnail summaries for videos, which allows users to see previews or snapshots quickly.

Video will be covered in Chapter 3, *Analyzing Videos*.

Video Indexer

Using the **Video Indexer** API, one can start indexing videos immediately upon upload. This means you can get video insights without using experts or custom code. Content discovery can be improved, utilizing the powerful artificial intelligence of this API. This allows you to make your content more discoverable.

Video indexer will be covered in Chapter 3, *Analyzing Videos*.

Content Moderator

The **Content Moderator** API utilizes machine learning to automatically moderate content. It can detect potentially offensive and unwanted images, videos, and text for over 100 languages. In addition, it allows you to review detected material to improve the service.

Content Moderator will be covered in Chapter 2, *Analyzing Images to Recognize a Face*.

Custom Vision Service

Custom Vision Service allows you to upload your own labeled images to a vision service. This means that you can add images that are specific to your domain to allow recognition using the Computer Vision API.

Custom Vision Service is not covered in this book.

Speech

Adding one of the **Speech** APIs allows your application to hear and speak to your users. The APIs can filter noise and identify speakers. Based on the recognized intent, they can drive further actions in your application.

Speech contains three APIs that are discussed as follows.

Bing Speech

Adding the **Bing Speech** API to your application allows you to convert speech to text and vice versa. You can convert spoken audio to text, either by utilizing a microphone or other sources in real time or by converting audio from files. The API also offers speech intent recognition, which is trained by **Language Understanding Intelligent Service** (**LUIS**) to understand the intent.

Speaker Recognition

The **Speaker Recognition** API gives your application the ability to know who is talking. By using this API, you can verify that the person speaking is who they claim to be. You can also determine who an unknown speaker is based on a group of selected speakers.

Custom Recognition

To improve speech recognition, you can use the **Custom Recognition** API. This allows you to fine-tune speech recognition operations for anyone, anywhere. By using this API, the speech recognition model can be tailored to the vocabulary and speaking style of the user. In addition, the model can be customized to match the expected environment of the application.

Translator Speech API

The **Translator Speech** API is a cloud-based automatic translation service for spoken audio. Using this API, you can add end-to-end translation across web apps, mobile apps, and desktop applications. Depending on your use cases, it can provide you with partial translations, full translations, and transcripts of the translations.

We will cover all speech related APIs in Chapter 5, *Speak with Your Application*.

Language

APIs related to language allow your application to process natural language and learn how to recognize what users want. You can add textual and linguistic analysis to your application, as well as natural language understanding.

The following five APIs can be found in the Language area.

Bing Spell Check

The **Bing Spell Check** API allows you to add advanced spell checking to your application.

This API will be covered in Chapter 6, *Understanding Text*.

Language Understanding Intelligent Service (LUIS)

LUIS is an API that can help your application understand commands from your users. Using this API, you can create language models that understand intents. By using models from Bing and Cortana, you can make these models recognize common requests and entities (such as places, times, and numbers). You can add conversational intelligence to your applications.

LUIS will be covered in Chapter 4, *Let Applications Understand Commands*.

Linguistic Analysis

The **Linguistic Analysis** API lets you parse complex text to explore the structure of text. By using this API, you can find nouns, verbs, and more in text, which allows your application to understand who is doing what to whom.

We will see more of Linguistic Analysis in Chapter 6, *Understanding Text*.

Text Analysis

The **Text Analysis** API will help you in extracting information from text. You can find the sentiment of a text (whether the text is positive or negative). You will be able to detect language, topic, and key phrases used throughout the text.

We will also cover Text Analysis in Chapter 6, *Understanding Text*.

Web Language Model

By using the **Web Language Model** (**WebLM**) API, you are able to leverage the power of language models trained on web-scale data. You can use this API to predict which words or sequences follow a given sequence or word.

Web Language Model API will be covered in Chapter 6, *Understanding Text*.

Translator Text API

By adding the **Translator Text** API, you can get textual translations for over 60 languages. It can detect languages automatically, and you can customize the API to your needs. In addition, you can improve translations by creating user groups, utilizing the power of crowd-sourcing.

Translator Text API will not be covered in this book.

Knowledge

When talking about **Knowledge** APIs, we are talking about APIs that allow you to tap into rich knowledge. This may be knowledge from the web. It may be from academia or it may be your own data. Using these APIs, you will be able to explore different nuances of knowledge.

The following four APIs are contained in the Knowledge API area.

Academic

Using the **Academic** API, you can explore relationships among academic papers, journals, and authors. This API allows you to interpret natural language user query strings, which allow your application to anticipate what the user is typing. It will evaluate said expression and return academic knowledge entities.

This API will be covered more in `Chapter 8`, *Query Structured Data in a Natural Way*.

Entity Linking

Entity Linking is the API you would use to extend knowledge of people, places, and events based on the context. As you may know, a single word may be used differently based on the context. Using this API allows you to recognize and identify each separate entity within a paragraph, based on the context.

We will go through Entity Linking API in `Chapter 7`, *Extending Knowledge Based on Context*.

Knowledge Exploration

The **Knowledge Exploration** API will let you add the possibility of using interactive search for structured data in your projects. It interprets natural language queries and offers auto-completions to minimize user effort. Based on the query expression received, it will retrieve detailed information about matching objects.

Details on this API will be covered in `Chapter 8`, *Query Structured Data in a Natural Way*.

Recommendations

The **Recommendations** API allows you to provide personalized product recommendations for your customers. You can use this API to add a frequently bought together functionality to your application. Another feature you can add is item-to-item recommendations, which allows customers to see what other customers like. This API will also allow you to add recommendations based on the prior activity of the customer.

We will go through this API in `Chapter 7`, *Extending Knowledge Based on Context*.

QnA Maker

The **QnA Maker** is a service to distill information for Frequently Asked Questions (FAQ). Using existing FAQs, either online or per document, you can create question and answer pairs. Pairs can be edited, removed, and modified, and you can add several similar questions to match a given pair.

We will cover QnA Maker in `Chapter 8`, *Query Structured Data in a Natural Way*.

Custom Decision Service

Custom Decision Service is a service designed to use reinforced learning to personalize content. The service understands any context and can provide context-based content.

This book does not cover Custom Decision Service.

Search

Search APIs give you the ability to make your applications more intelligent with the power of Bing. Using these APIs, you can use a single call to access data from billions of web pages, images, videos, and news.

The following five APIs are in the search domain.

Bing Web Search

With **Bing Web Search**, you can search for details in billions of web documents indexed by Bing. All the results can be arranged and ordered according to a layout you specify, and the results are customized to the location of the end user.

Bing Image Search

Using the **Bing Image Search** API, you can add an advanced image and metadata search to your application. Results include URL to images, thumbnails, and metadata. You will also be able to get machine-generated captions, similar images, and more. This API allows you to filter the results based on image type, layout, freshness (how new the image is), and license.

Bing Video Search

Bing Video Search will allow you to search for videos and return rich results. The results contain metadata from the videos, static or motion-based thumbnails, and the video itself. You can add filters to the result based on freshness, video length, resolution, and price.

Bing News Search

If you add **Bing News Search** to your application, you can search for news articles. Results can include authoritative images, related news and categories, information on the provider, URL, and more. To be more specific, you can filter news based on topics.

Bing Autosuggest

The **Bing Autosuggest** API is a small, but powerful one. It will allow your users to search faster with search suggestions, allowing you to connect a powerful search to your apps.

All Search APIs will be covered in Chapter 9, *Adding Specialized Search*.

Bing Entity Search

Using the **Bing Entity Search** API, you can enhance your searches. The API will find the most relevant entity based on your search terms. It will find entities such as famous people, places, movies, and more.

We will not cover Bing Entity Search in this book.

Getting feedback on detected faces

Now that we have seen what else Microsoft Cognitive Services can offer, we are going to add an API to our face detection application. Through this part, we will add the Bing Speech API to make the application say the number of faces out loud.

This feature of the API is not provided in the NuGet package, and as such we are going to use the REST API.

To reach our end goal, we are going to add two new classes, `TextToSpeak` and `Authentication`. The first class will be in charge of generating correct headers and making the calls to our service endpoint. The latter class will be in charge of generating an authentication token. This will be tied together in our ViewModel, where we will make the application speak back to us.

We need to get our hands on an API key first. Head over to the Microsoft Azure Portal. Create a new service for Bing Speech.

To be able to call the Bing Speech API, we need to have an authorization token. Go back to Visual Studio and create a new file called `Authentication.cs`. Place this in the `Model` folder.

We need to add two new references to the project. Find `System.Runtime.Serialization` and `System.Web` packages in the **Assembly** tab in the **Add References** window and add them.

In our `Authentication` class, define four private variables and one public property as follows:

```
private string _requestDetails;
private string _token;
private Timer _tokenRenewer;

private const int TokenRefreshInterval = 9;

public string Token { get { return _token; } }
```

The constructor should accept one string parameter, `clientSecret`. The `clientSecret` parameter is the API key you signed up for.

In the constructor, assign the `_clientSecret` variable as follows:

```
_clientSecret = clientSecret;
```

Create a new function called `Initialize` as follows:

```
public async Task Initialize()
{
    _token = GetToken();

    _tokenRenewer = new Timer(new
TimerCallback(OnTokenExpiredCallback), this,
```

```
            TimeSpan.FromMinutes(TokenRefreshInterval),
            TimeSpan.FromMilliseconds(-1));
    }
```

We then fetch the access token, in a method we will create shortly.

Finally, we create our `timer` class, which will call the `callback` function in 9 minutes. The `callback` function will need to fetch the access token again and assign it to the `_token` variable. It also needs to assure that we run the timer again in 9 minutes.

Next we need to create the `GetToken` method. This method should return a `Task<string>`object, and it should be declared as private and marked as async.

In the method, we start by creating an `HttpClient` object, pointing to an endpoint that will generate our token. We specify the root endpoint and add the token issue path as follows:

```
    using(var client = new HttpClient())
    {
        client.DefaultRequestHeaders.Add ("Opc-Apim-Subscription-Key",
    _clientSecret);
        UriBuilder uriBuilder = new UriBuilder
    (https://api.cognitive.microsoft.com/sts/v1.0");
        uriBuilder.Path = "/issueToken";
```

We then go on to make a POST call to generate a token as follows:

```
    var result = await client.PostAsync(uriBuilder.Uri.AbsoluteUri, null);
```

When the request has been sent, we expect there to be a response. We want to read this response and return the response string:

```
    return await result.Content.ReadAsStringAsync();
```

Add a new file called `TextToSpeak.cs` if you have not already done so. Put this file in the `Model` folder.

Beneath the newly created class (but inside the namespace), we want to add two event argument classes. These will be used to handle audio events, which we will see later.

The `AudioEventArgs` class simply takes a generic `stream`, and you can imagine it being used to send the audio stream to our application:

```
    public class AudioEventArgs : EventArgs
    {
        public AudioEventArgs(Stream eventData)
        {
            EventData = eventData;
```

```
    }

    public StreamEventData { get; private set; }
}
```

The next class allows us to send an event with a specific error message:

```
public class AudioErrorEventArgs : EventArgs
{
    public AudioErrorEventArgs(string message)
    {
        ErrorMessage = message;
    }

    public string ErrorMessage { get; private set; }
}
```

We move on to start on the `TextToSpeak` class, where we start off by declaring some events and class members as follows:

```
public class TextToSpeak
{
    public event EventHandler<AudioEventArgs>OnAudioAvailable;
    public event EventHandler<AudioErrorEventArgs>OnError;

    private string _gender;
    private string _voiceName;
    private string _outputFormat;
    private string _authorizationToken;
    private AccessTokenInfo _token;

    private List<KeyValuePair<string, string>> _headers = new
List<KeyValuePair<string, string>>();
```

The first two lines in the class are events using the event argument classes we created earlier. These events will be triggered if a call to the API finishes, and returns some audio, or if anything fails. The next few lines are string variables, which we will use as input parameters. We have one line to contain our access token information. The last line creates a new list, which we will use to hold our request headers.

We add two constant strings to our class as follows:

```
private const string RequestUri =
"https://speech.platform.bing.com/synthesize";

private const string SsmlTemplate =
    "<speak version='1.0'xml:lang='en-US'>
        <voice xml:lang='en-US'xml:gender='{0}'
```

```
        name='{1}'>{2}
    </voice>
</speak>";
```

The first string contains the request URI. That is the REST API endpoint we need to call to execute our request. Next we have a string defining our **Speech Synthesis Markup Language** (**SSML**) template. This is where we will specify what the speech service should say, and a bit on how it should say it.

Next we create our constructor as follows:

```
public TextToSpeak()
{
    _gender = "Female";
    _outputFormat = "riff-16khz-16bit-mono-pcm";
    _voiceName = "Microsoft Server Speech Text to Speech Voice (en-
US, ZiraRUS)";
}
```

Here we are just initializing some of our variables declared earlier. As you may see, we are defining the voice to be female and we define it to use a specific voice. In terms of gender, naturally it can be either female or male. In terms of voice name, it can be one of a long list of options. We will look more into the details of that list when we go through this API in a later chapter.

The last line specifies the output format of the audio. This will define the format and codec in use by the resulting audio stream. Again, this can be a number of varieties, which we will look into in a later chapter.

Following the constructor, there are three public methods we will create. These will generate an authentication token, generate some HTTP headers, and finally execute our call to the API. Before we create these, you should add two helper methods to be able to raise our events. Call them the `RaiseOnAudioAvailable` and `RaiseOnError` methods. They should accept `AudioEventArgs` and `AudioErrorEventArgs` as parameters.

Next, add a new method called the `GenerateHeaders` method as follows:

```
public void GenerateHeaders()
{
    _headers.Add(new KeyValuePair<string, string>("Content-Type",
"application/ssml+xml"));
    _headers.Add(new KeyValuePair<string, string>("X-Microsoft-
OutputFormat", _outputFormat));
    _headers.Add(new KeyValuePair<string, string>("Authorization",
_authorizationToken));
    _headers.Add(new KeyValuePair<string, string>("X-Search-AppId",
```

```
Guid.NewGuid().ToString("N")));
            _headers.Add(new KeyValuePair<string, string>("X-Search-
ClientID", Guid.NewGuid().ToString("N")));
            _headers.Add(new KeyValuePair<string, string>("User-Agent",
"Chapter1"));
        }
```

Here we add the HTTP headers to our previously created list. These headers are required for the service to respond, and if any is missing, it will yield an **HTTP/400** response. What we are using as headers is something we will cover in more detail later. For now, just make sure they are present.

Following this, we want to add a new method called GenerateAuthenticationToken as follows:

```
        public bool GenerateAuthenticationToken(string clientSecret)
        {
            Authentication auth = new Authentication(clientSecret);
```

This method accepts one string parameter, the client secret (your API key). First we create a new object of the Authentication class, which we looked at earlier, as follows:

```
        try
        {
            _token = auth.Token;

            if (_token != null)
            {
                _authorizationToken = $"Bearer {_token}";

                return true;
            }
            else
            {
                RaiseOnError(new AudioErrorEventArgs("Failed to generate
authentication token."));
                return false;
            }
        }
```

We use the authentication object to retrieve an access token. This token is used in our authorization token string, which, as we saw earlier, is being passed on in our headers. If the application for some reason fails to generate the access token, we trigger an error event.

Finish this method by adding the associated catch clause. If any exceptions occur, we want to raise a new error event.

The last method that we need to create in this class is going to be called the `SpeakAsync` method. This method will be actually performing the request to the Speech API:

```
public Task SpeakAsync(string textToSpeak,
CancellationTokencancellationToken)
    {
        varcookieContainer = new CookieContainer();
        var handler = new HttpClientHandler() {
            CookieContainer = cookieContainer
        };
        var client = new HttpClient(handler);
```

The method takes two parameters. One is the string, that will be the text we want to get spoken. The next is a cancellation token. This can be used to propagate that the given operation should be cancelled.

When entering the method, we create three objects which we will use to execute the request. These are classes from the .NET library, and we will not be going through them in any more detail.

We generated some headers earlier and we need to add these to our HTTP client. We do this by adding the headers in the preceding `foreach` loop, basically looping through the entire list:

```
foreach(var header in _headers)
        {
            client.DefaultRequestHeaders.TryAddWithoutValidation
(header.Key, header.Value);
        }
```

Next we create an `HTTP Request Message`, specifying that we will send data through the `POST` method and specifying the request URI. We also specify the content using the SSML template we created earlier and adding the correct parameters (gender, voice name, and the text we want to be spoken):

```
var request = new HttpRequestMessage(HttpMethod.Post,
RequestUri)
        {
            Content = new StringContent(string.Format(SsmlTemplate,
_gender, _voiceName, textToSpeak))
        };
```

We use the HTTP client to send the HTTP request asynchronously as follows:

```
var httpTask = client.SendAsync(request,
HttpCompletionOption.ResponseHeadersRead, cancellationToken);
```

The following code is a continuation of the asynchronous send call we made previously. This will run asynchronously as well and check the status of the response. If the response is successful, it will read the response message as a stream and trigger the audio event. If everything succeeded, then that stream should contain our text in spoken words:

```
var saveTask = httpTask.ContinueWith(async (responseMessage, token) =>
    {
        try
        {
            if (responseMessage.IsCompleted &&
                responseMessage.Result != null &&
                responseMessage.Result.IsSuccessStatusCode) {
                var httpStream = await responseMessage.
Result.Content.ReadAsStreamAsync().ConfigureAwait(false);
                RaiseOnAudioAvailable(new AudioEventArgs (httpStream));
            } else {
                RaiseOnError(new AudioErrorEventArgs($"Service returned
{responseMessage.Result.StatusCode}"));
            }
        }
        catch(Exception e)
        {
            RaiseOnError(new AudioErrorEventArgs
(e.GetBaseException().Message));
        }
    }
```

If the response indicates anything other than success, we will raise the error event.

We also want to add a catch clause as well as a `finally` clause to this. Raise an error if an exception is caught, and dispose of all objects used in the `finally` clause.

The final code we need is to specify that the continuation task is attached to the parent task. Also, we need to add the cancellation token to this task as well. Go on to add the following code to finish off the method:

```
    }, TaskContinuationOptions.AttachedToParent, cancellationToken);
    return saveTask;
}
```

With that in place, we are now able to utilize this class in our application, and we are going to do that now. Open the `MainViewModel.cs` file and declare a new class variable as follows:

```
private TextToSpeak _textToSpeak;
```

Add the following code in the constructor to initialize the newly added object. We also need to call a function to generate the authentication token as follows:

```
_textToSpeak = new TextToSpeak();
_textToSpeak.OnAudioAvailable +=
_textToSpeak_OnAudioAvailable;
_textToSpeak.OnError += _textToSpeak_OnError;

GenerateToken();
```

After we have created the object, we hook up the two events to event handlers. Then we generate an authentication token by creating a function GenerateToken with the following content:

```
public async void GenerateToken()
{
    if (await
_textToSpeak.GenerateAuthenticationToken("BING_SPEECH_API_KEY_HERE"))
        _textToSpeak.GenerateHeaders();
}
```

Then we generate an authentication token, specifying the API key for the Bing Speech API. If that call succeeds, we generate the HTTP headers required.

We need to add the event handlers, so create the method called `_textToSpeak_OnError` first as follows:

```
private void _textToSpeak_OnError(object sender,
AudioErrorEventArgs e)
{
    StatusText = $"Status: Audio service failed -
{e.ErrorMessage}";
}
```

It should be rather simple, just to output the error message to the user, in the status text field.

Next, we need to create a `_textToSpeak_OnAudioAvailable` method as follows:

```
        private void _textToSpeak_OnAudioAvailable(object sender,
AudioEventArgs e)
        {
            SoundPlayer player = new SoundPlayer(e.EventData);
            player.Play();
            e.EventData.Dispose();
        }
```

Here we utilize the `SoundPlayer` class from the .NET framework. This allows us to add the stream data directly and simply play the message.

The last part we need for everything to work is to make the call to the `SpeakAsync` method. We can make that by adding the following at the end of our `DetectFace` method:

```
    await _textToSpeak.SpeakAsync(textToSpeak, CancellationToken.None);
```

With that in place, you should now be able to compile and run the application. By loading a photo and clicking on **Detect face**, you should be able to get the number of faces spoken back to you. Just remember to have audio on!

Summary

In this chapter, you got a brief introduction to Microsoft Cognitive Services. We started off by creating a template project to easily create new projects for the coming chapters. We tried this template by creating an example project for this chapter. Then you learned how to detect faces in images by utilizing the Face API. From there, we took a quick tour of what Cognitive Services has to offer. We finished off by adding text-to-speech capabilities to our application by using the Bing Speech API.

The next chapter will go into more detail of the Vision part of the APIs. There you will learn how to analyze images using the Computer Vision API. You will dive more into the Face API and will learn how to detect emotions in faces by using the Emotion API. Some of this will be used to start building our smart-house application.

2
Analyzing Images to Recognize a Face

"We can use the Computer Vision API to prove to our clients the reliability of the data, so they can be confident making important business decisions based on that information."

- Leendert de Voogd, CEO Vigiglobe

In the previous chapter, you were briefly introduced to Microsoft Cognitive Services. Throughout this chapter, we will dive into image-based APIs from the Vision API. We will learn how to do image analysis. Moving on, we will dive deeper into the Face API, which we briefly looked at in the previous chapter. We will end this chapter by looking at how you can identify people.

In this chapter, we will cover the following topics:

- Analyzing images to identify content, metadata, and adult rating
- Recognizing celebrities in images and reading text in images
- Diving into the Face API:
    1. Learning to find the likelihood of two faces belonging to the same person
    2. Grouping faces based on visual similarities and searching similar faces
    3. Identifying a person from a face

Learning what an image is about using the Computer Vision API

The Computer Vision API allows us to process an image and retrieve information about it. It relies on advanced algorithms to analyze the content of the image in different ways, based on our needs.

Throughout this section, we will learn how to take advantage of this API. We will look at the different ways to analyze an image through standalone examples. Some of the features we will cover will also be incorporated into our end-to-end application in a later chapter.

Calling any of the APIs will return one of the following response codes:

Code	Description
200	Information of the extracted features in JSON format
400	Typically, this means bad request. It may be an invalid image URL, too small or too large an image, an invalid image format, or otherwise errors around the request body
415	Unsupported media type
500	Possible errors may be a failure to process the image, image processing timed out, or an internal server error

Setting up a chapter example project

Before we go into the API specifics, we need to create an example project for this chapter. This project will contain all examples, which are not put into the end-to-end application at this stage:

> If you have not already done so, sign up for an API key for Computer Vision by visiting `https://portal.azure.com`.

1. Create a new project in Visual Studio using the template we created in `Chapter 1`, *Getting Started with Microsoft Cognitive Services*.

2. Right-click on the project and choose **Manage NuGet Packages**. Search for the `Microsoft.ProjectOxford.Vision` package and install it into the project, as shown in the following screenshot:

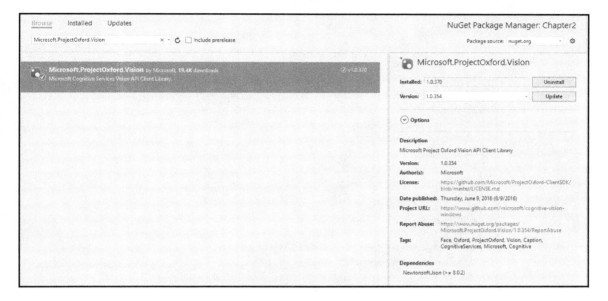

3. Create the following `UserControls` files and add them into the `ViewModel` folder:

- `CelebrityView.xaml`
- `DescriptionView.xaml`
- `ImageAnalysisView.xaml`
- `OcrView.xaml`
- `ThumbnailView.xaml`

   Also, add the corresponding ViewModels into the `ViewModel` folder:

- `CelebrityViewModel.cs`
- `DescriptionViewModel.cs`
- `ImageAnalysisViewModel.cs`
- `OcrViewModel.cs`
- `ThumbnailViewModel.cs`

Go through the newly created ViewModels and make sure all classes are public.

We will switch between the different views using a `TabControl` tag. Open the `MainView.xaml` file and add the following in the precreated `Grid` tag:

```
<TabControl x: Name = "tabControl"
                HorizontalAlignment = "Left"
                VerticalAlignment = "Top"
                Width = "810" Height = "520">
    <TabItem Header="Analysis" Width="100">
        <controls:ImageAnalysisView />
    </TabItem>
    <TabItem Header="Description" Width="100">
        <controls:DescriptionView />
    </TabItem>
    <TabItem Header="Celebs" Width="100">
        <controls:CelebrityView />
    </TabItem>
    <TabItem Header="OCR" Width="100">
        <controls:OcrView />
    </TabItem>
    <TabItem Header="Thumbnail" Width="100">
        <controls:ThumbnailView />
    </TabItem>
</TabControl>
```

This will add a tab bar at the top of the application and will allow you to navigate between the different views.

Next, we will add the properties and members required in our `MainViewModel.cs` file, as follows:

```
private IVisionServiceClient _visionClient;
```

The following is the variable used to access the Computer Vision API:

```
private CelebrityViewModel _celebrityVm;
public CelebrityViewModel CelebrityVm
{
    get { return _celebrityVm; }
    set
    {
        _celebrityVm = value;
        RaisePropertyChangedEvent("CelebrityVm");
    }
}
```

This declares a private variable holding the `CelebrityViewModel` object. It also declares the `public` property that we use to access the ViewModel in our View. Following the same pattern, add properties for the rest of the created ViewModels, as follows:

```
public MainViewModel()
{
    _visionClient = new VisionServiceClient("VISION_API_KEY_HERE",
"ROOT_URI");

    CelebrityVm = new CelebrityViewModel(_visionClient);
    DescriptionVm = new DescriptionViewModel(_visionClient);
    ImageAnalysisVm= new ImageAnalysisViewModel(_visionClient);
    OcrVm = new OcrViewModel(_visionClient);
    ThumbnailVm = new ThumbnailViewModel(_visionClient);
}
```

With all the properties in place, we create the ViewModels in our constructor. Notice how we first create the `VisionServiceClient` object, with the API key we signed up for earlier and the root URI, as described in `Chapter 1`, *Getting Started with Microsoft Cognitive Services*. This is then injected into all the ViewModels to be used there.

This should now compile and present you with the following application:

Generic image analysis

We start by adding some UI to the `ImageAnalysis.xaml` file. All the Computer Vision example UIs will be built in the same manner:

```
<Grid.ColumnDefinitions>
    <ColumnDefinition Width="*" />
    <ColumnDefinition Width="*" />
</Grid.ColumnDefinitions>
```

The UI should have two columns. The first one will contain the image selection, while the second one will display our results.

In the left-hand column, we create a vertically oriented `StackPanel` label. In this, we add a label and a `ListBox` label. The listbox will display a list of visual features we can add to our analysis query. Notice how we have a `SelectionChanged` event hooked up in the `ListBox` label. This will be added behind the code and will be covered shortly:

```
<StackPanel Orientation="Vertical"Grid.Column="0">

<TextBlock Text="Visual Features:"
           FontWeight="Bold"
           FontSize="15"
           Margin="5, 5" Height="20" />

<ListBox: Name = "VisualFeatures"
     ItemsSource = "{Binding ImageAnalysisVm.Features}"
     SelectionMode = "Multiple" Height="150" Margin="5, 0, 5, 0"
     SelectionChanged = "VisualFeatures_SelectionChanged" />
```

The listbox will be able to select multiple items, and the items are gathered in the ViewModel.

In the same stack panel, we also add a button element and an image element. These will allow us to browse for an image, show it, and analyze it. Both the `Button` command and the image source are bound to the corresponding properties in the ViewModel:

```
<Button Content = "Browse and analyze"
        Command = "{Binding
ImageAnalysisVm.BrowseAndAnalyzeImageCommand}"
        Margin="5, 10, 5, 10" Height="20" Width="120"
        HorizontalAlignment="Right" />
<Image Stretch = "Uniform"
       Source="{Binding ImageAnalysisVm.ImageSource}"
       Height="280" Width="395" />
</StackPanel>
```

We also add another vertically-oriented stack panel. This will be placed in the right-hand column. It contains a title label, as well as a textbox, bound to the analysis result in our ViewModel:

```
<StackPanel Orientation= "Vertical"Grid.Column="1">
    <TextBlock Text="Analysis Results:"
            FontWeight = "Bold"
            FontSize="15" Margin="5, 5" Height="20" />
    <TextBox Text = "{Binding ImageAnalysisVm.AnalysisResult}"
            Margin="5, 0, 5, 5" Height="485" />
</StackPanel>
```

Next, we want to add our `SelectionChanged` event handler to our code-behind. Open the `ImageAnalysisView.xaml.cs` file and add the following:

```
private void VisualFeatures_SelectionChanged(object sender,
SelectionChangedEventArgs e) {
    var vm = (MainViewModel) DataContext;
    vm.ImageAnalysisVm.SelectedFeatures.Clear();
```

The first line of the function will give us the current `DataContext`, which is the `MainViewModel` class. We access the `ImageAnalysisVm` property, which is our ViewModel, and clear the selected visual features list.

From there, we loop through the selected items from our listbox. All items will be added to the `SelectedFeatures` list in our ViewModel:

```
    foreach(VisualFeature feature in VisualFeatures.SelectedItems)
    {
        vm.ImageAnalysisVm.SelectedFeatures.Add(feature);
    }
}
```

Open the `ImageAnalysisViewModel.cs` file. Make sure the class inherits the `ObservableObject` class.

Declare a `private` variable, as follows:

```
private IVisionServiceClient _visionClient;
```

This will be used to access the Computer Vision API, and it is initialized through the constructor.

Next, we declare a private variable and the corresponding property for our list of visual features, as follows:

```
private List<VisualFeature> _features=new List<VisualFeature>();
public List<VisualFeature> Features {
    get { return _features; }
    set {
        _features = value;
        RaisePropertyChangedEvent("Features");
    }
}
```

In a similar manner, create a `BitmapImage` variable and property called `ImageSource`. Create a list of `VisualFeature` types called `SelectedFeatures` and a string called `AnalysisResult`.

We also need to declare the property for our button, as follows:

```
public ICommandBrowseAndAnalyzeImageCommand {get; private set;}
```

With that in place, we create our constructor, as follows:

```
public ImageAnalysisViewModel(IVisionServiceClientvisionClient) {
    _visionClient = visionClient;
    Initialize();
}
```

The constructor takes one parameter, the `IVisionServiceClient` object, which we have created in our `MainViewModel` file. It assigns that parameter to our variable created earlier. Then we call an `Initialize` function, as follows:

```
private void Initialize() {
    Features = Enum.GetValues(typeof(VisualFeature))
                    .Cast<VisualFeature>().ToList();

    BrowseAndAnalyzeImageCommand = new
DelegateCommand(BrowseAndAnalyze);
}
```

In the `Initialize` function, we fetch all the values from the `VisualFeature` variable of the `enum` type. These values are added to the features list, which is displayed in the UI. We have also created our button, and now we need to create the corresponding action, as follows:

```
private async void BrowseAndAnalyze(object obj)
{
    var openDialog = new Microsoft.Win32.OpenFileDialog();

    openDialog.Filter = "JPEG Image(*.jpg)|*.jpg";
    bool? result = openDialog.ShowDialog();

    if (!(bool)result) return;

    string filePath = openDialog.FileName;

    Uri fileUri = new Uri(filePath);
    BitmapImage image = new BitmapImage(fileUri);

    image.CacheOption = BitmapCacheOption.None;
    image.UriSource = fileUri;

    ImageSource = image;
```

The preceding first lines are similar to what we did in Chapter 1, *Getting Started with Microsoft Cognitive Services*. We open a file browser and get the selected image.

With an image selected, we want to run an analysis on it, as follows:

```
try {
    using (StreamfileStream = File.OpenRead(filePath)) {
        AnalysisResult analysisResult = await
_visionClient.AnalyzeImageAsync(fileStream, SelectedFeatures);
```

We call the `AnalyzeImageAsync` function of our `_visionClient`. This function has four overloads, all of which are quite similar. In our case, we pass on the image as a `Stream` type, and the `SelectedFeatures` list, containing the `VisualFeatures` variable to analyze.

The request parameters are as follows:

Parameter	Description
Image (required)	• Can be uploaded in the form of a raw image binary or URL. • Can be JPEG, PNG, GIF, or BMP. • File size must be less than 4 MB. • Image dimensions must be at least 50 x 50 pixels.
Visual features (optional)	A list indicating the visual feature types to return. It can include categories, tags, descriptions, faces, image types, color, and adult.
Details (optional)	A list indicating what domain-specific details to return.

The response to this request is the `AnalysisResult` string.

We check to see if the result is null. If it is not, we call a function to parse it and assign the result to our `AnalysisResult` string, as follows:

```
if (analysisResult != null)
    AnalysisResult = PrintAnalysisResult(analysisResult);
```

Remember to close the `try` clause and finish the method with the corresponding `catch` clause.

The `AnalysisResult` string contains data according to the visual features requested in the API call.

Data in the `AnalysisResult` variable is described in the following table:

Visual feature	Description
Categories	Images are categorized according to a defined taxonomy. This includes everything from animals, buildings, and outdoors, to people.
Tags	Images are tagged with a list of words related to the content.
Description	This contains a full sentence describing the image.
Faces	This detects faces in images and contains face coordinates, gender, and age.
ImageType	This detects if an image is clipart or a line drawing.
Color	This contains information about dominant colors, accent colors, and whether or not the image is in black and white.
Adult	This detects if an image is pornographic in nature and whether or not it is racy.

To retrieve data, such as the first description, you can do the following:

```
if (analysisResult.Description != null) {
    result.AppendFormat("Description: {0}\n",
analysisResult.Description.Captions[0].Text);
    result.AppendFormat("Probability: {0}\n\n",
analysisResult.Description.Captions[0].Confidence);
    }
```

A successful call can present us with the following result:

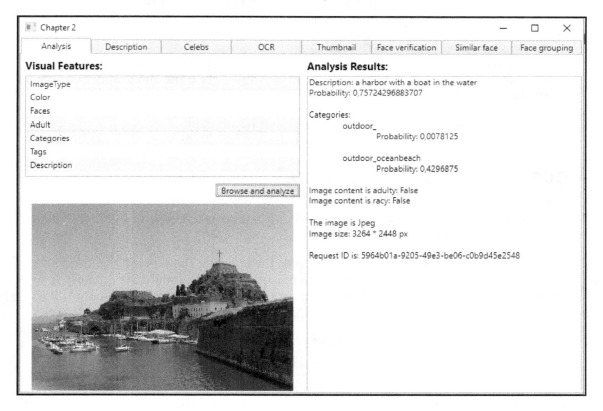

Sometimes, you may only be interested in the image description. In those cases, it is wasteful to ask for the full analysis we have just done. By calling the following function, you will get an array of descriptions:

```
AnalysisResultdescriptionResult = await
_visionClient.DescribeAsync(ImageUrl, NumberOfDescriptions);
```

In this call, we have specified a URL for the image and the number of descriptions to return. The first parameter must always be included, but it may be an image upload instead of a URL. The second parameter is optional, and, in cases where it is not provided, it defaults to one.

A successful query will result in an `AnalysisResult` object, which is the same as described in the preceding code. In this case, it will only contain the request ID, image metadata, and an array of captions. Each caption contains an image description and the confidence of that description.

We will add this form of image analysis to our smart-house application in a later chapter.

Recognizing celebrities using domain models

One of the features of the Computer Vision API is the possibility to recognize domain-specific content. At the time of writing, the API only supports celebrity recognition, where it is able to recognize around 200,000 celebrities.

For this example, we choose to use an image from the internet. The UI will then need a textbox to input the URL. It will need a button to load the image and do the domain analysis. An image element should be there to see the image, and a textbox to output the result.

The corresponding ViewModel should have two `string` properties, for the URL and the analysis result. It should have a `BitmapImage` property for the image, and an `ICommand` property for our button.

Add a private variable for the `IVisionServiceClient` type at the start of the ViewModel, as follows:

```
private IVisionServiceClient _visionClient;
```

This should be assigned in the constructor, which will take a parameter of the `IVisionServiceClient` type.

As we need a URL to fetch an image from the internet, we need to initialize the `Icommand` property with both an action and a predicate. The latter checks if the URL property is set or not:

```
public CelebrityViewModel(IVisionServiceClient visionClient) {
    _visionClient = visionClient;
    LoadAndFindCelebrityCommand = new
DelegateCommand(LoadAndFindCelebrity, CanFindCelebrity);
    }
```

The `LoadAndFindCelebrity` load creates a `Uri`, with the given URL. Using this, it creates a `BitmapImage` and assigns this to `ImageSource`, the `BitmapImage` property. The image should be visible in the UI:

```
private async void LoadAndFindCelebrity(object obj) {
    UrifileUri = new Uri(ImageUrl);
    BitmapImage image = new BitmapImage(fileUri);

    image.CacheOption = BitmapCacheOption.None;
    image.UriSource = fileUri;

    ImageSource = image;
```

We call the `AnalyzeImageInDomainAsync` type with the given URL. The first parameter we pass in is the image URL. Alternatively, this could have been an image opened as a `Stream` type:

```
try {
    AnalysisInDomainResultcelebrityResult = await
_visionClient.AnalyzeImageInDomainAsync(ImageUrl, "celebrities");

    if (celebrityResult != null)
        Celebrity = celebrityResult.Result.ToString();
    }
```

The second parameter is the domain model name, which is in `string` format. As an alternative, we could have used a specific `Model` object, which can be retrieved by calling the following:

```
VisionClient.ListModelsAsync();
```

That would return an array of `Models`, which we can display and select from. As there is only one available at this time, there is no point in doing so.

The result from `AnalyzeImageInDomainAsync` is an object of type `AnalysisInDomainResult`. This object will contain the request ID, metadata of the image, and the result, containing an array of celebrities. In our case, we simply output the entire result array. Each item in this array will contain the name of the celebrity, the confidence of a match, and the face rectangle in the image. Do try it in the example code provided.

Utilizing Optical Character Recognition

For some tasks, **Optical Character Recognition** (**OCR**) can be very useful. You can imagine taking a photo of a receipt. Using OCR, you can get the amount and have it automatically added to accounting.

OCR will detect text in images and extract machine-readable characters. It will automatically detect language. Optionally, the API will detect image orientation and correct it before reading the text.

To specify a language, you need to use the **BCP-47** language code. At the time of writing, the following languages are supported: Chinese Simplified, Chinese Traditional, Czech, Danish, Dutch, English, Finnish, French, German, Greek, Hungarian, Italian, Japanese, Korean, Norwegian, Polish, Portuguese, Russian, Spanish, Swedish, and Turkish.

In the code example, the UI will have an image element. It will also have a button to load the image and detect text. The result will be printed to a textbox element.

The ViewModel will need a `string` property for the result, a `BitmapImage` property for the image, and an `ICommand` property for the button.

Add a private variable to the ViewModel for the Computer Vision API, as follows:

```
private IVisionServiceClient _visionClient;
```

The constructor should have one parameter of the `IVisionServiceClient` type, which should be assigned to the preceding variable.

Create a function as a command for our button. Call it `BrowseAndAnalyze` and have it accept `object` as the parameter. We open a file browser and find an image to analyze. With the image selected, we run the OCR analysis, as follows:

```
using (StreamfileStream = File.OpenRead(filePath)) {
    OcrResultsanalysisResult = await _visionClient.RecognizeTextAsync
```

```
(fileStream);

        if(analysisResult != null)
            OcrResult = PrintOcrResult(analysisResult);
    }
```

With the image opened as a `Stream` type, we call the `RecognizeTextAsync` method. In this case, we pass on the image as a `Stream` type, but we could just as easily have passed on an URL to an image.

Two more parameters may be specified in this call. First, you can specify the language of the text. The default is unknown, which means that the API will try to detect the language automatically. Second, you can specify whether or not the API should detect the orientation of the image or not. The default is set to `false`.

If the call succeeds, it will return data in the form of an `OcrResults` object. We send this result to a function, the `PrintOcrResult` function, where we will parse it and print the text:

```
private string PrintOcrResult(OcrResultsocrResult)
{
    StringBuilder result = new StringBuilder();

    result.AppendFormat("Language is {0}\n", ocrResult.Language);
    result.Append("The words are:\n\n");
```

First, we create a `StringBuilder` object, which will hold all text. The first content we add to it is the language of the text in the image, as follows:

```
foreach(var region in ocrResult.Regions) {
    foreach(var line in region.Lines) {
        foreach(var text in line.Words) {
            result.AppendFormat("{0} ", text.Text);
        }
        result.Append("\n");
    }
    result.Append("\n\n");
}
```

The result has an array, containing the `Regions` property. Each item represents recognized text, and each region contains multiple lines. The `line` variables are arrays, where each item represents recognized text. Each line contains an array of `Words` property. Each item in this array represents a recognized word.

With all the words appended to the `StringBuilder` function, we return it as a string. This will then be printed in the UI, as shown in the following screenshot:

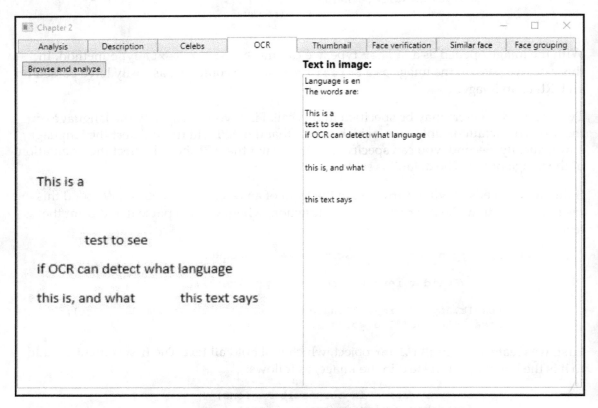

The result also contains the orientation and angle of the text. Combining this with the bounding box, also included, you can mark each word in the original image.

Generating image thumbnails

In today's world, we, as developers, have to consider different screen sizes when displaying images. The Computer Vision API offers some help in that it can generate thumbnails.

Thumbnail generation, in itself, is not that big a deal. What makes the API clever is that it analyzes the image and determines the region of interest.

It will also generate smart cropping coordinates. This means that if the specified aspect ratio differs from the original, it will crop the image, with a focus on the interesting regions.

In the example code, the UI consists of two image elements and one button. The first image is the image in its original size. The second is for the generated thumbnail, which we specify to be 250x250 pixels in size.

The View model will need corresponding properties, two `BitmapImages` methods to act as image sources, and one `ICommand` property for our button command.

Define a private variable in the ViewModel, as follows:

```
private IVisionServiceClient _visionClient;
```

This will be our API access point. The constructor should accept an `IVisionServiceClient` object, which should be assigned to the preceding variable.

For the `ICommand` property, we create a function, `BrowseAndAnalyze`, accepting an `object` parameter. We do not need to check if we can execute the command or not. We will browse for an image each time.

In the `BrowseAndAnalyze` function, we open a file dialog and select an image. When we have the image file path, we can generate our thumbnail, as follows:

```
using (StreamfileStream = File.OpenRead(filePath))
{
    byte[] thumbnailResult = await
_visionClient.GetThumbnailAsync(fileStream, 250, 250);

    if(thumbnailResult != null &&thumbnailResult.Length != 0)
        CreateThumbnail(thumbnailResult);
}
```

We open the image file so that we have a `Stream` type. This stream is the first parameter in our call to the `GetThumbnailAsync` method. The next two parameters indicate the width and height we want for our thumbnail.

By default, the API call will use smart cropping, so we do not have to specify it. If we have a case where we do not want smart cropping, we could add a `bool` variable as the fourth parameter.

If the call succeeds, we get a `byte` array back. This is the image data. If it contains data, we pass it on to a new function, `CreateThumbnail`, to create a `BitmapImage` object from it as follows:

```
private void CreateThumbnail(byte[] thumbnailResult)
{
    try {
        MemoryStreamms = new MemoryStream(thumbnailResult);
        ms.Seek(0, SeekOrigin.Begin);
```

To create an image from a `byte` array, we create a `MemoryStream` object from it. We make sure that we start at the beginning.

Next, we create a `BitmapImage` object and start the initialization of it. We specify the `CacheOption` and set the `StreamSource` to the `MemoryStream` variables we created earlier. Finally, we stop the `BitmapImage` initialization and assign the image to our `Thumbnail` property:

```
BitmapImage image = new BitmapImage();
image.BeginInit();
image.CacheOption = BitmapCacheOption.None;
image.StreamSource = ms;
image.EndInit();

Thumbnail = image;
```

Close up the `try` clause and add the corresponding `catch` clause, and you should be able to generate thumbnails.

Diving deep into the Face API

The Face API has two main features. The first one is face detection and the other is face recognition.

Face detection allows one to detect up to 64 faces in one image. We have already seen the basic usage. The features of face recognition are implied in its name. Using it, we can detect if two faces belong to the same person. We can find similar faces, or one in particular, and we can group similar faces. We will learn how to do all of this in the following pages.

When calling any of the APIs, it will respond with one of the following responses:

Code	Description
200	Successful call. Returns an array containing data related to the API call.
400	Request body is invalid. Can be a number of errors, depending on the API call. Typically, the request code is invalid.
401	Access denied due to invalid subscription key. The key may be wrong or the account/subscription plan is blocked.
403	Out of call volume data. You have made all the available calls to the API for this month.
415	Invalid media type.
429	Rate limit is exceeded. You will need to wait a period of time (<1 minute in the free preview) before you try again.

Retrieving more information from the detected faces

In Chapter 1, *Getting Started with Microsoft Cognitive Services*, we learned the very basic form of face detection. In the example, we retrieved a Face array. This contained information on all faces found in an image. In that specific example, we obtained information about the face rectangle, face ID, face landmarks, and age.

When calling the API, there are four request parameters:

Parameter	Description
image	• Image in which to search for faces. Either in the form of a URL or binary data. • Supported formats are JPEG, PNG, GIF, and BMP. • Max file size is 4 MB. • The size of detectable faces is between 36 x 36 pixels and 4,096 x 4,096 pixels.
return FaceId (optional)	Boolean value. Specifies if the response should include the face ID or not.
return FaceLandmarks (optional)	Boolean value. Specifies if the response should include FaceLandmarks in detected faces.

`return FaceAttributes` (optional)	• String value. Comma-separated string with all face attributes to analyze. • Supported attributes are age, gender, head pose, smile, facial hair, and glasses. • These attributes are still experimental and should be treated as such.

If a face is successfully discovered, it will expire in 24 hours. When calling other parts of the Face API, it is often required to have a face ID as an input. In those cases, we need to detect a face first followed by the actual API call we are supposed to do.

Using this knowledge, I challenge you to play around with the example in Chapter 1, *Getting Started with Microsoft Cognitive Services*. Draw a rectangle around the face. Mark the eyes in the image.

Deciding whether two faces belong to the same person

To decide if two faces belong to the same person, we are going to call the Verify function of the API. The API allows us to detect when two faces are of the same person, called face-to-face verification. Detecting if a face belongs to a specific person is called **face-to-person verification**.

The UI will consist of three button elements, two image elements, and one text block element. Two of the buttons will be used to browse for images, which are then shown in each image element. The last button will run the verification. The text block will output the result.

Lay out the UI how you want and bind the different elements to properties in the ViewModel, as we have done previously. In the ViewModel, there should be two BitmapImage properties for the image elements. There should be one string property, containing the verification result. Finally, there should be three ICommand properties, one for each of our buttons.

Remember to add the UI to the `MainView.xaml` file as a new `TabItem`. Also, add the ViewModel to the `MainViewModel.cs` file, where you will also need to add a new variable for the `FaceServiceClient` variable. This should be created with the Face API key, which we signed up for in `Chapter 1`, *Getting Started with Microsoft Cognitive Services.*

In the ViewModel, we need to declare the following three private variables:

```
private FaceServiceClient _faceServiceClient;
private Guid _faceId1 = Guid.Empty;
private Guid _faceId2 = Guid.Empty;
```

We have seen the first one before; it will access the Face API. The two `Guid` variables will be assigned when we have run the face detection.

The constructor accepts one parameter, which is our `FaceServiceClient` object. This is assigned to the previously created variable:

```
public FaceVerificationViewModel (FaceServiceClientfaceServiceClient)
{
    _faceServiceClient = faceServiceClient;
    Initialize();
}
```

From the constructor, we call the `Initialize` function to create the `DelegateCommand` properties, as follows:

```
private void Initialize()
{
    BrowseImage1Command = new DelegateCommand(BrowseImage1);
    BrowseImage2Command = new DelegateCommand(BrowseImage2);
    VerifyImageCommand = new DelegateCommand(VerifyFace,
CanVerifyFace);
}
```

The browse commands do not need to be disabled at any point, so we just pass on the command function, as follows:

```
private async void BrowseImage1(object obj) {
    Image1Source = await BrowseImageAsync(1);
}
```

Both functions will look similar. We call another function to browse for an image and detect a face. To separate each image, we pass on the image number.

The `BrowseImageAsync` function will accept an `int` type as a parameter. It returns a `BitmapImage` object, which we assign to the `BitmapImage` property bound to our UI. The first part opens a browse dialog and returns the selected image. We will jump in when we have the image and the path to that image.

We open the image as a `Stream` object. The `Stream` object is used in the API call to detect faces. When we call the API, we can use the default call, as it will return the value we are interested in:

```
try {
    using (Stream fileStream = File.OpenRead(filePath)) {
        Face[] detectedFaces = await
_faceServiceClient.DetectAsync(fileStream);
```

When the detection completes, we check to see which image this is and assign the `FaceId` parameter to the correct `Guid` variable. For this example, we are assuming that there will be only one face per image:

```
        if (imagenumber == 1)
            _faceId1 = detectedFaces[0].FaceId;
        else
            _faceId2 = detectedFaces[0].FaceId;
    }
}
```

Finish off the function by adding catch clauses as you see fit. Also, you need to create and return a `BitmapImage` parameter from the selected image.

Before the button to the face verification is enabled, we do a check to see if both face IDs have been set:

```
private bool CanVerifyFace(object obj)
{
    return !_faceId1.Equals(Guid.Empty) &&!
_faceId2.Equals(Guid.Empty);
}
```

The `VerifyFace` function is not a complex one:

```
private async void VerifyFace(object obj) {
    try {
        VerifyResultverificationResult = await
_faceServiceClient.VerifyAsync(_faceId1, _faceId2);
```

With the face IDs set, we can make a call to the `VerifyAsync` function of the API. We pass on the face IDs as a parameters and get a `VerifyResult` object in return. We use this object to provide the output, as follows:

```
            FaceVerificationResult = $"The two provided faces is identical:
    {verificationResult.IsIdentical}, with confidence:
    {verificationResult.Confidence}";
        }
```

A successful call will return a code-200 response. The response data is a `bool` type variable, `isIdentical`, and a number, `confidence`:

At the time of writing, the `NuGet` package for the Face API only allows for face-to-face verification. If we were calling directly to the REST API, we could have utilized face-to-person verification as well.

To use the face-to-person verification, only one image is required. You will need to pass on the face ID for that image. You will also need to pass on a person-group ID, and a person ID. These are to specify a specific person group to search in and a certain person within that groups. We will cover person group and persons later in this chapter.

Finding similar faces

Using the Face API, you can find faces similar to a provided face. The API allows for two search modes. The match person is the default one. This will match faces to the same person, according to an internal same-person threshold. The other is match face, which will ignore the same-person threshold. This returns matches that are similar, but the similarity may be low.

In the example code provided, we have three buttons in our UI: one for generating a face list, another for adding faces to the list, and, finally, one to find similar faces. We need a textbox to specify a name for the face list. For convenience, we add a listbox, outputting the persisted face IDs from the face list. Also, we add an image element to show the image we are checking, and a textbox outputting the result.

In the corresponding ViewModel, we need to add a `BitmapImage` property for the image element. We need two `string` properties: one for our face-list name and one for the API call result. To get data to our listbox, we need an `ObservableCollection` property containing `Guids`. The buttons need to be hooked up to individual `ICommand` properties.

We declare two private variables at the start of the ViewModel. The first one is a `bool` variable to indicate whether or not the face list already exists. The other is used to access the Face API:

```
private bool _faceListExists = false;
private FaceServiceClient _faceServiceClient;
```

The constructor should accept the `FaceServiceClient` parameter, which it assigns to the preceding variable. It will then call an `Initialize` function, as follows:

```
private async void Initialize()
{
    FaceListName = "Chapter2";

    CreateFaceListCommand = new DelegateCommand(CreateFaceListAsync,
CanCreateFaceList);
    FindSimilarFaceCommand = new DelegateCommand(FindSimilarFace);
    AddExampleFacesToListCommand = new
DelegateCommand(AddExampleFacesToList, CanAddExampleFaces);
```

First, we initialize the `FaceListName` property to `Chapter2`. Next, we create the command objects, specifying actions and predicates, as follows:

```
        await DoesFaceListExistAsync();
        UpdateFaceGuidsAsync();
    }
```

We finish the `Initialize` function by calling two functions. One checks if the face list exists, while the second updates the list of face IDs:

```
    private async Task DoesFaceListExistAsync()
    {
        FaceListMetadata[] faceLists = await
_faceServiceClient.ListFaceListsAsync();
```

To check if a given face list exists, we first need to get a list of all face lists. We do so by calling the `ListFaceListsAsync` method, which will return a `FaceListMetadata` array. We make sure that the result has data before we loop through the array:

```
    foreach (FaceListMetadatafaceList in faceLists) {
        if (faceList.Name.Equals(FaceListName)) {
            _faceListExists = true;
            break;
        }
    }
```

Each `FaceListMetadata` array, from the resulting array, contains a face-list ID, a name of the face list, and user-provided data. For this example, we are just interested in the name. If the face-list name we have specified is the name of any face list returned, we set the `_faceListExists` parameter to true. If the face list exists, we can update the list of face IDs.

To get the faces in a face list, we need to get the face list first. This is done with a call to the Face API's function, the `GetFaceListAsync` method. This requires the face-list ID to be passed as a parameter. The face-list ID needs to be in lowercase or digits and can contain a maximum of 64 characters. For the sake of simplicity, we use the face-list name as the face ID, as follows:

```
    private async void UpdateFaceGuidsAsync() {
        if (!_faceListExists) return;

    try {
        FaceListfaceList = await
_faceServiceClient.GetFaceListAsync(FaceListName.ToLower());
```

The result of this API call is a `FaceList` object, containing the face-list ID and face-list name. It also contains user-provided data and an array of persisted faces:

```
if (faceList == null) return;

PersonFace[] faces = faceList.PersistedFaces;

foreach (PersonFace face in faces) {
    FaceIds.Add(face.PersistedFaceId);
}
```

We check if we have any data and then get the array of persisted faces. Looping through this array, we are able to get the `PersistedFaceId` parameter (as a `guid` variable) and user-provided data of each item. The persisted face ID is added to the `FaceIds` `ObservableCollection`. Finish the function by adding the corresponding `catch` clause.

If the face list does not exist, and we have specified a face-list name, we can create a new face list, as follows:

```
private async void CreateFaceListAsync(object obj) {
    try {
        if (!_faceListExists) {
            await _faceServiceClient.CreateFaceListAsync (
FaceListName.ToLower(), FaceListName, string.Empty);
            await DoesFaceListExistAsync();
        }
    }
```

First, we check to see that the face list does not exist. Using the `_faceServiceClient` parameter, you are required to pass on a face-list ID, a face-list name, and user data. As seen previously, the face-list ID needs to be lowercase characters or digits.

Using the REST API, the user parameter is optional, and as such, you would not have to provide it.

After we have created a face list, we want to ensure that it exists. We do this by a call to the previously created `DoesFaceListExistAsync` function. Add the `catch` clause to finish the function.

If the named face list exists, we can add faces to this list. Add the `AddExampleFacesToList` function. It should accept `object` as a parameter. I will leave the details of adding the images up to you. In the provided example, we get a list of images from a given directory and loop through it. With the file path of a given image, we do the following.

We open the image as a `Stream`. To optimize for our similarity operation, we find the `FaceRectangle` parameter in an image. As there should be only one face per image in the face list, we select the first element in the `Face` array, as follows:

```
using (StreamfileStream = File.OpenRead(image))
{
    Face[] faces = await _faceServiceClient.DetectAsync(fileStream);
    FaceRectanglefaceRectangle = faces[0].FaceRectangle;
```

Adding the face to the face list is as simple as calling the `AddFaceToFaceListAsync` function. We need to specify the face-list ID and the image. The image may come from a `Stream` (as in our case) or a URL. Optionally, we can add user data and the face rectangle of the image, as follows:

```
AddPersistedFaceResult addFacesResult = await
_faceServiceClient.AddFaceToFaceListAsync(FaceListName.ToLower(),
fileStream, null, faceRectangle);
    UpdateFaceGuidsAsync();
```

The result of the API call is an `AddPersistedFaceResult` variable. This contains the persisted face ID, which is different from a face ID in the `DetectAsync` call. A face added to a face list will not expire until it is deleted.

We finish the function by calling the `UpdateFaceGuidsAsync` method.

Finally, we create our `FindSimilarFace` function, also accepting `object` as a parameter. To be able to search for similar faces, we need a face ID (the `Guid` variable) from the `DetectAsync` method. This can be called with a local image or from a URL. The example code opens a file browser and allows the user to browse for an image.

With the face ID, we can search for similar faces:

```
try {
    SimilarPersistedFace[] similarFaces = await
_faceServiceClient.FindSimilarAsync (findFaceGuid, FaceListName.ToLower(),
3);
```

We call the `FindSimilarAsync` function. The first parameter is the face ID of the face we specified. The next parameter is the face-list ID, and the final parameter is the number of candidate faces returned. The default for this is 20, so it is often best to specify a number.

Instead of using a face list to find similar faces, you can use an array of the `Guid` variable. That array should contain face IDs retrieved from the `DetectAsync` method.

At the time of writing, the NuGet API package only supports, match-person mode. If you are using the REST API directly, you can specify the mode as a parameter.

Depending on the mode selected, the result will contain either the face ID or the persisted face ID of similar faces. It will also contain the confidence of similarity of the given face.

To delete a face from the face list, call the following function in the Face API:

```
DeleteFaceFromFaceListAsync(FACELISTID, PERSISTEDFACEID)
```

To delete a face list, call the following function in the Face API:

```
DeleteFaceListAsync(FACELISTID)
```

To update a face list, call the following function in the Face API:

```
UpdateFaceListAsync(FACELISTID, FACELISTNAME, USERDATA)
```

Grouping similar faces

If you have several images of faces, one thing you may want to do is group the faces. Typically, you will want to group faces based on similarity, which is a feature the Face API provides.

By providing the API with a list of face IDs, it will respond with one or more groups. One group consists of faces that are similar looking. Usually, this means that the faces belong to the same person. Faces that cannot find any similar counterparts are placed in a group we'll call MessyGroup.

Create a new View called FaceGroupingView.xaml. The View should have six image elements, with corresponding titles and textboxes for face IDs. It should also have a button for our group command, and a textbox to output the grouping result.

In the corresponding FaceGroupingViewModel.xaml View model, you should add the BitmapImage properties for all images. You should also add the string properties for the face IDs, and one for the result. There is also a need for an ICommand property.

At the start of the ViewModel, we declare some private variables, as follows:

```
private FaceServiceClient _faceServiceClient;
private List<string> _imageFiles = new List<string>();
private List<Guid> _faceIds = new List<Guid>();
```

The first one is used to access the Face API. Second, we have a list of strings containing the location of our images. The last list contains the detected face IDs.

The constructor accepts a parameter of the `FaceServiceClient` type. It assigns it to the corresponding variable and calls the `Initialize` function. This creates our `ICommand` object and calls a function to add our images to the application.

In the function to add images, we add hardcoded image paths to our `_imageFiles` list. For this example, we add six. Using a `for` loop, we generate each `BitmapImage` property. When we have an image, we want to detect faces in it:

```
try {
    using (Stream fileStream = File.OpenRead(_imageFiles[i])) {
        Face[] faces = await
        _faceServiceClient.DetectAsync(fileStream);
```

We do not need any more data than the generated face ID, which we know is stored for 24 hours after detection:

```
        _faceIds.Add(faces[0].FaceId);
        CreateImageSources(image, i, faces[0].FaceId);
    }
}
```

Assuming there is only one face per image, we add that face ID to our `_faceIds` list. The image, face ID, and current iteration number in the loop are passed on to a new function, `CreateImageSources`. This function contains a `switch` case based on the iteration number. Based on the number, we assign the image and face ID to the corresponding image and image ID property. This is then shown in the UI.

We have a button to group the images. To group the images, we call the Face API's `GroupAsync` method, passing on an array of face IDs. The array of face IDs must contain at least two elements, and it cannot contain more than 1,000 elements:

```
private async void GroupFaces(object obj) {
    try {
        GroupResultfaceGroups = await
_faceServiceClient.GroupAsync(_faceIds.ToArray());
```

The response is a `GroupResult` type, which may contain one or more groups, as well as the messy group:

```
        if (faceGroups != null)
            FaceGroupingResult = ParseGroupResult(faceGroups);
    }
```

We check to see if there is a response and then we parse it. Before looking at the `ParseGroupResult` method, add the corresponding `catch` clause and close-up `GroupFaces` function, as follows:

```
private string ParseGroupResult(GroupResultfaceGroups) {
    StringBuilder result = new StringBuilder();
    List<Guid[]>groups = faceGroups.Groups;
    result.AppendFormat("There are {0} group(s)\n", groups.Count);
```

When parsing the results, we first create a `StringBuilder` class to hold our text. Then we get the `groups` from the result. A group is an array of face IDs of the images in that group. All groups are stored in a list, and we append the number of groups to the `StringBuilder` class.

We loop through the lists of groups. Inside this loop, we loop through each item in the group. For the sake of readability, we have a helper function to find the image name from the ID. It finds the index in our `_faceIds` list. This is then used in the image name, so if the index is 2, the image name would be `Image 3`. For this to give the intended effect, you must have placed the images in a logical order, as follows:

```
result.Append("Groups:\t");

foreach(Guid[] guid in groups)
{
    foreach(Guid id in guid)
    {
        result.AppendFormat("{0} - ", GetImageName(id));
    }
    result.Append("\n");
}
```

The `GroupResult` method may also contain a `MessyGroup` array. This is an array of `Guid` variables containing the face IDs in that group. We loop through this array and append the image name, the same way we did with the regular groups:

```
result.Append("Messy group:\t");

Guid[] messyGroup = faceGroups.MessyGroup;
foreach(Guidguid in messyGroup)
{
    result.AppendFormat("{0} - ", GetImageName(guid));
}
```

We end the function by returning the `StringBuilder` function's text, which will output it to the screen, as follows:

```
    return result.ToString();
}
```

Make sure that the ViewModels have been created in the `MainViewModel.cs` file. Also, make sure that the View has been added as a `TabItem` property in the `MainView.xaml` file. Compile and test the application.

If you are using the sample images provided, you may end up with something like the following:

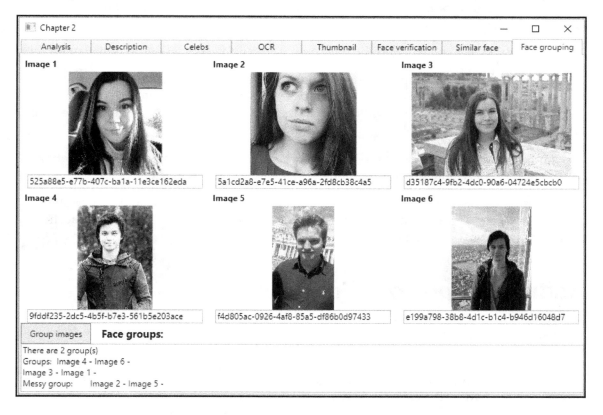

Adding identification to our smart-house application

As a part of our smart-house application, we want the application to recognize who we are. Doing so opens up the opportunity to get responses and actions from the application, tailored to you.

Creating our smart-house application

Create a new project for the smart-house application, based on the MVVM template we created earlier.

With the new project created, add the `Microsoft.ProjectOxford.Face` NuGet package.

As we will be building this application throughout this book, we will start small. In the `MainView.xaml` file, add a `TabControl` property containing two items. The two items should be two user controls, one called the `AdministrationView.xaml` file and the other called the `HomeView.xaml` file.

The administration control will be where we administer different parts of the application. The home control will be the starting point and the main control to use.

Add corresponding ViewModels to the Views. Make sure they are declared and created in `MainViewModel.cs`, as we have seen throughout this chapter. Make sure the application compiles and runs before moving on.

Adding people to be identified

Before we can go on to identify a person, we need to have something to identify them from. To identify a person, we need a `PersonGroup` property. This is a group that contains several `Persons` properties.

In the administration control, we will execute several operations in this regard. The UI should contain two textbox elements, two listbox elements, and six buttons. The two textbox elements will allow us to input a name for the person group and a name for the person. One listbox will list all person groups we have available. The other will list all the persons in any given group.

We have buttons for each of the operations we want to execute, which are as follows:

- Add person group
- Delete person group
- Train person group
- Add person
- Delete person
- Add person face

The View model should have two `ObservableCollection` properties: one of `PersonGroup` type and the other of `Person` type. We should also add three `string` properties. One will be for our person-group name, the other for our person name. The last will hold some status text. We also want a `PersonGroup` property for the selected person group. Finally, we want a `Person` property holding the selected person.

In our View model, we want to add a private variable for the `FaceServiceClient` method:

```
private FaceServiceClient _faceServiceClient;
```

This should be assigned in the constructor, which should accept a parameter of the `FaceServiceClient` type. It should also call an initialization function, which will be six `ICommand` properties that we should add. The initialization function should call the `GetPersonGroups` function to list all person groups available:

```
private async void GetPersonGroups() {
    try {
        PersonGroup[] personGroups = await
        _faceServiceClient.ListPersonGroupsAsync();
```

The `ListPersonGroupsAsync` function does not take any parameters and returns an array of `PersonGroup` array if successfully executed:

```
if(personGroups == null || personGroups.Length == 0)
{
    StatusText = "No person groups found.";
    return;
}

PersonGroups.Clear();

foreach (PersonGrouppersonGroup in personGroups)
{
    PersonGroups.Add(personGroup);
```

```
            }
        }
```

We check to see if the array contains any elements. If it does, we clear out the existing `PersonGroups` list. Then we loop through each item of the `PersonGroup` array and add them to the `PersonGroups` list.

If no person groups exist, we can add a new one by filling in a name. The name you fill in here will also be used as a person-group ID. This means it can include numbers and English lowercase letters, "-" (hyphen), and "_" (underscore). The maximum length is 64 characters. When it is filled in, we can add a person group:

```
        private async void AddPersonGroup(object obj) {
            try {
                if(await DoesPersonGroupExistAsync(PersonGroupName.ToLower()))
    {
                    StatusText = $"Person group {PersonGroupName} already
    exist";
                    return;
                }
```

First, we call the `DoesPersonGroupExistAsync` function, specifying `PersonGroupName` as a parameter. If this is true, the name we have given already exists, and as such we are not allowed to add it. Note how we call the `ToLower` function on the name. This is so we are sure the ID is in lowercase:

```
                await _faceServiceClient.CreatePersonGroupAsync
    (PersonGroupName.ToLower(), PersonGroupName);
                StatusText = $"Person group {PersonGroupName} added";
                GetPersonGroups();
            }
```

If the person group does not exist, we call the `CreatePersonGroupAsync` function. Again, we specify the `PersonGroupName` as lowercase in the first parameter. This represents the ID of the group. The second parameter indicates the name we want. We end the function by calling the `GetPersonGroups` function again, so we get the newly added group in our list.

The `DoesPersonGroupExistAsync` function makes one API call. It tries to call the `GetPersonGroupAsync` function, with the person-group ID specified as a parameter. If the resulting `PersonGroup` list is anything but null, we return `true`.

To delete a person group, a group must be selected as follows:

```
private async void DeletePersonGroup(object obj)
{
    try
    {
        await _faceServiceClient.DeletePersonGroupAsync
(SelectedPersonGroup.PersonGroupId);
        StatusText = $"Deleted person group
{SelectedPersonGroup.Name}";

        GetPersonGroups();
    }
```

The API call to the `DeletePersonGroupAsync` function requires a person-group ID as a parameter. We get this from the selected person group. If no exception is caught, the call has completed successfully, and we call the `GetPersonGroups` function to update our list.

When a person group is selected from the list, we make sure to call the `GetPersons` function. This will update the list of persons, as follows:

```
private async void GetPersons()
{
    if (SelectedPersonGroup == null)
        return;

    Persons.Clear();

    try
    {
        Person[] persons = await _faceServiceClient.GetPersonsAsync
(SelectedPersonGroup.PersonGroupId);
```

We make sure the selected person group is not null. If it is not, we clear our `persons` list. The API call to the `GetPersonsAsync` function requires a person-group ID as a parameter. A successful call will result in a `Person` array:

```
        if (persons == null || persons.Length == 0)
        {
            StatusText = $"No persons found in
{SelectedPersonGroup.Name}.";
            return;
        }

        foreach (Person person in persons)
        {
            Persons.Add(person);
```

```
            }
        }
```

If the resulting array contains any elements, we loop through it. Each `Person` object is added to our `persons` list.

If no persons exist, we can add new ones. To add a new one, a person group must be selected, and a name of the person must be filled in. With this in place, we can click on the add button:

```
        private async void AddPerson(object obj)
        {
            try
            {
                CreatePersonResultpersonId = await
_faceServiceClient.CreatePersonAsync(SelectedPersonGroup.PersonGroupId,
PersonName);
                StatusText = $"Added person {PersonName} got ID:
{personId.PersonId.ToString()}";
                GetPersons();
            }
```

The API call to the `CreatePersonAsync` function requires a person-group ID as the first parameter. The next parameter is the name of the person. Optionally, we can add user data as a third parameter. In that case, it should be a string. When a new person has been created, we update the `persons` list by calling the `GetPersons` function again.

If we have selected a person group and a person, we are able to delete that person:

```
        private async void DeletePerson(object obj)
        {
            try
            {
                await _faceServiceClient.DeletePersonAsync
(SelectedPersonGroup.PersonGroupId, SelectedPerson.PersonId);

                StatusText = $"Deleted {SelectedPerson.Name} from
{SelectedPersonGroup.Name}";

                GetPersons();
            }
```

To delete a person, we make a call to the `DeletePersonAsync` function. This requires the person-group ID of the person group the person lives in. It also requires the ID of the person we want to delete. If no exceptions are caught, the call succeeded, and we call the `GetPersons` function to update our person list.

Our administration control now looks similar to the following:

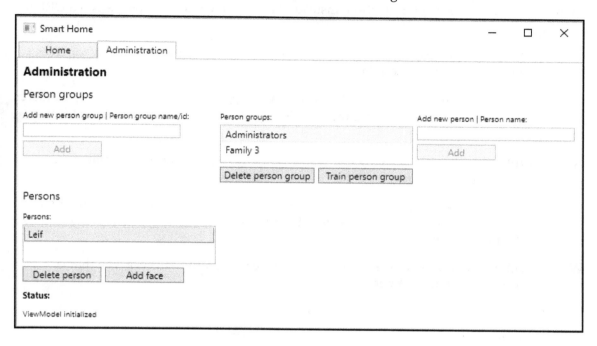

Before we can identify a person, we need to associate faces with that person. With a given person group, and person selected, we can add faces. To do so, we open a file dialog. When we have an image file, we can add the face to the person, as follows:

```
using (StreamimageFile = File.OpenRead(filePath))
{
    AddPersistedFaceResultaddFaceResult = await
_faceServiceClient.AddPersonFaceAsync(
    SelectedPersonGroup.PersonGroupId,
    SelectedPerson.PersonId, imageFile);

    if (addFaceResult != null)
    {
        StatusText = $"Face added for {SelectedPerson.Name}.
Remember to train the person group!";
    }
}
```

We open the image file as a `Stream`. This file is passed on as the third parameter in our call to the `AddPersonFaceAsync` function. Instead of a stream, we could have passed a URL to an image.

The first parameter in the call is the person-group ID of the group where the person lives. The next parameter is the person ID.

Optional parameters are user data, in the form of a string, and a `FaceRectangle` parameter for the image. The `FaceRectangle` parameter is required if there is more than one face in the image.

A successful call will result in an `AddPersistedFaceResult` object. This contains the persisted face ID for the person.

Each person can have a maximum of 248 faces associated. The more faces you can add, the more likely it is that you will receive a solid identification later. Also, you should add faces from slightly different angles.

With enough faces associated, we need to train the person group. This is a task that is required after any change to a person or person group.

We can train a person group when one has been selected:

```
private async void TrainPersonGroup(object obj)
{
    try
    {
        await _faceServiceClient.TrainPersonGroupAsync(
SelectedPersonGroup.PersonGroupId);
```

The call to the `TrainPersonGroupAsync` function takes a person-group ID as a parameter. It does not return anything, and it may take a while to execute:

```
while(true)
{
    TrainingStatustrainingStatus = await
_faceServiceClient.GetPersonGroupTrainingStatusAsync
(SelectedPersonGroup.PersonGroupId);
```

We want to ensure that the training completed successfully. To do so, we call the `GetPersonGroupTrainingStatusAsync` function inside a `while` loop. This call requires a person-group ID, and a successful call results in a `TrainingStatus` object:

```
        if(trainingStatus.Status != Status.Running)
        {
            StatusText = $"Person group finished with status:
{trainingStatus.Status}";
            break;
        }

        StatusText = "Training person group...";
        await Task.Delay(1000);
    }
}
```

We check the status, and we show the result if it is not running. If the training is still running, we wait for one second and run the check again.

When the training has succeeded, we are ready to identify people.

There are a few API calls we have not looked at, which will be mentioned briefly here:

- To update a person group, call the following and the function returns nothing:

```
UpdatePersonGroupAsync(PERSONGROUPID, NEWNAME, USERDATA)
```

- To get a person's face, call the following:

```
GetPersonFaceAsync(PERSONGROUPID, PERSONID, PERSISTEDFACEID)
```

A successful call returns the persisted face ID and user-provided data.

- To delete a person's face, call the following; this call does not return anything:

```
DeletePersonFaceAsync(PERSONGROUPID, PERSONID, PERSISTEDFACeID)
```

- To update a person, call the following; this call does not return anything:

```
UpdatePersonAsync(PERSONGROUPID, PERSONID, NEWNAME, USERDATA)
```

- To update a person's face, call the following; this call does not return anything:

```
UpdatePersonFaceAsync(PERSONGROUID, PERSONID, PERSISTEDFACEID,
USERDATA)
```

Identifying a person

To identify a person, we are going to do so by uploading an image. Open the `HomeView.xaml` file and add a `ListBox` element to the UI. This will contain the person groups to choose from when identifying a person. We will need to add a button element to find an image, upload it, and identify the person. A `TextBox` element is added to show the working response. For our own convenience, we also add an image element to show the image we are using.

In the View model, add an `ObservableCollection` property of the `PersonGroup` type. We need to add a property for the selected `PersonGroup` type. Also, add a `BitmapImage` property for our image, and a string property for the response. We will also need an `ICommand` property for our button.

Add a private variable for the `FaceServiceClient` type, as follows:

```
private FaceServiceClient _faceServiceClient;
```

This will be assigned in our constructor, which should accept a parameter of the `FaceServiceClient` type. From the constructor, call on the `Initialize` function to initialize everything:

```
private void Initialize()
{
    GetPersonGroups();
    UploadOwnerImageCommand = new
DelegateCommand(UploadOwnerImage, CanUploadOwnerImage);
}
```

First we call the `GetPersonGroups` function to retrieve all the person groups. This function makes a call to the `ListPersonGroupsAsync` API, which we saw earlier. The result is added to our `PersonGroup` list's `ObservableCollection` parameter.

Next we create our `ICommand` object. The `CanUploadOwnerImage` function will return `true` if we have selected an item from the `PersonGroup` list. If we have not, it will return `false`, and we will not be able to identify anyone.

In the `UploadOwnerImage` function, we first browse to an image and then load it. With an image loaded and a file path available, we can start to identify the person in the image:

```
using (StreamimageFile = File.OpenRead(filePath))
{
    Face[] faces = await _faceServiceClient.DetectAsync(imageFile);
    Guid[] faceIds = faces.Select(face =>face.FaceId).ToArray();
```

We open the image as a `Stream` type. Using this, we detect faces in the image. From the detected faces, we get all the face IDs in an array:

```
IdentifyResult[] personsIdentified = await
_faceServiceClient.IdentifyAsync (SelectedPersonGroup.PersonGroupId,
faceIds, 1);
```

The array of face IDs will be sent as the second parameter to the `IdentifyAsync` API call. Remember that when we detect a face, it is stored for 24 hours. Proceeding to use the corresponding face ID will make sure the service knows which face to use for identification.

The first parameter used is the ID of the person group we have selected. The last parameter in the call is the number of candidates returned. As we do not want to identify more than one person at a time, we specify one. Because of this, we should ensure that there is only one face in the image we upload.

A successful API call will result in an array of the `IdentifyResult` parameter. Each item in this array contains candidates:

```
foreach(IdentifyResultpersonIdentified in personsIdentified) {
    if(personIdentified.Candidates.Length == 0) {
        SystemResponse = "Failed to identify you.";
        break;
    }
    GuidpersonId = personIdentified.Candidates[0].PersonId;
```

We loop through the array of results. If we do not have any candidates, we just break out of the loop. If, however, we do have candidates, we get the `PersonId` parameter of the first candidate (we asked for only one candidate earlier, so this is okay):

```
    Person person = await faceServiceClient.GetPersonAsync(
SelectedPersonGroup.PersonGroupId, personId);

    if(person != null) {
        SystemResponse = $"Welcome home, {person.Name}";
        break;
    }
  }
}
```

With the `personId` parameter, we get a single `Person` object, using the API call the `GetPersonAsync` function. If the call is successful, we print a welcome message to the correct person and break out of the loop:

Automatically moderating user content

Using the **Content Moderator** API, we can add monitoring to user-generated content. The API is created to assist with flags and to assess and filter offensive and unwanted content.

The content to moderate

We will quickly go through the key features of the moderation APIs in this section.

 A reference to the documentation for all APIs can be found at https://docs.microsoft.com/nb-no/azure/cognitive-services/content-moderator/api-reference.

Image moderation

The **Image Moderation** API allows you to moderate images for adult and racy content. It can also extract textual content and detect faces in images.

When using the API to evaluate adult and racy content, the API will take an image as input. Based on the image, it will return a Boolean value, indicating if the image is either adult or racy. It will also contain a corresponding confidence score between 0 and 1. The Boolean value is set based on a set of default thresholds.

If the image contains any text, the API will use OCR to extract the text. It will then detect the same information, as text moderation, which we will get to shortly.

Some content-based applications may not want to display any personally identifiable information, in which case it can be wise to detect faces in images. Based on the information retrieved in the face-detection evaluation, you can ensure that no user content contains images of people.

Text moderation

Using the Text Moderation API, you can screen text against custom and shared lists of text. It is able to detect personally identifiable information and profanity in text. In this case, personally identifiable information is the presence of information such as email, phone, and mailing address.

When you submit a text to be moderated, the API can detect the language used, if not stated. Screening text will automatically correct any misspelled words (to catch deliberately misspelled words). The results will contain the location of profanities in the text and personal identifiable information, as well as the original text, auto-corrected text and language. Using these results, you can moderate content appropriately.

Moderation tools

There are three ways to moderate content, enabled by the Content Moderator:

- **Human moderation**: Using teams and community to manually moderate all content.
- **Automated moderation**: Utilizing machine learning and AI to moderate at scale with no human interaction
- **Hybrid moderation**: A combination of the preceding two, where people typically do reviews on occasion

The common scenario used is the last one. This is where machine learning is used to automate the moderation process, and teams of people can review the moderation. Microsoft have created a review tool to ease this process. This allows you to see through all the items for review in a web browser while using the APIs in your application. We will look into this tool now.

Using the review tool

To get started with the review tool, head over to `https://contentmoderator.cognitive.microsoft.com/`. From here, you can sign in using your Microsoft account. On your first sign in, you will need to register by adding your name to the account. You will then go on to create a *review team*, as shown in the following screenshot:

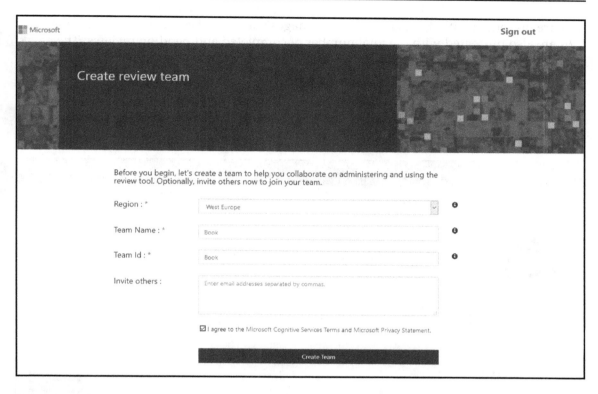

Do so by selecting the region and entering a team name. Optionally, you can enter email addresses of other people who should be a part of the team. Click on **Create Team**.

Once in, you will be presented with the following dashboard:

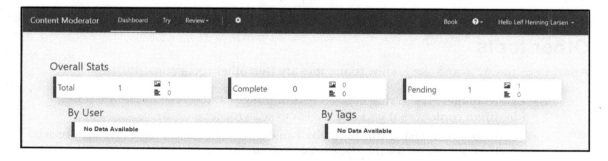

You are presented with the total number of images and textual content that is for review. You are also presented with the total number of completed and pending reviews. The dashboard also lists the users that have completed reviews, and any tags used for content.

By selecting the **Try** option in the menu, you have the option to upload images or text to execute moderation online. Do so by either uploading an image or entering sample text in the textbox. Once done, you can select the **Review** option, where you will be presented with the following:

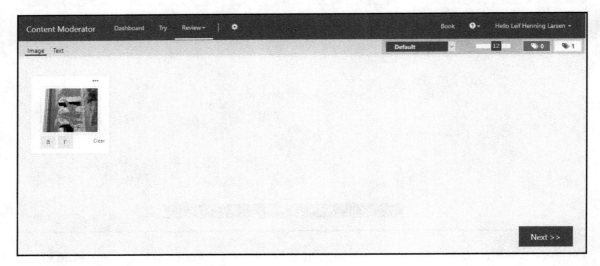

If the given content is either adult content or racist, you can click on the **a** or **r** buttons, respectively. For text, any profanities will be displayed. Once you are done marking reviews, click on **Next**. This will go through a process of moderating the given content.

Other tools

Apart from the APIs and the review tool, there are two other tools you can use:

- **List Manager API**: Using custom lists of images and text to moderate pre-identified content that you don't wish to scan for repeatedly
- **Workflow API**: Using this API, you can define conditional logic and actions to specify the policies used by your specific content

To use any of these APIs, or to use the moderator APIs, you can make calls to specific REST APIs. To do so, you will need to use an API key and a base URL. These settings can be found in **Settings | Credentials** on the review tool website, as shown in the following screenshot:

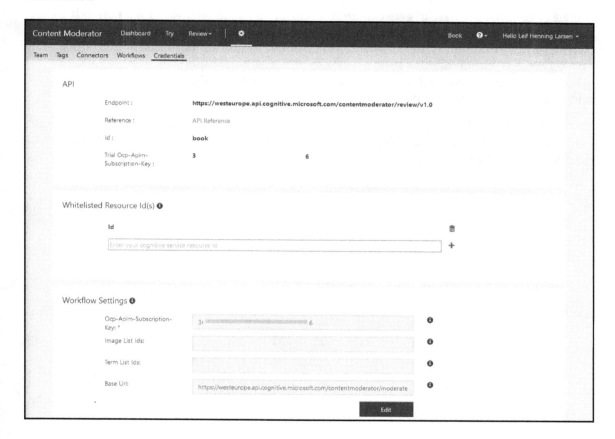

Summary

In this chapter, we took a deep dive into a big part of the Vision APIs. You learned how to get good descriptions of images. Next you learned how to recognize celebrities and text in images. We saw how we can generate thumbnails. Following this, we moved on to the Face API, where we got more information about detected faces. We found out how to verify if two faces were the same. After this, you learned how to find similar faces and group similar faces. Then we added identification to our smart-house application, allowing it to know who we are. Finally, we took a quick look into the Content Moderator to see how you can add automatic moderation to user-generated content.

The next chapter will continue with the final two Vision APIs. You will learn how to detect emotion in images and videos. Moving on from there, we will focus more on videos, discovering what the Video API has to offer.

3
Analyzing Videos

In the previous chapter, we looked into different APIs for processing images. In this chapter, we will cover two new APIs: the Emotion API and the Video API. Working our way through this chapter, we will add emotion recognition to our smart-house application. We will also learn how to detect emotions in videos. Additionally, we will learn how to use the different operations of the Video API.

In this chapter, we will cover the following topics:

- Recognizing emotions in images
- Retrieving an aggregated summary of emotion from videos
- Stabilizing and smoothing shaky videos
- Detecting and tracking faces in videos
- Detecting motion in videos with a stationary background
- Automatically generating video thumbnail summaries

Knowing your mood using the Emotion API

The Emotion API allows you to recognize emotions from faces, both in images and in videos.

Research has shown that there are some key emotions that can be classified as cross-cultural. These are happiness, sadness, surprise, anger, fear, contempt, disgust, and neutral. All of these are detected by the API, which allows your applications to respond in a more personalized way, by knowing the user's mood.

We will learn how to recognize emotions from images first, so our smart-house application can know our mood.

Getting images from a web camera

Imagine that there are several cameras around your house. The smart-house application can see how your mood is at any time. By knowing this, it can utilize the mood to better predict your needs.

We are going to add web-camera capabilities to our application. In case you do not have a web camera, you can follow along, but load images using the techniques we have already seen.

First we need to add a NuGet package to our smart-house application. Search for OpenCvSharp3-AnyCPU and install the package by **shimat**. This is a package that allows for the processing of images and is utilized by the next dependency we are going to add.

In the example code provided, there is a project called VideoFrameAnalyzer. This is a project written by Microsoft, which allows us to grab frame-by-frame images from a web camera. Using this, we are able to analyze emotions in our application. The use case we will execute is as follows:

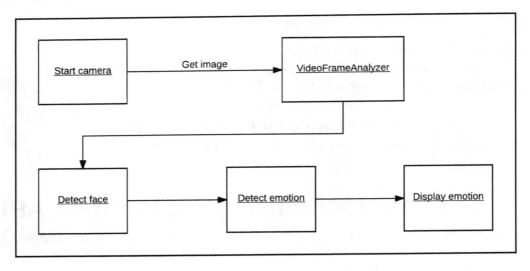

In our HomeView.xaml file, add two new buttons. One will be to start the web camera, while the other will be to stop it.

In the corresponding view model, add two `ICommand` properties for each of the buttons. Also add the following private members:

```
private FrameGrabber<CameraResult> _frameGrabber;
private static readonly ImageEncodingParam[] s_jpegParams = {
    new ImageEncodingParam(ImwriteFlags.JpegQuality, 60)
};
```

The first one is a `FrameGrabber` object, which is from the `VideoFrameAnalyzer` project. The static member is an array of parameters for images and is used when fetching web camera images. Additionally, we need to add a `CameraResult` class, which should be internal within the view model file:

```
internal class CameraResult {
    public EmotionScores[] EmotionScores { get; set; } = null;
}
```

We initialize the array of `EmotionScores` to null. This is done as we always will get the emotion scores assigned from the analysis result.

Add initialization of the `_frameGrabber` member in the constructor and add the following in the `Initialization` function:

```
_frameGrabber.NewFrameProvided += OnNewFrameProvided;
```

Each time a new frame is provided, from the camera, an event is raised:

```
private void OnNewFrameProvided(object sender,
FrameGrabber<CameraResult>.NewFrameEventArgs e) {
    Application.Current.Dispatcher.Invoke(() => {
        BitmapSource bitmapSource = e.Frame.Image.ToBitmapSource();

        JpegBitmapEncoder encoder = new JpegBitmapEncoder();
        MemoryStream memoryStream = new MemoryStream();
        BitmapImage image = new BitmapImage();
```

When we receive new frames, we want to create a `BitmapImage` from it to show it in the UI. To do so requires us to invoke the action from the current dispatcher, as the event is triggered from a background thread.

We get the `BitmapSource` of the `Frame` and create some needed variables, as follows:

```
encoder.Frames.Add(BitmapFrame.Create(bitmapSource));
encoder.Save(memoryStream);
```

Using the *encoder* we created, we add the `bitmapSource` and save it to the `memoryStream`, as follows:

```
memoryStream.Position = 0;
image.BeginInit();
image.CacheOption = BitmapCacheOption.OnLoad;
image.StreamSource = memoryStream;
image.EndInit();

memoryStream.Close();
ImageSource = image;
```

This `memoryStream` is then assigned to the `BitmapImage` we created. This is in turn assigned to the `ImageSource`, which will show the frame in the UI.

As this event will be triggered a lot, we will get a fluent stream in the UI, and it will seem like it is a direct video feed.

In our `Initialization` function, we will also need to create our `ICommand` for the buttons, as follows:

```
StopCameraCommand = new DelegateCommand(StopCamera);
StartCameraCommand = new DelegateCommand(StartCamera, CanStartCamera);
```

To be able to start the camera, we need to have selected a person group, and we need to have at least one camera available:

```
private bool CanStartCamera(object obj) {
    return _frameGrabber.GetNumCameras() > 0 && SelectedPersonGroup !=
null;
}
```

To start a camera, we need to specify which camera to use, and how often we want to trigger an analysis:

```
private async void StartCamera(object obj) {
    _frameGrabber.TriggerAnalysisOnInterval
(TimeSpan.FromSeconds(5));
    await _frameGrabber.StartProcessingCameraAsync();
}
```

If no camera is specified in `StartProcessingCameraAsync`, the first one available is chosen by default.

We will get back to the analysis part soon.

To stop the camera, we run the following command:

```
private async void StopCamera(object obj) {
    await _frameGrabber.StopProcessingAsync();
}
```

Letting the smart-house know your mood

We now have a video from the web camera available for our use. To be able to analyze emotions from it, we first need to add the Emotion API NuGet client package. Find and install the `Microsoft.ProjectOxford.Emotion` NuGet client package to the application.

 If you have not already done so, sign up for an API key for the Emotion API here: `https://portal.azure.com`.

Next we want to add a new private member, which will be used to access the API features:

```
private EmotionServiceClient _emotionServiceClient;
```

This should be assigned in the constructor. As with the `FaceServiceClient`, we create a new object of this type in the `MainViewModel.cs` and pass it in through the constructor.

In the `FrameGrabber` class, there is a `Func`, which will be used for analysis functions. We need to create the function that will be passed on this, where the emotions will be recognized.

Create a new function, `EmotionAnalysisAsync`, accepting a `VideoFrame` as a parameter. The return type should be `Task<CameraResult>`, and the function should be marked as `async`:

```
private async Task<CameraResult> EmotionAnalysisAsync (VideoFrame
frame) {
        MemoryStream jpg = frame.Image.ToMemoryStream(".jpg",
s_jpegParams);
        try {
            Emotion[] emotions = await
_emotionServiceClient.RecognizeAsync(jpg);
```

The `frame` we get as a parameter is used to create a `MemoryStream` containing the current frame. This will be in the JPG file format and will be passed on to the `RecognizeAsync` API function.

There are three overloads for `RecognizeAsync`. Instead of specifying a stream, we can pass on a URL. For both the stream and the URL, we can pass on a `FaceRectangle` as the second parameter. This will guide the service, as to which face to use. Adding the `FaceRectangle` parameter will require you to call `DetectAsync` from the Face API first.

Calling `RecognizeAsync` will, if successful, return an array of the `Emotion` type. Each item contains the `FaceRectangle` parameter and the current scores of each emotion. The scores are what we want to return:

```
return new CameraResult {
    EmotionScores = emotions.Select(e => e.Scores).ToArray()
};
```

Catch any exceptions that may be thrown, and return null in that case.

In our `Initialize` function, we need to assign this function to the `Func`. We also need to add an event handler each time we have a new result:

```
_frameGrabber.NewResultAvailable += OnResultAvailable;
_frameGrabber.AnalysisFunction = EmotionAnalysisAsync;
private void OnResultAvailable(object sender,
FrameGrabber<CameraResult>.NewResultEventArgs e)
{
    var analysisResult = e.Analysis.EmotionScores;
    if (analysisResult == null || analysisResult.Length == 0)
        return;
```

When a new result is in, we grab the `EmotionScore` that is received. If it is null, or does not contain any elements, we do not want to do anything else:

```
string emotion = AnalyseEmotions(analysisResult[0]);

Application.Current.Dispatcher.Invoke(() => {
    SystemResponse = $"You seem to be {emotion} today.";
});
}
```

As we only expect one face in each frame, we select the first emotion score to be parsed. We parse it in `AnalyseEmotions`, which we will look at in a bit.

Using the result from `AnalyseEmotions`, we print a string to the result to indicate the current mood. This will need to be invoked from the current dispatcher, as the event has been triggered in another thread.

To get the current mood in a readable format, we parse the emotion scores in `AnalyseEmotions` as follows:

```
private string AnalyseEmotions(Scores analysisResult) {
    string emotion = string.Empty;
    var sortedEmotions = analysisResult.ToRankedList();
    string currentEmotion = sortedEmotions.First().Key;
```

With the `Scores` we get, we call a `ToRankedList` function. This will return a list of `KeyValuePair`, containing each emotion, with the corresponding confidence. The first one will be the most likely and so on. We only care about the top one, so we select it.

With the top emotion score selected, we go through a `switch` statement to find the correct emotion. This is returned and printed to the result:

```
switch(currentEmotion)
{
    case "Anger":
        emotion = "angry";
        break;
    case "Contempt":
        emotion = "contempt";
        break;
    case "Disgust":
        emotion = "disgusted";
        break;
    case "Fear":
        emotion = "scared";
        break;
    case "Happiness":
        emotion = "happy";
        break;
    case "Neutral":
        default:
        emotion = "neutral";
        break;
    case "Sadness":
        emotion = "sad";
        break;
    case "Suprise":
```

```
                emotion = "suprised";
                break;
        }
        return emotion;
}
```

The last piece in the puzzle is to make sure the analysis is being executed at a specified interval. In the `StartCamera` function, add the following line, just before calling `StartProcessingCamera`:

```
_frameGrabber.TriggerAnalysisOnInterval(TimeSpan.FromSeconds(5));
```

This will trigger emotion analysis to be called every fifth second.

With a happy smile on my face, the application now knows I am happy and can provide further interaction accordingly. If we compile and run the example, we should get results like those shown in the following screenshots:

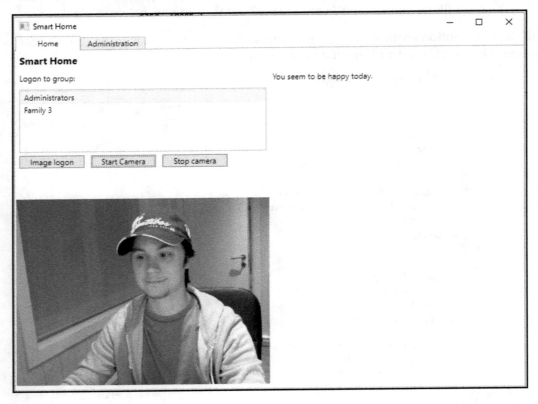

As my mood changes to neutral, the application detects this as well:

Diving into the Video API

The Video API provides advanced algorithms for video processing. Using this API, you can build more personalized and intelligent applications.

There are four main features of this API, which we will look into. They are as follows:

- Face detection and tracking
- Motion detection
- Stabilizing shaky videos
- Generating intelligent video thumbnails

 If you have not already done so, register for an API key for the Video API at `https://azure.microsoft.com/en-us/try/cognitive-services/`. Click on **Get API Key** next to the Video API.

Microsoft has created a NuGet package, containing the Video API, which allows us to utilize all the features available. Let us start by creating a new project in Visual Studio, based off our MVVM template.

In the newly created project, add `Microsoft.ProjectOxford.Video` through the NuGet Package Manager.

As this example project will have a lot of common functionality, we just need one View. The example code provided has added a View, `VideoView.xaml`, to the `View` folder, and a corresponding view model. You can, however, just use the `MainView.xaml`, if that is what you prefer.

Split the View into two columns, adding a `StackPanel` in each. The left one should have a button for browsing video files. It should have a `ComboBox` element for selecting video operations. Additionally, it should have a button for executing the selected operation, and a `MediaElement` for showing the selected video.

The right-hand `StackPanel` should have a `TextBox` element to show the status and textual responses. It should also have a `MediaElement` to be able to show resulting videos.

The corresponding view model should have two `Uri` properties as the source for each `MediaElement`. It should have a `string` property for the textual result. It will need an `IEnumerable` property, returning the values from an `enum`, which we will define in a bit, and also the selected video operation to execute. Last but not least, it will need two `ICommand` properties for each of our buttons.

In the `Interface` folder, add a new file called `AvailableOperations.cs`. Add the following content to it:

```
namespace Chapter3.Interface
{
    public enum AvailableOperations
    {
        FaceDetection,
        MotionDetection,
        Stabilization,
        Thumbnail
    }
}
```

Here we define an `enum` type variable called `AvailableOperations`. This holds all the video operations we can execute, which are face detection, motion detection, video stabilization, and video thumbnail generation.

Back in the view model, the `IEnumerable` variable we defined should return the values from `AvailableOperations`:

```
public IEnumerable<AvailableOperations> VideoOperations {
    get {
        return Enum.GetValues(typeof(AvailableOperations))
.Cast<AvailableOperations>();
    }
}
```

Create a new file called `VideoOperations.cs` in the `Model` folder. We will come back to this later. For now, all you need to know is that this is where we gather all API calls.

The ViewModel should define three private members as follows:

```
private string _videoExtension = ".mp4";
private string _filePath;
private VideoOperations _videoOperations;
```

The first is a string, containing the file format of the input video. You will see why later. The second string just contains the file path of our input video. The last one will allow us to call various video operations.

Depending on whether or not you have created a new View and ViewModel, the constructor of the view model may be a bit different. In the example code, we have a view model separate from the `MainViewModel.cs` file, and as such, we pass on the `VideoOperations` object in the constructor. The constructor then assigns this to the member created earlier and creates the `ICommand` properties, as follows:

```
public VideoViewModel(VideoOperations videoOperations) {
    _videoOperations = videoOperations;

    BrowseVideoCommand = new DelegateCommand(BrowseVideo);
    ExecuteVideoOperationCommand = new
DelegateCommand(ExecuteVideoOperation,
    CanExecuteVideoCommand);
}
```

As we work our way through the rest of the chapter, we will see the command actions for both `BrowseVideoCommand` and `ExecuteVideoOperationCommand`.

Compiling and running this application should present you with something similar to the following:

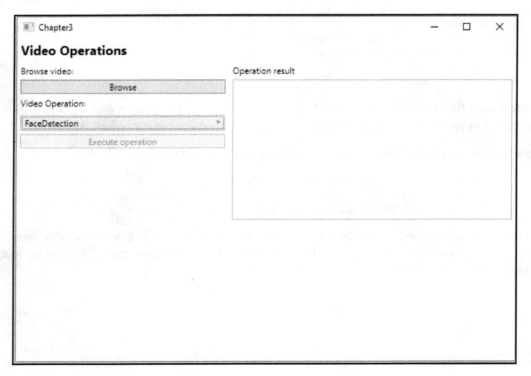

Video operations as common code

Before we dive into the different features of the API, we will write some code that can be used by all four of them. Using the NuGet client package, we are able to use the same function to execute all video operations. The difference lies in which operation type we specify.

Open the `VideoOperations.cs` file and add the following class beneath the `VideoOperations` class:

```
public class VideoOperationStatusEventArgs : EventArgs {
    public string Status { get; private set; }
    public string Message { get; private set; }

    public VideoOperationStatusEventArgs(string status, string message)
{
        Status = status;
        Message = message;
    }
}
```

In case any operation throws an exception or fails, we want to be able to raise an event. The event should contain a `Status`, and a `Message`, explaining the situation.

Back in the `VideoOperations` class, define the following member and event:

```
private VideoServiceClient _videoServiceClient;
public event EventHandler<VideoOperationStatusEventArgs>
OnVideoOperationStatus;
```

The first one is the Video API client object, while the second one is the event, as mentioned previously.

In the constructor, we create a new `VideoServiceClient` object, as follows:

```
public VideoOperations() {
    _videoServiceClient = new VideoServiceClient("API_KEY_HERE");
}
```

When we want to execute a video operation, we need to specify the video-operation settings to use. To do so, we create a function, `CreateVideoOperationSettings`, accepting an `AvailableOperations` object as a parameter. The return type should be of the type `VideoOperationSettings`, which is the base class for all operation settings:

```
    public VideoOperationSettings
  CreateVideoOperationSettings(AvailableOperations operation) {
        VideoOperationSettings videoOperationSettings = null;
        switch (operation) {
```

In the preceding function, we create a local variable, `videoOperationSettings`, which will act as the return object. Based on the `AvailableOperations` object, we assign the `videoOperationSettings` to the correct type, as follows:

```
        case AvailableOperations.FaceDetection:
        videoOperationSettings = new FaceDetectionOperationSettings();
        break;
```

The first case is face detection and/or face tracking. In that case, we need a `FaceDetectionOperationSettings` object. This does not contain any properties to set:

```
        case AvailableOperations.Stabilization:
        videoOperationSettings = new VideoStabilizationOperationSettings();
        break;
```

The next case is for video stabilization. Here we create a new `VideoStabilizationOperationSettings`, which again does not contain any properties to set:

```
        case AvailableOperations.MotionDetection:
        videoOperationSettings = new MotionDetectionOperationSettings()
        {
            DetectLightChange = true,
            FrameSamplingValue = 10,
            MergeTimeThreshold = 10,
            SensitivityLevel = MotionDetectionOperationSettings.
SensitivityLevels.Medium
        };
        break;
```

For motion detection, we create a `MotionDetectionOperationSettings` object, which is a bit more interesting. Here we can specify several values, which are explained in the following table:

Property	Description
DetectLightChange	This specifies whether or not the motion detection should be triggered on a change in light from frame to frame.
FrameSamplingValue	This specifies which frames to be detected. In our case, we want to detect from every 10th frame.
MergeTimeThreshold	This specifies if successive motions should be merged as one.
SensitivityLevel	This specifies the level of sensitivity on a scale of low, medium, and high. Higher sensitivity will cause more false alarms.
DetectionZones	An array of `MotionPolygon`, which allows you to specify certain regions in the video, where motion should be detected.

The last case is for `VideoThumbnailOperationSettings`, which allows us to generate intelligent video thumbnails:

```
case AvailableOperations.Thumbnail:
videoOperationSettings = new VideoThumbnailOperationSettings()
{
    FadeInFadeOut = true,
    MaxMotionThumbnailDurationInSecs = 10,
    OutputAudio = true,
    OutputType = VideoThumbnailOperationSettings .OutputTypes.Video
};
break;
```

This is again a bit more interesting, as we can specify properties for the object. These are explained in the following table:

Property	Description
FadeInFadeOut	This specifies whether or not to fade in and fade out between different scenes.
MaxMotionThumbnailDurationInSecs	This specifies the maximum length of the thumbnail. If this is not specified, the algorithm defaults to optimized durations.

OutputAudio	This specifies whether or not audio present in the video should be present in the thumbnail.
OutputType	This specifies the output type. Currently, only video is available.

If no valid `AvailableOperations` is put in, we return `null` as the `videoOperationSettings`:

```
        default:
        break;
    }
    return videoOperationSettings;
}
```

With that function created, we will add a helper function to raise the status event:

```
    private void RaiseVideoOperationStatus (VideoOperationStatusEventArgs
args) {
        OnVideoOperationStatus?.Invoke(this, args);
    }
```

All this does is to take in the event arguments `VideoOperationStatusEventArgs`, and fire off the event if someone listens to it.

Next, we add a function that will actually create and execute a video operation. Call it `ExecuteVideoOperations` and let it accept a `Stream` object and a `VideoOperationSettings` object. This function should be `async` and have `Task` as the return type:

```
    public async Task ExecuteVideoOperation(Stream stream,
VideoOperationSettings videoOperationSettings) {
        try {
            Operation operation = await
_videoServiceClient.CreateOperationAsync (stream, videoOperationSettings);
```

In a `try` clause, we call the `CreateOperationAsync` function using the `_videoServiceClient`. This function accepts the `Stream` and `VideoOperationSettings` given in the function arguments. The response from the call is an object of the type `Operation`. This contains the URL, where we can get the operation status.

Executing either API call will result in a 202 status code. This contains a URL for the operation location, which you can use to query the operation status.

The CreateOperationAsync function does come with two overloads. One accepts a string for the URL of a video online. The other contains a byte array of the video. No matter which function you call, the following code applies:

```
if (operation == null) {
        RaiseVideoOperationStatus(new
VideoOperationStatusEventArgs("Failed", "Failed to create video
operation"));
        return;
    }
    await Task.Run(() => GetVideoOperationResultAsync(operation));
}
```

If the resulting operation object is null, we raise the status event, as the operation failed. We also do not bother to do anything more in the function, as it would be pointless.

If the API call succeeds, we start a new thread, which will check the operation status. We specify the operation object as a parameter, as we will need the URL it provides.

Before we look at it, make sure you catch any exceptions and raise the status event in that case.

Getting operation results

Before we check the operation status, we want to add a new EventArgs class. Add the following at the bottom of the file:

```
public class VideoOperationResultEventArgs : EventArgs {
    public string Status { get; set; }
    public string Message { get; set; }
    public string ProcessingResult { get; set; }
    public string ResourceLocation { get; set; }
}
```

This class will contain a status, a message, and either the processing result or the resource location. We will learn more about the latter two as we progress.

Additionally, we want to add another event to the `VideoOperations` class, as follows:

```
public event EventHandler<VideoOperationResultEventArgs>
OnVideoOperationCompleted;
```

Add a helper function to raise this event, as follows:

```
private void RaiseVideoOperationCompleted
(VideoOperationResultEventArgs args) {
    OnVideoOperationCompleted?.Invoke(this, args);
}
```

This will accept the newly created `VideoOperationResultEventArgs` as an argument and raise the event if anyone listens to it.

Now let us create the `GetVideoOperationResultAsync` function. This is the function we saw earlier, being started in its own thread:

```
private async void GetVideoOperationResultAsync (Operation
videoOperation)
    {
        try
        {
            while(true)
            {
                OperationResult operationResult = await
_videoServiceClient.GetOperationResultAsync (videoOperation);
```

This function must be marked as `async`, and it accepts an object of the type `Operation`. We start a `while` loop, which will run until we break out of it.

The first thing we do in this loop is to request the operation status, calling `GetOperationResultAsync`, specifying the `videoOperation`. This call will result in a `OperationResult` object, containing data such as creation and last action time, status message, operation status, processing result, and resource location:

```
bool isCompleted = false;
switch(operationResult.Status)
{
    case OperationStatus.Failed:RaiseVideoOperationStatus(new
VideoOperationStatusEventArgs("Failed", $"Video operation failed:
{operationResult.Message}"));
    isCompleted = true;
    break;
```

Using the `Status` field in the `operationResult` object, we can check the status using a `switch` statement. If the status is `Failed`, we raise a status event, specifying the reason for failure. In that case, we will set a `bool`, `IsCompleted`, to `true` so that we can break out of the `while` loop.

If the status is `NotStarted`, `Uploading`, or `Running`, we raise an event, stating as such. We also define the latter to be the `default` state. None of these states will break out of the `while` loop:

```
    case OperationStatus.NotStarted: RaiseVideoOperationStatus(new
VideoOperationStatusEventArgs("Not started", "Video operation has not
started yet"));
        break;

    case OperationStatus.Running: default: RaiseVideoOperationStatus(new
VideoOperationStatusEventArgs("Running", "Video operation is running"));
        break;

    case OperationStatus.Uploading: RaiseVideoOperationStatus(new
VideoOperationStatusEventArgs("Uploading", "Video is uploading"));
        break;
```

If the status is `Succeeded`, we raise the completed video-operation event. We make sure to specify the processing result and resource location, as follows:

```
    case OperationStatus.Succeeded: RaiseVideoOperationCompleted (new
VideoOperationResultEventArgs
    {
        Status = "Succeeded",
        Message = "Video operation completed successfully",
        ProcessingResult = operationResult.ProcessingResult,
        ResourceLocation = operationResult.ResourceLocation,
    });
    isCompleted = true;
    break;
```

If we are executing face detection/tracking or motion detection operations, the processing result will contain data. This will, in these cases, be JSON data in a string format.

If we are executing stabilization or generate-thumbnail operations, the resource location will contain data. In these cases, this will contain a link to the resulting videos.

When we come out of the `switch` statement, we check to see if the operation has completed. If it has, we break out of the `while` loop. If it has not, we wait for 20 seconds before we try again:

```
            if (isCompleted)
                break;
            else
                await Task.Delay(TimeSpan.FromSeconds(20));
        }
    }
```

There are a couple of reasons why we wait for 20 seconds. The first is that we are currently using the preview version. The API key for this only allows five calls to `GetOperationResultAsync` every minute. The second reason is that video processing is naturally going to take a while. Therefore, there is no point in spamming the service, checking if the operation has completed.

Make sure you catch any exceptions before moving on. Raise a status event, specifying the exception, if any is caught.

The last function we want to add in the `VideoOperations` class is one to retrieve resulting videos. Call this function `GetResultVideoAsync` and let it accept a `string` as a parameter. This will be the video URL. The function should return a `Task<Stream>` object and should be marked as `async`:

```
        public async Task<Stream> GetResultVideoAsync(string url) {
            try {
                Stream resultStream = await
    _videoServiceClient.GetResultVideoAsync(url);
                return resultStream;
            }
```

In this function, we make a call to `GetResultVideoAsync`, specifying `url` as an argument. A successful call will result in a `Stream` object, containing the resulting video. This is then returned to the caller. If any exception is thrown, we catch it and return null.

All the API calls we have made can result in different errors. These are described in the following table:

Code	Description
400	This can be `InvalidVideoSize` or `BadArgument`. The first means the video is too small or too big. The latter means the JSON request failed to serialize.
401	Unauthorized. The subscription key is invalid.
403	`QuotaLimitExceeded`. The volume quote has been exceeded.
415	Content type is wrong. This should not occur using the NuGet client package.
429	`RateLimitExceeded`. The rate limit has been exceeded, so wait a bit before trying again.

Wiring up the execution in the ViewModel

With the `VideoOperations` class completed, it is time to wire up the actions in our ViewModel.

Earlier, we created the `ICommand` objects. Let us start by looking at the `BrowseVideo` function:

```
private void BrowseVideo(object obj)
{
    Microsoft.Win32.OpenFileDialog openDialog = new
Microsoft.Win32.OpenFileDialog();
    openDialog.Filter = "Video files (*.mp4, *.mov,
*.wmv)|*.mp4;*.mov;*.wmv";

    bool? result = openDialog.ShowDialog();
    if (!(bool)result) return;

    _filePath = openDialog.FileName;
    _videoExtension = Path.GetExtension(_filePath);
}
```

None of this code should be new, as we have done the same in previous chapters. We create an `OpenFileDialog`, with only allowed video files filtered. The allowed video files for all operations are .mp4, .mov, and .wmv.

If we have a file selected, we assign the file path to our _filePath member. We also find the file extension and assign it to the _videoExtension member.

The other `ICommand` we have, `ExecuteVideoOperationCommand`, needs to make sure we have selected a file before allowing execution:

```
private bool CanExecuteVideoCommand(object obj) {
    return !string.IsNullOrEmpty(_filePath);
}
```

We do so by simply checking that the `_filePath` member is not null or empty.

To execute a video operation, we have an async function, `ExecuteVideoOperation`:

```
private async void ExecuteVideoOperation(object obj)
{
    VideoOperationSettings operationSettings =
_videoOperations.CreateVideoOperationSettings (SelectedVideoOperation);
```

The first thing we want to do is create `VideoOperationSettings`. We do so by calling `CreateVideoOperationSettings` created earlier, specifying the `SelectedVideoOperation`:

```
using (FileStream originalVideo = new FileStream (_filePath,
FileMode.Open, FileAccess.Read))
    {
        if (operationSettings == null) return;
        await _videoOperations.ExecuteVideoOperation (originalVideo,
operationSettings);
    }
```

With the video-operation settings created, we create a new `FileStream` from our video. If the stream is null, we leave the function.

If the stream has data, we call the `ExecuteVideoOperation`. We pass on the video stream and the operation settings:

```
VideoSource = new Uri(_filePath);
    }
```

To end the function, we want to update the `VideoSource` property, with the `_filePath`. This sets the source of the `MediaElement` in the view and plays the videos.

Before we can test anything, we need to hook onto the events in the `VideoOperations` class. Add the following in the constructor, beneath the assignment or creation of `_videoOperations`:

```
_videoOperations.OnVideoOperationCompleted +=
OnVideoOperationCompleted;
    _videoOperations.OnVideoOperationStatus += OnVideoOperationStatus;
```

While we're at it, let's create the `OnVideoOperationStatus`:

```
private void OnVideoOperationStatus(object sender,
VideoOperationStatusEventArgs e)
    {
        Application.Current.Dispatcher.Invoke(() =>
        {
            StringBuilder sb = new StringBuilder();
            sb.AppendFormat("{0}\n", e.Status);
            sb.AppendFormat("{0}\n", e.Message);
            Result = sb.ToString();
        });
    }
```

This is a fairly simple function, which prints the status and status message to the UI. As the event has been raised in a different thread, we need to invoke an action from the current dispatcher.

The other event handler, `OnVideoOperationCompleted`, is similar but has some additional code to it:

```
private async void OnVideoOperationCompleted(object sender,
VideoOperationResultEventArgs e)
    {
        await Application.Current.Dispatcher.Invoke(async () =>
        {
            StringBuilder sb = new StringBuilder();
            sb.AppendFormat("{0}\n", e.Status);
            sb.AppendFormat("{0}\n", e.Message);
```

Again, we need to invoke an action on the current dispatcher. Doing so, we want to add the status and the message to the resulting view.

Moving on, we check to see if we have data in the `ProcessingResult` field. If we have, we format the string as JSON and print it to the resulting View. The `JsonFormatter` is a class you can find in the `Model` folder in the example project:

```
if (!string.IsNullOrEmpty(e.ProcessingResult))
    {
        sb.Append("Results: \n");
        sb.AppendFormat("{0}\n",
        JsonFormatter.FormatJson(e.ProcessingResult));
    }
```

Next, we check to see if we have a resulting video, using the `ResourceLocation`. If we have, we print out the URL to the resulting view and call the `GetResultVideoAsync` to get the video. If we do not have a video, we leave the function:

```
if (!string.IsNullOrEmpty(e.ResourceLocation))
{
    sb.AppendFormat("Video can be fetched at: {0}\n",
e.ResourceLocation);
    Stream resultVideo = await
    _videoOperations.GetResultVideoAsync(e.ResourceLocation);
    if (resultVideo == null) return;
```

If we have a result video, we generate a new temporary file, which we open as a `FileStream`. Using the `resultVideo` stream, we write to the temporary file, which will be of the same format as the original video file:

```
string tempFilePath = Path.GetTempFileName() + _videoExtension;
using (FileStream stream = new FileStream(tempFilePath,
FileMode.Create))
    {
        byte[] b = new byte[2048];
        int lenght = 0;
        while((lenght = await resultVideo.ReadAsync(b, 0, b.Length)) >
0) {
            await stream.WriteAsync(b, 0, lenght);
        }
    }
```

When we have written to the temporary file, we create a new `Uri` and assign this to the `ResultVideoSource`. This will make the resulting video, `MediaElement`, play the resulting video, in the right `StackPanel`. We also make sure that all resulting text is printed to the UI before we close the video:

```
    Uri fileUri = new Uri(tempFilePath);
    ResultVideoSource = fileUri;
    }
    Result = sb.ToString();
});
```

When testing with videos the following bullet points describes a few considerations you need to make in regard to video files:

- They cannot be larger than 100 MB
- They must be either MP4, MOV, or WMV
- The resolution should be less than or equal to 4K
- Detectable faces are in the range of 24x24 to 2,048x2,048 pixels
- The maximum number of detectable faces per video is 64

A test run with a resulting video will look something like the following screenshots:

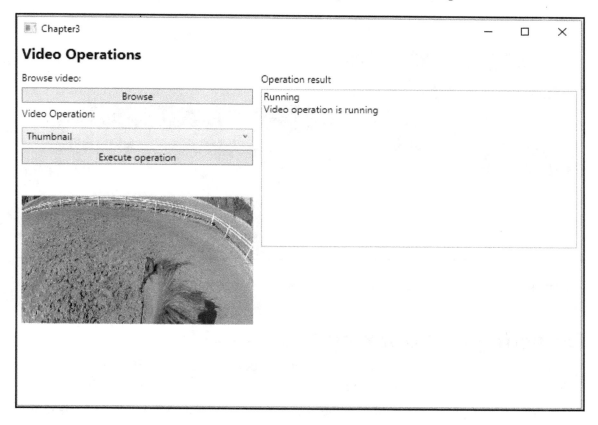

When a video has been uploaded, the processing is running:

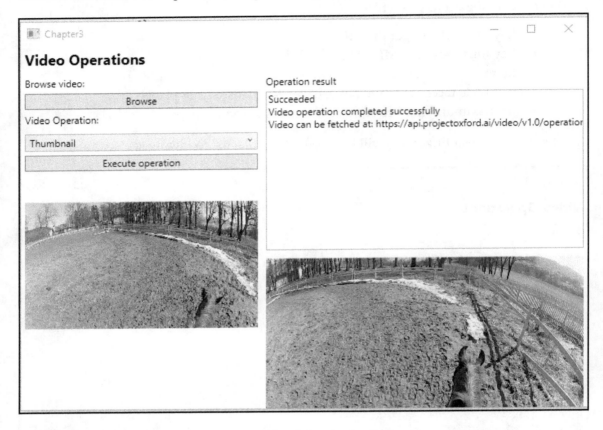

All resulting videos and output files will be deleted after 24 hours.

Detecting and tracking faces in videos

When detecting and tracking faces, you will get a response containing JSON data. This will consist of faces detected, the times they have been detected, and where in each frame.

Frontal and near-frontal faces will give the best result, while large face angles may be more challenging to detect.

The result will look as follows:

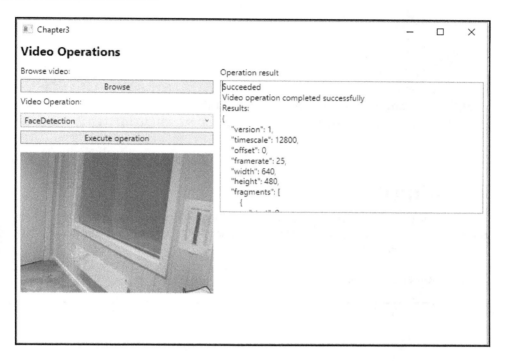

The basics of the JSON returned are as follows:

```
{
    "version": 1,
    "timescale": 12800,
    "offset": 0,
    "framerate": 25,
    "width": 640,
    "height": 480,
    "fragments": [{
        "start": 0,
        "duration": 48640
    }, {
        "start": 48640,
        "duration": 25600,
        "interval": 512,
        "events": [[{
            "id": 0,
            "x": 0,
            "y": 0.14375,
            "width": 0.16875,
```

```
                    "height": 0.225
                }],
            },],
            "facesDetected": [{
            "faceId": 0
        }]
    }
```

From the JSON, you can see the faces detected, with `faceId`. Each face will have a position in the video, per event, and width and height. This allows you to map each face with a rectangle.

Detecting motion

When detecting motion in a video, the response will contain the frame and duration of the motion that was detected. If motion is detected in several places in the video, the result will specify each region of detection.

The result will look as follows:

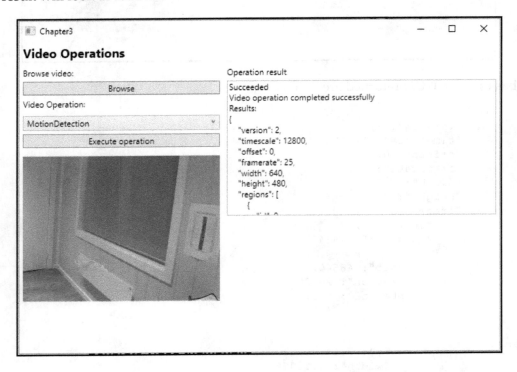

The basics of the JSON returned are as follows:

```
{
    "version": 2,
    "timescale": 12800,
    "offset": 0,
    "framerate": 25,
    "width": 640,
    "height": 480,
    "regions": [
        "id": 0,
        "type": "polygon",
        "points": [
        {
            "x": 0.000000,
            "y": 0.000000
        },},
        "fragments": [{
        "start": 0,
        "duration": 143360
},{
        "start": 143360,
        "duration": 20992,
        "interval": 512,
        "events": [
            "type": 2,
            "typeName": "motion",
            "locations": [{
                "x": 0.004184,
                "y": 0.525140,
                "width": 0.558333,
                "height": 0.350000
            }],
            "regionId": 0
        }],
    }
}
```

In the preceding code, you can clearly see you get defined regions of movement. You can also find the start of movements, the location of the movement in the video, and which region each movement is in.

Stabilizing shaky videos

Stabilizing shaky videos requires the width and height of the video to be even numbers. It is optimized for small camera motions, such as holding a static camera and walking at a slow speed.

The results of this operation will not contain any JSON data, as you will get a resulting video as the response.

Generating video thumbnails

Generating video thumbnails will not result in any JSON data. The result will be a video, where the duration is either set as a parameter in `VideoThumbnailOperationSettings` or selected by default.

The processing algorithm defines the following as optimal thumbnail durations:

Video duration	< 3 min	3 min - 15 min	15 min - 30 min	> 30 min
Thumbnail duration	15 sec	30 sec	60 sec	90 sec

Analyzing emotions in videos

Earlier, we looked at analyzing emotions in images. We can do the same analysis with videos as well.

To be able to do this, we can modify the existing example for the Video API.

Start by adding `Microsoft.ProjectOxford.Emotion` as a NuGet client package.

Next we add `Emotion` to the `AvailableOperations` enum. In the `VideoOperations` class, add a new case for this value in `CreateVideoOperationSettings`. Return null, as we do not need any video-operation settings for this.

Add a private member to `VideoOperations`:

```
private EmotionServiceClient _emotionServiceClient;
```

Initialize this in the constructor, using the API key you registered earlier.

In the `VideoOperationResultEventArgs`, add a new property called `EmotionResult`. This should be of the type `VideoAggregateRecognitionResult`.

Back in the `VideoOperations` class, copy the `GetVideoOperationResultAsync` function. Rename it to `GetVideoEmotionResultAsync` and change the accepted parameter to `VideoEmotionRecognitionOperation`. Inside the function, you need to change the first line in the `while` loop to the following:

```
var operationResult = await
_emotionServiceClient.GetOperationResultAsync(videoOperation);
```

This will get the current operation status, like we saw for the Video API calls.

Change the `Succeeded` case to the following:

```
case VideoOperationStatus.Succeeded:
    var result = operationResult as
VideoOperationInfoResult<VideoAggregateRecognitionResult>;
    RaiseVideoOperationCompleted(new VideoOperationResultEventArgs
    {
        Status = "Succeeded",
        Message = "Video operation completed successfully",
        EmotionResult = result.ProcessingResult,
    });
    isCompleted = true;
    break;
```

As you can see, we cast the `operationResult` into a `VideoOperationInfoResult<VideoAggregateRecognitionResult>` object. This is so we can access the `ProcessingResult`, containing an aggregate of the emotions in the video.

At the time of writing, when using the NuGet API, the result will only be an aggregate of the emotions. If you are calling the REST API directly, you can specify that you want emotions on a per-frame basis.

Before we leave the `VideoOperations` class, let us add a new function, `ExecuteVideoEmotionAnalysis`. Let this accept a `Stream` as a parameter and let the return type be `Task`. Mark the function as `async`:

```
public async Task ExecuteVideoEmotionAnalysis(Stream videoStream) {
    try
    {
        VideoEmotionRecognitionOperation operation = await
_emotionServiceClient.RecognizeInVideoAsync(videoStream);
```

Here we are calling the `RecognizeInVideoAsync` function in the `_emotionServiceClient`. We pass on the `videoStream` containing the video to analyze. As with the functions in the Video API, this also has two overloads: one accepting a URL as a `string` and the other accepting a `byte` array.

The result is a `VideoEmotionRecognitionOperation` object, which we pass on to get the operation status:

```
    if (operation == null) {
        RaiseVideoOperationStatus(new
VideoOperationStatusEventArgs("Failed", "Failed to analyze emotions in
video"));
        return;
    }
    await Task.Run(() => GetVideoEmotionResultAsync(operation));
}
```

Again, we check to see if the operation contains anything. If it does, we start a new thread, querying the operation status.

The final part we need is to modify the `OnVideoOperationCompleted` event handler in the view model.

After the `if`, check for `ResourceLocation` and add a new `if`:

```
if(e.EmotionResult != null) {
    sb.Append("Emotion results:\n");
    foreach(var fragment in e.EmotionResult.Fragments) {
        if (fragment.Events == null) continue;
```

We check to see if we have any emotion results. There is some data in the `EmotionResult`; however, we want to loop through the `Fragments`, where the emotions can be found.

Each fragment contains an `Event`, and we want to access those that are not null:

```
foreach(var aggregate in fragment.Events) {
    if (aggregate == null)
        continue;
```

Each `Event` in turn contains aggregates. We do not care about aggregates that do not exist:

```
foreach(var emotion in aggregate) {
    if (emotion == null)
        continue;
    var emotionScores = emotion.WindowMeanScores.ToRankedList();

    foreach(var score in emotionScores) {
        sb.AppendFormat("Emotion: {0} / Score: {1}\n", score.Key,
score.Value);
    }
}
```

In each aggregate, there is an emotion, containing `WindowMeanScores` for that fragment. We get a ranked list of this data and loop through it to print out the mean scores of all emotions.

The result can look something like the following:

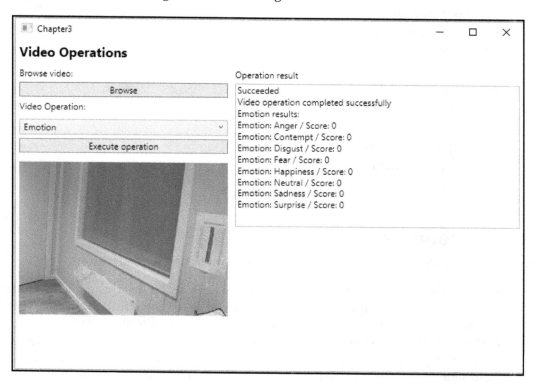

Unlocking video insights using Video Indexer

The Video Indexer is a service that allows you to upload videos and gain insights from the videos. This insight can be used to make the videos (and by extension your content) more discoverable. It can also be used to improve engagement from the users.

General overview

Using artificial intelligence technologies, the Video Indexer enables you to extract a great deal of information. It can gain insights from the following list of features:

- Audio transcript
- Face tracking and identification
- Speaker indexing
- Visual-text recognition
- Voice-activity detection
- Scene detection
- Keyframe extraction
- Sentiment analysis
- Translation
- Visual content moderation
- Keywords extraction
- Annotations

Typical scenarios

There are a few typical scenarios where one might want to use Video Indexer:

- **Search**: If you have a library of videos, you can use the insights gained to index each video. Indexing by spoken words or where two specific people were seen together can provide a much better search experience for the users.
- **Monetization**: The value of each video can be improved by using the insights. For example, you can deliver more relevant ads by using the video insights to present ads that are contextually correct. For instance, by using the insights, you can display ads for sports shoes in the middle of a football match instead of a swimming competition.

- **User engagement**: By using the insights, you can improve the user engagement by displaying relevant video moments. If you have a video covering different material for 60 minutes, placing video moments over that time allows the user to jump straight to the relevant section.

Key concepts

The following topics are key concepts that are important to understand when discussing the Video Indexer.

Breakdowns

This is a complete list with all details of all the insights. This is where a full video transcript comes from; however, it is mostly too detailed for users. Instead, you would want to use summarized insights to gain the interesting knowledge before looking up more details in breakdowns.

Summarized insights

Instead of going through several thousands of time ranges and checking for given data in them, one can use the summarized insights. This will provide you with an aggregated view of data, such as faces, keywords and sentiments, and the time ranges it appears in.

Keywords

From any transcribed audio in the video, Video Indexer will extract a list of keywords and topics that may be relevant to the video.

Sentiments

When a video is transcribed, it is also analyzed for sentiment. This means you can gauge whether or not the video is more positive or negative.

Blocks

Blocks are used to move through the data in an easier manner. If there are changes to speakers or long pauses between audio, these might be indexed as separate blocks.

How to use Video Indexer

We are going to take a quick look at how you can utilize the Video Indexer.

Through a web portal

To use the prebuilt tool from Microsoft, head over to `https://www.videoindexer.ai/`. Log in with your Microsoft account. When you have signed in, you will be asked to register the account by filling out some information, as shown in the following screenshot:

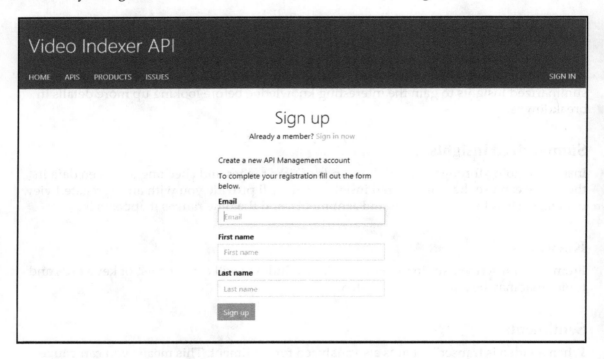

Once you have logged in, you will find yourself at the dashboard, as shown in the following screenshot:

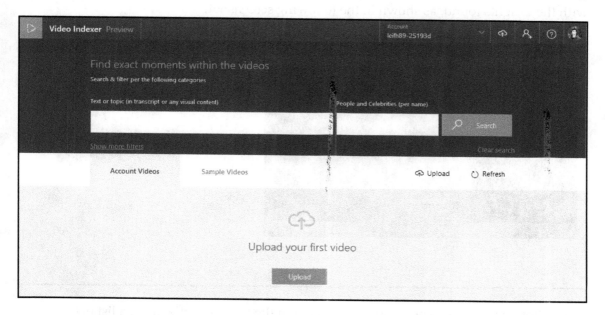

To get started, you can upload your videos by clicking on **Upload**. This will open a popup to either upload a video or enter a URL to a video. Alternatively, you can get started quickly by selecting a sample video by clicking on **Sample Videos** in the menu.

When you have chosen a video, or the video you uploaded has completed its indexing, you will be taken to a page to see the insights. This page will show you the video in full, along with the insights found, as shown in the following screenshot:

In addition to keywords and people discovered in the videos, you will get a list of annotations and sentiment of the speech throughout the video, as shown in the following screenshot:

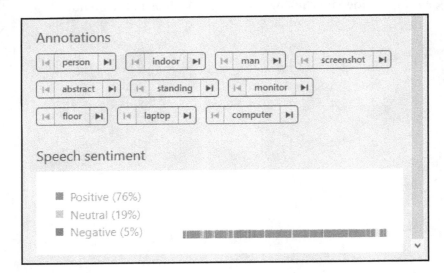

The Video Indexer will also create a transcript of all audio through the video, which you can follow along with by selecting **Transcript** at the top of the insights frame, as shown in the following screenshot:

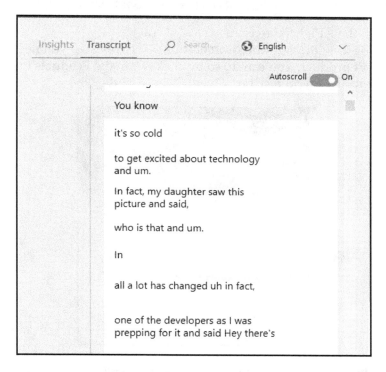

This transcript will automatically move forward as the video moves forward.

Video Indexer API

Apart from the premade Video Indexer site, there is also a Video Indexer API present. This allows you to gain the exact same insights as the web tool from your own application.

To get started with the API, head over to `https://videobreakdown.portal.azure-api.net/`. Once here, log in with your Microsoft account. The first step you need to take is to subscribe to the API product. You can do so by clicking on the **Products** tab, selecting **Production**, and clicking on **Subscribe**:

Once you have subscribed to the product, you will be taken to a page to see the API keys, as shown in the following screenshot. This can always be reached by going to the **Products** tab and selecting the product you subscribe to:

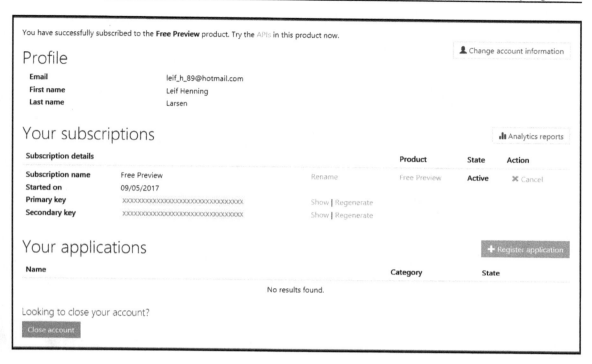

Once you have the key, select the **APIs** tab and select your subscribed product. This will present all the API calls that are available to use. The entire API is REST based, and as such you are able to use it from any application as long as you provide the correct request parameters and API keys.

Summary

Throughout this chapter, we covered the Emotion API and the Video API. We started by making the smart-house application see what kind of mood you are in. Following this, we dived deep into the Video API, where you learned how to detect and track faces, detect motion, stabilize videos, and generate intelligent video thumbnails. Next, we moved back to the Emotion API, where you learned how to do emotion analysis on videos. Finally, we closed the chapter by taking a quick look at the Video Indexer and how it can be used to gain insights from videos.

In the next chapter, we will move away from the Vision APIs and into the first Language API. You will learn how to understand intent in sentences, using the power of LUIS.

4
Letting Applications Understand Commands

"LUIS saved us tremendous time while going from a prototype to production."

- Eyal Yavor, Co-founder and CTO, Meekan

Throughout the previous chapters, we have focused on Vision APIs. Starting with this chapter, we move on to the Language APIs, where we will start with **Language Understanding Intelligent Service (LUIS)**. Throughout this chapter, you will see how to create and maintain language-understanding models. Finally, you will see how to complete actions on the user's behalf.

By the end of this chapter, we will have covered the following topics:

- Creating language-understanding models
- Handling common requests using prebuilt models from Bing and Cortana
- Executing actions based on intent

Creating language-understanding models

Often, we wish that our computer could understand what we want. As we go on with our day-to-day business, we would like to be able to talk to the computer, or mobile phone, using regular sentences. With no help at all, this is hard to do.

Utilizing the power of LUIS, we can now solve this problem. By creating language-understanding models, we allow applications to understand what users want. We can also recognize key data. This is, typically, data you want to be a part of a query or command. If you are asking for the latest news, key data may be the topic you are asking to get the news for.

Registering an account and getting a license key

To get started with LUIS, you should head over to `https://www.luis.ai`. This is where we will set up our application. Click on the **Sign in or create an account** button to get started.

Once inside, we want to make sure we have a subscription key. We can register for one using Microsoft Azure. Open a new tab in the browser and point it to `https://portal.azure.com`. If you do not have an account here, sign up for one. If you do have an account, sign in.

When you are inside the Azure Portal, click on the + sign in the menu on the left-hand side. This will present you with the **Marketplace**. Search for **Language Understanding Intelligent Service**. You should be presented with the screen shown in the following screenshot:

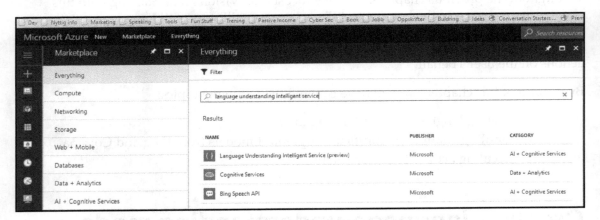

Select the **Language Understanding Intelligent Service (preview)** option. Click on the **Create** button. Enter the required parameters.

There are two price tiers to select from. One is standard, which allows for 10 calls per second. This costs an amount per 1,000 calls. The other one is free and allows for five calls per second and 10,000 calls per month.

When you have created the API account, you can get your subscription keys by clicking on the **Keys** option inside the **RESOURCE MANAGEMENT** category, as shown in the following screenshot:

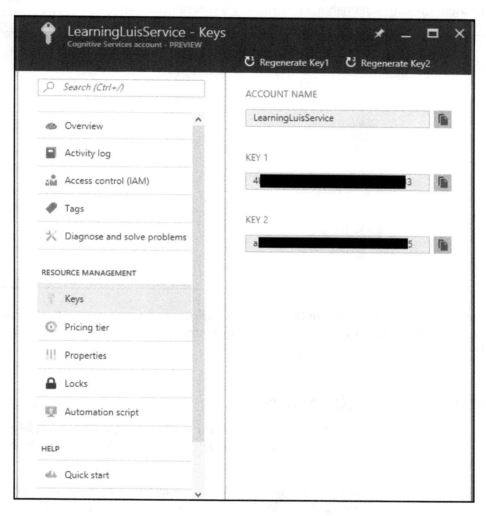

Copy either one of them.

Head back to the LUIS site. Click on the **ACCOUNT NAME** field, in the top-right corner, and go to the user settings. Add the newly created subscription key by selecting the **My Keys** tab. Click on **Add a new key** and paste in the new key into the **Key Value** field, as shown in the following screenshot. Give the key a meaningful name:

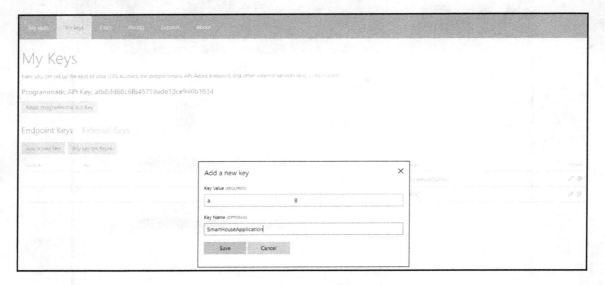

The **Programmatic API Key** seen in the screenshot allows us to programmatically create applications, intents, and entities, as well as train the models. However, we will not cover that in this book.

Creating an application

With the subscription keys in place, we can create our first application. Click on **My Apps** from the top menu. This should take you back to the application list, which should be empty. Click on **New App**.

In the form that is shown, we fill in the given information about our application. We are required to give the application a name. We also need to indicate an atypical usage scenario, which we will be set to be **Other (please specify)**. Specify this to be **SmartHouseApplication**. This application falls under the **Tools** domain, and we choose to use an English **Application Culture**.

Other languages that are available are Brazilian, Portuguese, Chinese, French, German, Italian, Japanese, and Spanish.

The following screenshot shows how we can define the application:

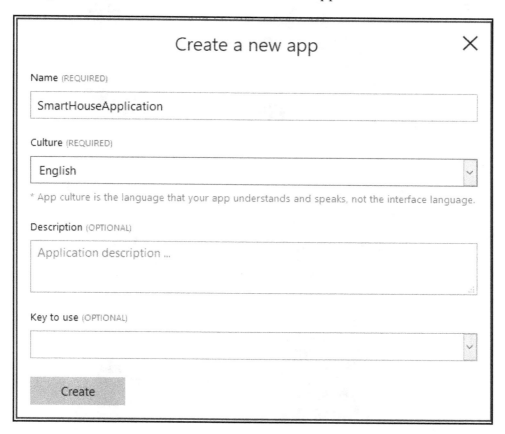

When you click on the **Create** button, the application will be created. This process will take about a minute or so to complete, so just be patient.

When the application has been created, you will be taken to the application's home base, as shown in the following screenshot:

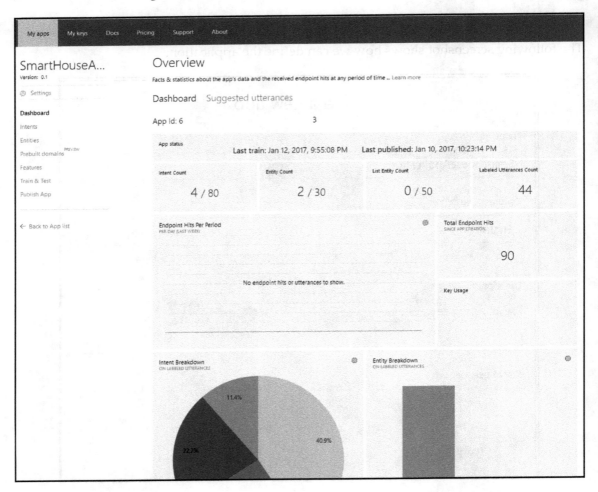

As you can see, we have a variety of features to use, and we will cover the important ones here.

The application we will build will be aimed at our smart house application. We will configure the application to recognize commands to set the temperature in different rooms. In addition, we would like it to tell us what the temperatures in the different rooms are.

Recognizing key data using entities

One of the key features of LUIS is the ability to recognize key data in sentences. This is known as entities. In a news application, an example of an entity would be the topic. If we ask to get the latest news, we could specify a topic for the service to recognize.

For our application, we want to add an entity for rooms. Do so by clicking on the selecting **Entities** in the left-hand pane. Then click on **Add custom entity**.

You will be presented with the following screen:

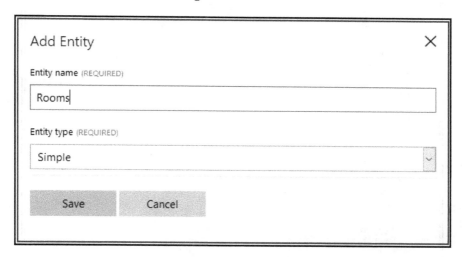

Enter the name of the entity and click on the **Save** button. That's it, you have now created the first entity. We will see how to use this in a bit.

As you may have noticed, there is a drop-down list called **Entity type** in the entity creation form. Entity types are a way to create hierarchical entities, which is basically about defining relationships between entities.

As an example, you can imagine searching for news inside a given timeframe. The generic top-level entity is `Date`. Going from there, you can define two children, **StartDate** and **EndDate**. These will be recognized by the service, where models will be built for the entity and its children.

To add an hierarchical child entity, check the checkbox and select **Hierarchical** from the selection. Click on the + button next to **Entity Children** for each child you want to add, as shown in the following screenshot. Enter the name of the child:

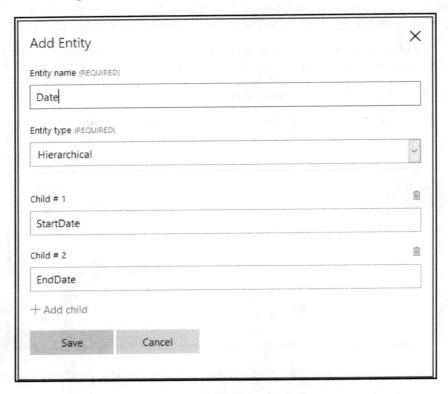

The other types of entities you can add are called **Composite entities**. This is a type of entity that is formed by a set of existing entities. This is what we would call a *has-a* relationship, so the components are children, but not in a parent-child relationship.

Composite entities do not share common traits as hierarchical entities do. When deleting the top-level entity, you do not delete components. Using composite entities, LUIS can identify groups of entities, which are then treated as a single entity.

An example of a composite entity is when you order a pizza. You can order by stating *I want a large pizza with mushrooms and pepperoni*. Here we can see the size as an entity, and we can also see the two toppings as entities. Combining these could make a composite entity, which is called an order.

The last type of entities you can add are called **List Entities**. This is a customized list of entity values to be used as keywords or identifiers within utterances.

When using entities, there may be times where an entity can consist of several words. For our case, with the entity `Rooms`, we may ask for the living room. To be able to identify such phrasings, we can define a feature list. This is a comma-separated list, which can contain some or all of the expected phrases.

Let us add one for our application. On the left-hand side, at the bottom of the pane, you will see **Features**. Select this and click on **Add phrase list** to create a new one. Call it `Rooms` and add different rooms you could expect to find in a house, as shown in the following screenshot:

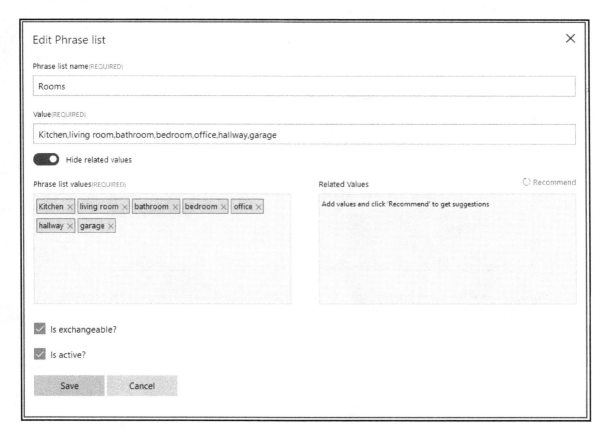

By clicking on **Recommend** on the right-hand side, LUIS will recommend more values related to the ones you have already entered.

We will see how this is utilized later.

In addition to creating phrase lists, we can create **Pattern features**. The typical use case is when you have data that matches patterns but is not feasible to enter as a phrase list. Typically, this can be product numbers.

Understanding what the user wants using intents

Now that we have defined an entity, it is time to see how it fits in with intents. An *intent* is basically the purpose of a sentence.

We can add intents to our application by selecting the **Intents** option in the left-hand pane. Click on **Add intent**. When we add an intent, we want to give it a name. The name should be descriptive of what the intent is. We want to add an intent named GetRoomTemperature, where the goal is to get the temperature of a given room, as shown in the following screenshot:

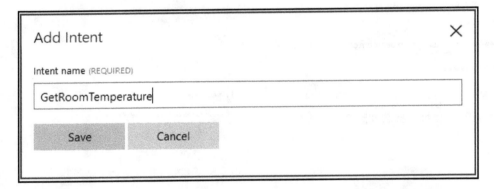

When you click on the **Save** button, you will be taken to the utterance page. Here we can add sentences that we can use for the intent, so let us add one. Enter what is the temperature in the kitchen? and press *Enter*. The sentence (or utterance, as it is called) will be ready for labeling. Labeling an utterance means that we define what intent it belongs to. We also make sure we mark entities with the correct type.

The following screenshot shows the labeling process for our first utterance:

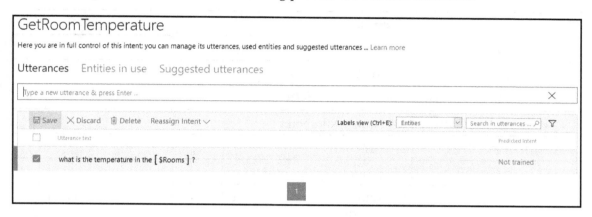

As you can see, the entity is marked. You can tell LUIS that a word is a given entity by holding the mouse over and clicking on the word. This will pop up the menu with all the available entities, and you will then select the correct one. Also, notice how the **GetRoomTemperature** intent is selected in the drop-down list. Click on the **Save** button when you are done labeling the utterance.

All applications are created with a default intent called **None**. This intent will get sentences that do not belong to our application at all. If we were to say, *Order a large pizza with mushrooms and pepperoni*, this would end up with None as the intent.

When you are creating intents, you should define at least three to five utterances. This will give LUIS something to work on, and as such, it can create better models. We will see how we can improve performance later in this chapter.

Simplifying development using prebuilt models

Building entities and intents can be easy, or it can be more advanced. Fortunately, LUIS provides a set of prebuilt entities that stem from Bing. These entities will be included in the applications, as well as on the web, while doing the labeling process.

The following table describes all the available prebuilt entities:

Entity	Example
builtin.number	Five/23.21
builtin.ordinal	Second/3rd
builtin.temperature	2 degrees Celsius/104 F
builtin.dimension	231 square kilometers
builtin.age	27 years old
builtin.geography	City/country/point of interest
builtin.encyclopedia	Person/organization/event/TV episodes/products/film (and many more)
builtin.datetime	Date/time/duration/set

The last three have several subentities, as described in the **Example** field.

We are going to add one of these prebuilt entities, so go to the **Entities** menu selection. Click on **Add prebuilt entity**. Select **temperature** from the list and click on **Save**.

With the newly created entity, we want to add a new intent called **SetTemperature**. If the example utterance is *Set the temperature in the kitchen to 22 degrees Celsius*, we can label the utterance as follows:

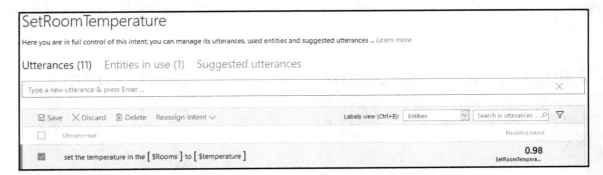

As you can see, we have a `room` entity. We also have the prebuilt `temperature` entity clearly labeled. As the correct intent should be selected in the drop-down menu, we can click on the **Save** button to save the utterance.

Prebuilt domains

In addition to using prebuilt entities, one can use prebuilt domains. These are entities and intents that are already existing, leveraging commonly used intents and entities from different domains. By using these intents/entities, you can use models that you would typically use in Windows. A very basic example is to set up appointments in the calendar.

To use Cortana's prebuilt domain, you can select **Prebuilt domains** from the left-hand menu. This will open a list of available domains. By selecting either one, you will be asked if you would like to add the domain to the application, as shown in the following screenshot:

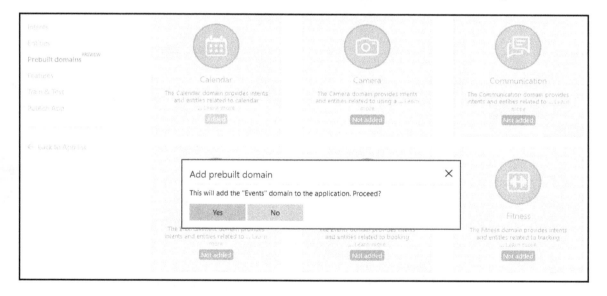

This will add intents and entities for that specific domain to the list of entities and intents already defined, as shown in the following screenshot:

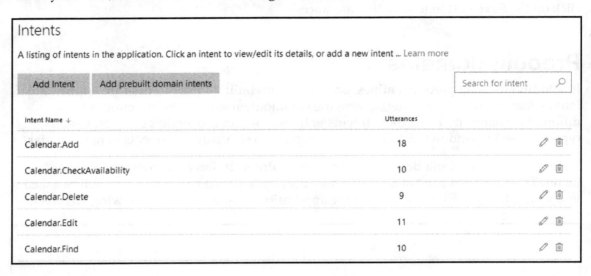

The following list shows the top-level domains that are available with Cortana prebuilt domains. For a complete list of available prebuilt domains, please refer to `Appendix A`, *LUIS Entities and Intents*:

- `Calendar`
- `Camera`
- `Communication`
- `Entertainment`
- `Events`
- `Fitness`
- `Gaming`
- `HomeAutomation`
- `MovieTickets`
- `Music`
- `Note`
- `OnDevice`

- Places
- Reminder
- RestaurantReservation
- Taxi
- Translate
- Utilities
- Weather
- Web

Training a model

Now that we have a working model, it is time to put it into action.

Training and publishing the model

The first step to using the model is to make sure the model has some utterances to work with. As we have seen, we have added one utterance per intent for now. Before we deploy the application, we need more.

Think of three to four different ways to set or get the room temperature and add them, specifying the entities and intents. Also, add a couple of utterances that fall into the None intent, just for reference.

When we have added new utterances, we need to train the model. Doing so will make LUIS develop code to recognize relevant entities and intents in the future. This process is done periodically; however, it is wise to do it when you have made changes, before publication. This can be done by selecting **Train & Test** in the left-hand menu. Click on **Train application**.

To test the application, one can simply enter test sentences in the **Interactive Testing** tab. This will show you what any given sentence is labeled as and what intents the service has discovered, as shown in the following screenshot:

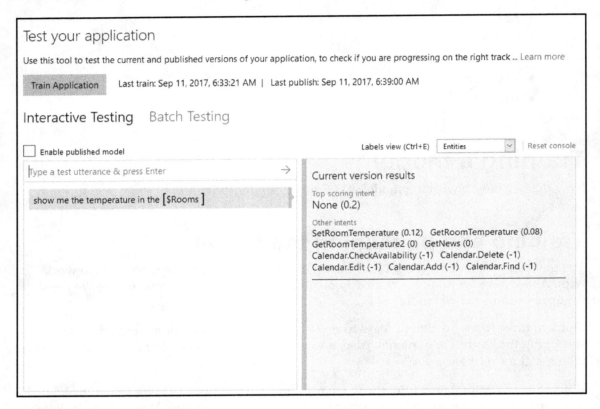

With the training completed, we can publish the application. This will deploy the models to an HTTP endpoint, which will interpret sentences we send to it.

Select **Publish** from the left-hand menu. This will present you with the following screen:

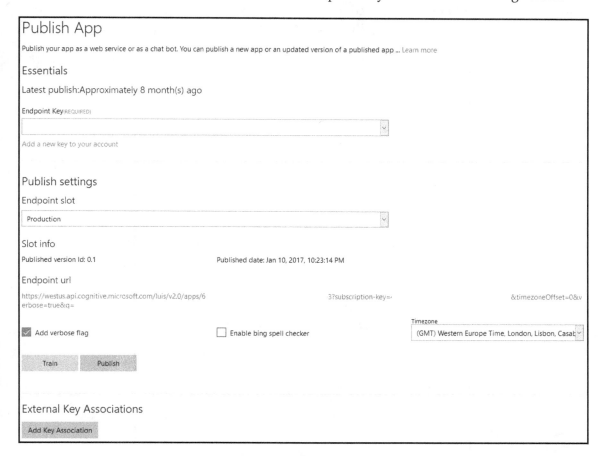

Click on the **Publish** button to deploy the application. The URL beneath the **Endpoint url** field is the endpoint where the model is deployed. As you can see, it specifies the application ID as well as the subscription key.

Before we go any further, we can verify that the endpoint actually works. Do so by entering a query into the text field (for instance, `get the bedroom temperature`) and clicking on the link. This should present you with something similar to the following screenshot:

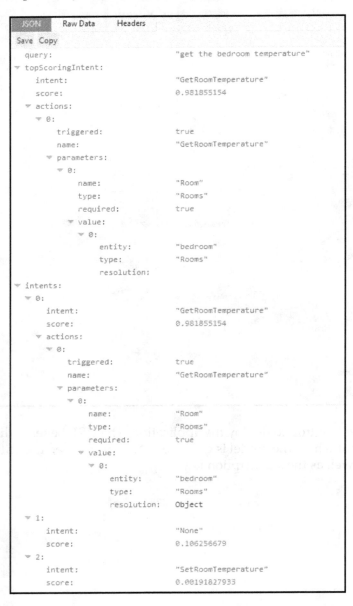

When the model has been published, we can move on to access it through the code.

Connecting to the smart-house application

To be able to easily work with LUIS, we will want to add the NuGet client package. In the smart-house application, go to the NuGet package manager and find the `Microsoft.Cognitive.LUIS` package. Install this to the project.

We will need to add a new class called `Luis`. Place the file under the `Model` folder. This class will be in charge of calling the endpoint and processing the result.

As we will need to test this class, we will need to add a View and a ViewModel. Add the files called `LuisView.xaml` to the `View` folder, and `LuisViewModel.cs` to the `ViewModel` folder.

The View should be rather simple. It should contain two `TextBox` elements, one for inputting requests and the other for displaying results. We do also need a button to execute commands.

Add the View as a `TabItem` in the `MainView.xaml` file.

The ViewModel should have two `string` properties, one for each of the `TextBox` elements. It will also need an `ICommand` property for the button command.

We will create the `Luis` class first, so open the `Luis.cs` file. Make the class `public`.

When we have made requests and received the corresponding result, we want to trigger an event to notify the UI. We want some additional arguments with this event, so below the `Luis` class, create a `LuisUtteranceResultEventArgs` class inheriting from the `EventArgs` class, as follows:

```
public class LuisUtteranceResultEventArgs : EventArgs {
    public string Status { get; set; }
    public string Message { get; set; }
    public bool RequiresReply { get; set; }
}
```

This will contain a `Status` string, a status `Message`, and the `Result` itself. Back to the class, `Luis`, add an event and a private member, as follows:

```
public event EventHandler<LuisUtteranceResultEventArgs>
OnLuisUtteranceResultUpdated;

private LuisClient _luisClient;
```

We have already discussed the first one. The private member is the API access object, which we installed from NuGet:

```
public Luis(LuisClientluisClient) {
    _luisClient = luisClient;
}
```

The constructor should accept the `LuisClient` object as a parameter and assign it to the member we previously created.

Let us create a helper method to raise the `OnLuisUtteranceResultUpdated` event, as follows:

```
private void RaiseOnLuisUtteranceResultUpdated(
LuisUtteranceResultEventArgsargs)
{
    OnLuisUtteranceResultUpdated?.Invoke(this, args);
}
```

This is purely for our own convenience.

To be able to make requests, we will create a function called `RequestAsync`. This will accept a `string` as a parameter and have `Task` as the return type. The function should be marked as `async`, as follows:

```
public async Task RequestAsync(string input) {
    try {
        LuisResult result = await _luisClient.Predict(input);
```

Inside the function, we make a call to the `Predict` function of `_luisClient`. This will send a query to the endpoint we published earlier. A successful request will result in a `LuisResult` object containing some data, which we will explore shortly.

We use the result in a new function, where we process it. We make sure we catch any exceptions and notify any listeners about it:

```
        ProcessResult(result);
    }
    catch(Exception ex) {
        RaiseOnLuisUtteranceResultUpdated(new
LuisUtteranceResultEventArgs
        {
            Status = "Failed",
            Message = ex.Message
        });
    }
}
```

In the `ProcessResult` function, we create a new object of the `LuisUtteranceResultEventArgs` type. This will be used when notifying listeners of any results. In this argument object, we add the status `Succeeded` and the `result` object. We also write out a message, stating the top identified intent. We also add the likelihood of this intent being the top one out of all the intents we have. Finally, we also add the number of intents identified:

```
private void ProcessResult(LuisResult result) {
    LuisUtteranceResultEventArgsargs = new
LuisUtteranceResultEventArgs();

    args.Result = result;
    args.Status = "Succeeded";
    args.Message = $"Top intent is {result.TopScoringIntent.Name} with
score {result.TopScoringIntent.Score}. Found {result.Entities.Count}
entities.";

    RaiseOnLuisUtteranceResultUpdated(args);
}
```

With that in place, we head to our view model. Open the `LuisViewModel.cs` file. Make sure the class is `public` and that it inherits from the `ObservableObject` class.

Declare a private member, as follows:

```
private Luis _luis;
```

This will hold the `Luis` object we created earlier:

```
public LuisViewModel() {
    _luis = new Luis(new LuisClient("APP_ID_HERE", "API_KEY_HERE"));
```

Our constructor creates the `Luis` object, making sure it is initialized with a new `LuisClient`. As you may see, this requires two parameters, the application ID and the subscription ID. There is also a third parameter, `preview`, but we will not need to set it at this time.

The application ID can be found either by looking at the URL in the publishing step or by going to the **Dashboard** on the application's site at `https://www.luis.ai`. There you will find the **App Id**, as shown in the following screenshot:

Overview

Facts & statistics about the app's data and the received endpoint hits at any period of time ... Learn more

Dashboard   Suggested utterances

App Id: 6   3

With the `Luis` object created, we complete the constructor as follows:

```
_luis.OnLuisUtteranceResultUpdated += OnLuisUtteranceResultUpdated;
ExecuteUtteranceCommand = new DelegateCommand(ExecuteUtterance,
CanExecuteUtterance);
}
```

This will hook up the `OnLuisUtteranceResultUpdated` event and create a new `DelegateCommand` event for our button. For our command to be able to run, we need to check that we have written any text in the input field. This is done in `CanExecuteUtterance`.

The command, `ExecuteUtterance`, is itself rather simple:

```
private async void ExecuteUtterance(object obj) {
    await _luis.RequestAsync(InputText);
}
```

All we do is make a call to the `RequestAsync` function in the `_luis` object. We do not need to wait for any results, as these will be coming from the event.

The event handler, `OnLuisUtteranceResultUpdated`, will format the results and print it to the screen.

First we make sure that we invoke the methods in the current dispatcher thread. This is done as the event is triggered in another thread. We create a `StringBuilder`, which will be used to concatenate all the results:

```
private void OnLuisUtteranceResultUpdated(object sender,
LuisUtteranceResultEventArgs e) {
    Application.Current.Dispatcher.Invoke(() => {
        StringBuilder sb = new StringBuilder();
```

First we append the `Status` and the status `Message`. We then check to see if we have any entities detected and append the number of entities, as follows:

```
sb.AppendFormat("Status: {0}\n", e.Status);
sb.AppendFormat("Summary: {0}\n\n", e.Message);

if(e.Result.Entities != null&&e.Result.Entities.Count != 0) {
    sb.AppendFormat("Entities found: {0}\n", e.Result.Entities.Count);
    sb.Append("Entities:\n");
```

If we do have any entities, we loop through each of them, printing out the entity name and the value:

```
        foreach(var entities in e.Result.Entities) {
            foreach(var entity in entities.Value) {
                sb.AppendFormat("Name: {0}\tValue: {1}\n",
                                entity.Name, entity.Value);
            }
        }
        sb.Append("\n");
    }
```

Finally, we add `StringBuilder` to our `ResultText` string, which should display it on screen, as follows:

```
        ResultText = sb.ToString();
    });
}
```

With everything compiling, the result should look something like the following screenshot:

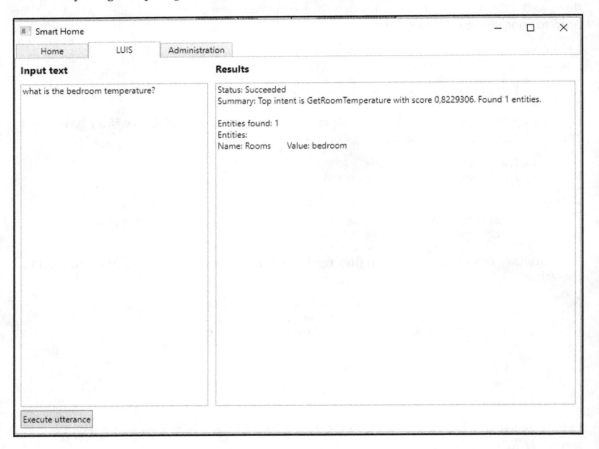

Model improvement through active usage

LUIS is a machine learning service. The applications we create, and the models that are generated, can therefore improve based on use. Through the development, it is a good idea to keep an eye on the performance. You may notice some intents that are often mislabeled or entities that are hard to recognize.

Visualizing performance

On the LUIS website, the dashboard displays information about intent and entity breakdowns. This is basically information on how the distribution of intents and entities is from the utterances that have been used.

The following image shows how the intent breakdown display looks:

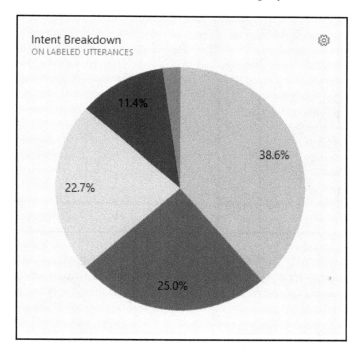

The next image shows how the entity breakdown looks:

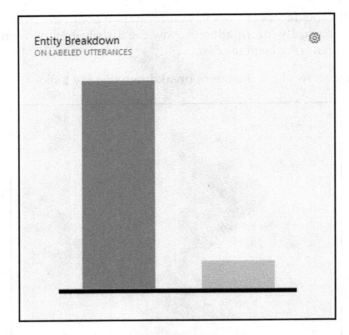

By hovering the mouse over the different bars (or sectors of the pie diagram), the name of the intent/entity will be displayed. In addition, the percentage number of the total number of intents/entities in use is displayed.

Resolving performance problems

If you notice an error in your applications, there are typically four options to resolve it:

- Adding model features
- Adding labeled utterances
- Looking for incorrect utterance labels
- Changing the schema

We will now look briefly into each of these.

Adding model features

This is typically something we can do if we have phrases that should be detected as entities, but are not. We have already seen an example of this with the room entity, where one room could be the living room.

The solution is, of course, to add phrase lists or Regex features. There are three scenarios where this will likely help:

- When LUIS fails to see words or phrases that are similar.
- When LUIS has trouble identifying entities. Adding all possible entity values in a phrase list should help.
- When rare or proprietary words are used.

Adding labeled utterances

Adding and labeling more utterances will always improve performance. This will most likely help in the following scenarios:

- When LUIS fails to differentiate between two intents.
- When LUIS fails to detect entities between surrounding words.
- If LUIS systematically assigns low scores to an intent.

Looking for incorrect utterance labels

A common mistake is mislabeling an utterance or entity. In that case, you will need to find the incorrect utterance and correct it. This will likely resolve problems in the following scenarios:

- If LUIS fails to differentiate between two intents, even when similar utterances have been labeled
- If LUIS consistently misses an entity

Changing the schema

If all the preceding solutions fail and you still have problems with the model, you may consider changing the schema, meaning combining, regrouping, and/or dropping intents and entities.

Keep in mind that if it is hard for humans to label an utterance, it is even harder for a machine.

Active learning

A very nice feature of LUIS is the power of active learning. When we are using the service actively, it will log all queries, and as such, we are then able to analyze usage. Doing so allows us to quickly correct errors and label utterances we have not seen before.

Using the application we have built, the smart-house application, if we run a query with the utterance, `can you tell me the bedroom temperature?`, the model will likely not recognize this. If we debug the process, stepping through the `ProcessResult` function, we can see the following values returned:

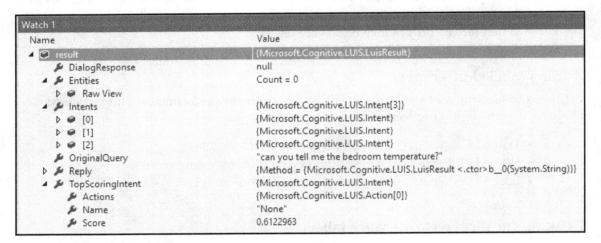

As you can see from the preceding screenshot, the top scoring intent is `None`, with a score of 0.61. No entities have been recognized either, so this is not good.

Head back into to the LUIS website. Move to the **Intents** page, which can be found in the left-hand menu. Select any intent and click on **Suggested Utterances**. Here we can see that the utterance we just tried has been added. We can now label the intent and entity correctly:

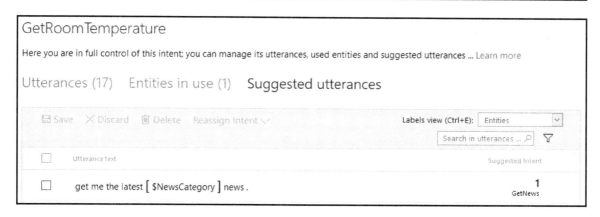

By labelling the utterance with the correct intent and entity, we will get a correct result next time we query in this way, as you can see in the following screenshot:

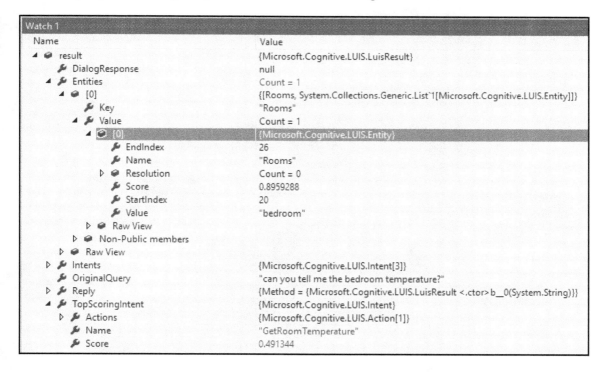

Summary

In this this chapter, we created a LUIS application. You saw how to create language-understanding models, which can recognize entities in sentences. You learned how to understand the user's intent and saw how we can trigger actions from this. An important step was to see how to improve the model in various ways.

In the next chapter, we will utilize what you have learned here, using LUIS when we learn about the Speech APIs, adding the possibility of speaking with our application.

Speaking with Your Application

5

In the previous chapter, we learned to discover and understand the intent of a user, based on utterances. In this chapter, we will learn how to add audio capabilities to our applications. We will learn to convert text to speech and speech to text. We will learn how to identify the person speaking. Throughout this chapter, we will learn how you can utilize spoken audio to verify a person. Finally, we will touch briefly on how to customize speech recognition, to make it unique for your application's usage.

By the end of this chapter, we will have covered the following topics:

- Converting spoken audio to text and text to spoken audio
- Recognizing intent from spoken audio, utilizing LUIS
- Verifying that the speaker is who they claim to be
- Identifying the speaker
- Tailoring the recognition API to recognize custom speaking styles and environments

Converting text to audio and vice versa

In Chapter 1, *Getting Started with Microsoft Cognitive Services*, we utilized a part of the Bing Speech API. We gave the example application the ability to speak sentences to us. We will use the code created in that example now, but we will dive a bit deeper into the details.

We will also go through the other feature of Bing Speech API, converting spoken audio to text. The idea is that we can speak to the Smart-House application, which will recognize what we are saying. Using the textual output, it will use LUIS to get the intent of our sentence. In case LUIS needs more information, the application will politely ask us with audio.

To get started, we want to modify the build definition of the Smart-House application. We need to specify whether we are running it on a 32-bit or a 64-bit OS. To utilize speech-to-text conversion, we want to install the Bing Speech NuGet client package. Search for `Microsoft.ProjectOxford.SpeechRecognition`, and install either the 32-bit version or the 64-bit version, depending on your system.

Further on, we need to add references to `System.Runtime.Serialization` and `System.Web`. These are needed to be able to make web requests and deserialize response data from the APIs.

Speaking to the application

Add a new file to the `Model` folder, called `SpeechToText.cs`. Beneath the automatically created `SpeechToText` class, we want to add an `enum` type variable called `SttStatus`. It should have two values, `Success` and `Error`.

In addition, we want to define an `EventArgs` class for events that we will raise during execution. Add the following class at the bottom of the file:

```
public class SpeechToTextEventArgs : EventArgs
{
    public SttStatus Status { get; private set; }
    public string Message { get; private set; }
    public List<string> Results { get; private set; }

    public SpeechToTextEventArgs(SttStatus status,
    string message, List<string> results = null)
    {
        Status = status;
        Message = message;
        Results = results;
    }
}
```

As you can see, the `event` argument will hold the operation status, a message of any kind, and a list of strings. This will be a list with potential speech-to-text conversions.

The `SpeechToText` class needs to implement `IDisposable`. This is done so that we can clean up the resources used for recording spoken audio, and be able to shut down the application properly. We will add the details later, so for now, make sure you add the `Dispose` function.

We need to define a few private members in the class, as well as an event:

```
public event EventHandler<SpeechToTextEventArgs> OnSttStatusUpdated;

private DataRecognitionClient _dataRecClient;
private MicrophoneRecognitionClient _micRecClient;
private SpeechRecognitionMode _speechMode =
SpeechRecognitionMode.ShortPhrase;

private string _language = "en-US";
private bool _isMicRecording = false;
```

The `OnSttStatusUpdated` event will be triggered whenever we have a new operation status. `DataRecognitionClient` and `MicrophoneRecognitionClient` are the two objects we can use to call the Bing Speech API. We will look at how they are created in a bit.

We define the `SpeechRecognitionMode` to be `ShortPhrase`. This means we do not expect any spoken sentences longer than 15 seconds. The alternative is `LongDictation`, which means that we can convert spoken sentences up to 2 minutes long.

Finally, we specify the language to be English, and define a `bool` type variable, which indicates whether or not we are currently recording anything.

In our constructor, we accept the Bing Speech API key as a parameter. We will use this in the creation of our API clients:

```
public SpeechToText(string bingApiKey)
{
    _dataRecClient = SpeechRecognitionServiceFactory.
CreateDataClientWithIntent (_language, bingApiKey, "LUIS_APP_ID",
"LUIS_API_KEY");

    _micRecClient = SpeechRecognitionServiceFactory.
CreateMicrophoneClient(_speechMode, _language, bingApiKey);

    Initialize();
}
```

As you can see, we create both the `_dataRecClient` and `_micRecClient` by calling the `SpeechRecognitionServiceFactory`. For the first client, we state that we want to use intent recognition as well. The parameters required are the language, Bing API key, the LUIS app ID, and the LUIS API key. By using a `DataRecognitionClient` object, we need to upload audio files with speech.

By using `MicrophoneRecognitionClient`, we can use a microphone for real-time conversion. For this, we do not want intent detection, so we call `CreateMicrophoneClient`. In this case, we only need to specify the speech mode, the language, and the Bing Speech API key.

Before leaving the constructor, we call an `Initialize` function. In this, we subscribe to certain events on each of the clients:

```
private void Initialize()
{
    _micRecClient.OnMicrophoneStatus += OnMicrophoneStatus;
    _micRecClient.OnPartialResponseReceived +=
OnPartialResponseReceived;
    _micRecClient.OnResponseReceived += OnResponseReceived;
    _micRecClient.OnConversationError += OnConversationErrorReceived;

    _dataRecClient.OnIntent += OnIntentReceived;
    _dataRecClient.OnPartialResponseReceived +=
OnPartialResponseReceived;
    _dataRecClient.OnConversationError += OnConversationErrorReceived;
    _dataRecClient.OnResponseReceived += OnResponseReceived;
}
```

As you can see, there are quite a few similarities between the two clients. The two differences are that `_dataRecClient` will get intents through the `OnIntent` event, and `_micRecClient` will get the microphone status through the `OnMicrophoneStatus` event.

We do not really care about partial responses. However, they may be useful in some cases, as they will continuously give the currently completed conversion:

```
private void OnPartialResponseReceived(object sender,
PartialSpeechResponseEventArgs e)
{
    Debug.WriteLine($"Partial response received:{e.PartialResult}");
}
```

For our application, we choose to output it to the debug console window. In this case, `PartialResult` is a string with the partially converted text:

```
private void OnMicrophoneStatus(object sender, MicrophoneEventArgs e)
{
    Debug.WriteLine($"Microphone status changed to recording:
{e.Recording}");
}
```

We do not care about the current microphone status either. Again, we output the status to the debug console window.

Before moving on, add a helper function, called `RaiseSttStatusUpdated`. This should raise the `OnSttStatusUpdated`, when called.

When we are calling `_dataRecClient`, we may recognize intents from LUIS. In these cases, we want to raise an event, where we output the recognized intent. This is done with the following code:

```
private void OnIntentReceived(object sender, SpeechIntentEventArgs e)
{
    SpeechToTextEventArgs args = new
SpeechToTextEventArgs(SttStatus.Success, $"Intent received:
{e.Intent.ToString()}.\n Payload: {e.Payload}");
    RaiseSttStatusUpdated(args);
}
```

We choose to print out intent information, and the `Payload`. This is a string containing recognized entities, intents, and actions triggered from LUIS.

If any errors occur during the conversion, there are several things we want to do. First and foremost, we want to stop any microphone recordings that may be running. There is really no point in trying to convert more in the current operation if it has failed:

```
private void OnConversationErrorReceived(object sender,
SpeechErrorEventArgs e)
{
    if (_isMicRecording) StopMicRecording();
```

We will create the `StopMicRecording` in a bit.

In addition, we want to notify any subscribers that the conversion failed. In such cases, we want to give details about error codes and error messages:

```
    string message = $"Speech to text failed with status
code:{e.SpeechErrorCode.ToString()}, and error message:
{e.SpeechErrorText}";
    SpeechToTextEventArgs args = new
SpeechToTextEventArgs(SttStatus.Error, message);

    RaiseSttStatusUpdated(args);
}
```

The OnConversationError event does, fortunately, provide us with detailed information about any errors.

Now let us look at the StopMicRecording method:

```
private void StopMicRecording()
{
    _micRecClient.EndMicAndRecognition();
    _isMicRecording = false;
}
```

This is a simple function, which calls EndMicAndRecognition on the _micRecClient MicrophoneRecognitionClient object. When this is called, we stop the client from recording any more.

The final event handler that we need to create is the OnResponseReceived handler. This will be triggered whenever we receive a complete converted response from the service.

Again, we want to make sure we do not record any more, if we are currently recording:

```
private void OnResponseReceived(object sender, SpeechResponseEventArgs
e)
{
    if (_isMicRecording) StopMicRecording();
```

The SpeechResponseEventArgs argument contains a PhraseResponse object. This contains an array of RecognizedPhrase, which we want to access. Each item in this array contains the confidence of correct conversion. It also contains the converted phrases as DisplayText. This uses inverse text normalization, proper capitalization, and punctuation, and it masks profanities with asterisks:

```
RecognizedPhrase[] recognizedPhrases = e.PhraseResponse.Results;
List<string> phrasesToDisplay = new List<string>();

foreach(RecognizedPhrase phrase in recognizedPhrases)
{
    phrasesToDisplay.Add(phrase.DisplayText);
}
```

We may also get the converted phrases in other formats, as described in the following table:

Format	Description
LexicalForm	This is the raw, unprocessed recognition result.
InverseTextNormalizationResult	This displays phrases such as *one two three four* as *1234*, so it is ideal for usages such as *go to second street*.
MaskedInverseTextNormalizationResult	Inverse text normalization and profanity mask. No capitalization or punctuation applied.

For our use, we are just interested in the `DisplayText`. With a populated list of recognized phrases, we raise the status update event:

```
    SpeechToTextEventArgs args = new
SpeechToTextEventArgs(SttStatus.Success, $"STT completed with status:
{e.PhraseResponse.RecognitionStatus.ToString()}", phrasesToDisplay);

    RaiseSttStatusUpdated(args);
}
```

To be able to use this class, we need a couple of public functions so we can start speech recognition:

```
    public void StartMicToText()
    {
        _micRecClient.StartMicAndRecognition();
        _isMicRecording = true;
    }
```

The `StartMicToText` method will call the `StartMicAndRecognition` method on the `_micRecClient` object. This will allow us to use the microphone to convert spoken audio. This function will be our main way to access this API:

```
    public void StartAudioFileToText(string audioFileName) {
        using (FileStream fileStream = new FileStream(audioFileName,
FileMode.Open, FileAccess.Read))
        {
            int bytesRead = 0;
            byte[] buffer = new byte[1024];
```

The second function will require a filename for the audio file, with the audio we want to convert. We open the file, with read access, and are ready to read it:

```
try {
    do {
        bytesRead = fileStream.Read(buffer, 0, buffer.Length);
        _dataRecClient.SendAudio(buffer, bytesRead);
    } while (bytesRead > 0);
}
```

As long as we have data available, we read from the file. We will fill up the `buffer`, and call the `SendAudio` method. This will then trigger a recognition operation in the service.

If any exceptions occur, we make sure to output the exception message to a debug window. Finally, we need to call the `EndAudio` method so that the service does not wait for any more data:

```
catch(Exception ex) {
    Debug.WriteLine($"Exception caught: {ex.Message}");
}
finally {
    _dataRecClient.EndAudio();
}
```

Before leaving this class, we need to dispose of our API clients. Add the following in the `Dispose` function:

```
if (_micRecClient != null) {
    _micRecClient.EndMicAndRecognition();
    _micRecClient.OnMicrophoneStatus -= OnMicrophoneStatus;
    _micRecClient.OnPartialResponseReceived -=
OnPartialResponseReceived;
    _micRecClient.OnResponseReceived -= OnResponseReceived;
    _micRecClient.OnConversationError -= OnConversationErrorReceived;

    _micRecClient.Dispose();
    _micRecClient = null;
}

if(_dataRecClient != null) {
    _dataRecClient.OnIntent -= OnIntentReceived;
    _dataRecClient.OnPartialResponseReceived -=
OnPartialResponseReceived;
    _dataRecClient.OnConversationError -= OnConversationErrorReceived;
    _dataRecClient.OnResponseReceived -= OnResponseReceived;

    _dataRecClient.Dispose();
```

```
        _dataRecClient = null;
    }
```

We stop microphone recording, unsubscribe from all events, and dispose and clear the client objects.

Make sure the application compiles before moving on. We will look at how to use this class a bit later.

Letting the application speak back

We have already seen how to make the application speak back to us. We are going to use the same classes we created in Chapter 1, *Getting Started with Microsoft Cognitive Services*. Copy Authentication.cs and TextToSpeech.cs from the example project from Chapter 1, *Getting Started with Microsoft Cognitive Services*, into the Model folder. Make sure the namespaces are changed accordingly.

As we have been through the code already, we will not go through it again. We will instead look at some of the details left out in Chapter 1, *Getting Started with Microsoft Cognitive Services*.

Audio output format

The audio output format can be one of the following formats:

- raw-8khz-8bit-mono-mulaw
- raw-16khz-16bit-mono-pcm
- riff-8khz-8bit-mono-mulaw
- riff-16khz-16bit-mono-pcm

Error codes

There are four possible error codes in calls to the API. These are described in the following table:

Code	Description
400 / BadRequest	A required parameter is missing, empty, or null. Alternatively, a parameter is invalid. An example may be a string longer than the allowed length.

401 / `Unauthorized`	The request is not authorized.
413 / `RequestEntityTooLarge`	The SSML input is larger than supported.
502 / `BadGateway`	Network-related or server-related issue.

Supported languages

The following languages are supported:

English (Australian), English (United Kingdom), English (United States), English (Canada), English (India), Spanish, Mexican Spanish, German, Arabic (Egypt), French, Canadian French, Italian, Japanese, Portuguese, Russian, Chinese (S), Chinese (Hong Kong), and Chinese (T).

Utilizing LUIS based on spoken commands

To utilize the features that we have just have added, we are going to modify `LuisView` and `LuisViewModel`. Add a new `Button` in the View, which will make sure we record commands. Add a corresponding `ICommand` in the ViewModel.

We also need to add a few more members to the class:

```
private SpeechToText _sttClient;
private TextToSpeech _ttsClient;
private string _bingApiKey = "BING_SPEECH_API_KEY";
```

The first two will be used to convert between spoken audio and text. The third is the API key for the Bing Speech API.

Make the ViewModel implement the `IDisposable`, and explicitly dispose the `SpeechToText` object.

Create the objects by adding the following in the constructor:

```
_sttClient = new SpeechToText(_bingApiKey);
_sttClient.OnSttStatusUpdated += OnSttStatusUpdated;

_ttsClient = new TextToSpeech();
_ttsClient.OnAudioAvailable += OnTtsAudioAvailable;
_ttsClient.OnError += OnTtsError;
GenerateHeaders();
```

This will create the client objects and subscribe to the required events. Finally it will call a function to generate authentication tokens for the REST API calls. This function should look like this:

```
private async void GenerateHeaders()
{
    if (await _ttsClient.GenerateAuthenticationToken(_bingApiKey))
    _ttsClient.GenerateHeaders();
}
```

If we receive any errors from _ttsClient, we want to output it to the debug console:

```
private void OnTtsError(object sender, AudioErrorEventArgs e)
{
    Debug.WriteLine($"Status: Audio service failed -
{e.ErrorMessage}");
}
```

We do not need to output this to the UI, as this feature is a nice-to-have feature.

If we have audio available, we want to make sure that we play it:

```
private void OnTtsAudioAvailable(object sender, AudioEventArgs e)
{
    SoundPlayer player = new SoundPlayer(e.EventData);
    player.Play();
    e.EventData.Dispose();
}
```

We do so by creating a SoundPlayer object. Using the audio stream we get from the event arguments, we can play the audio to the user.

If we have a status update from _sttClient, we want to display this in the textbox.

If we have successfully recognized spoken audio, we want to show the Message string, if it is available:

```
private void OnSttStatusUpdated(object sender, SpeechToTextEventArgs e)
{
    Application.Current.Dispatcher.Invoke(() => {
        StringBuilder sb = new StringBuilder();

        if(e.Status == SttStatus.Success) {
            if(!string.IsNullOrEmpty(e.Message)) {
                sb.AppendFormat("Result message: {0}\n\n", e.Message);
            }
```

We also want to show all recognized phrases. Using the first available phrase, we make a call to LUIS:

```
if(e.Results != null && e.Results.Count != 0) {
    sb.Append("Retrieved the following results:\n");
        foreach(string sentence in e.Results) {
            sb.AppendFormat("{0}\n\n", sentence);
        }
        sb.Append("Calling LUIS with the top result\n");
        CallLuis(e.Results.FirstOrDefault());
    }
}
```

If the recognition failed we print out any error messages that we may have. Finally, we make sure that the `ResultText` is updated with the new data:

```
else {
    sb.AppendFormat("Could not convert speech to text:{0}\n",
e.Message);
    }

    sb.Append("\n");
    ResultText = sb.ToString();
});
}
```

The newly created `ICommand` needs to have a function to start the recognition process:

```
private void RecordUtterance(object obj) {
    _sttClient.StartMicToText();
}
```

The function starts the microphone recording.

Finally, we need to make some modifications to `OnLuisUtteranceResultUpdated`. Make the following modifications, where we output any `DialogResponse`:

```
if (e.RequiresReply && !string.IsNullOrEmpty(e.DialogResponse))
{
    await _ttsClient.SpeakAsync(e.DialogResponse,
CancellationToken.None);
    sb.AppendFormat("Response: {0}\n", e.DialogResponse);
    sb.Append("Reply in the left textfield");
    RecordUtterance(sender);
}
else
{
    await _ttsClient.SpeakAsync($"Summary: {e.Message}",
```

```
CancellationToken.None);
    }
```

This will play the `DialogResponse`, if it exists. The application will ask you for more information, if required. It will then start the recording, so we can answer without clicking any buttons.

If no `DialogResponse` exists, we simply make the application speak the summary to us. This will contain data on intents, entities, and actions from LUIS.

Knowing who is speaking

Using the **Speaker Recognition** API we can identify who is speaking. By defining one or more speaker profiles, with corresponding samples, we can identify if any of these is speaking at any time.

To be able to utilize this feature, we need to go through a few steps:

1. We add one or more speaker profile to the service.
2. Each speaker profile enrolls several spoken samples.
3. We call the service to identify a speaker based on audio input.

 If you have not already done so, sign up for an API key for the Speaker Recognition API at `https://portal.azure.com`.

Start by adding a new NuGet package to your smart-house application. Search for and add `Microsoft.ProjectOxford.SpeakerRecognition`.

Add a new class called `SpeakerIdentification` to the `Model` folder of your project. This class will hold all the functionality related to speaker identification.

Beneath the class, we add another class, containing `EventArgs` for status updates:

```
public class SpeakerIdentificationStatusUpdateEventArgs : EventArgs
{
    public string Status { get; private set; }
    public string Message { get; private set; }
    public Identification IdentifiedProfile { get; set; }

    public SpeakerIdentificationStatusUpdateEventArgs (string status,
string message)
```

```
        {
            Status = status;
            Message = message;
        }
    }
```

The two first properties should be self-explanatory. The last one, `IdentificationProfile`, will hold the results of a successful identification process. We will look at what information this contains later.

We also want to send events for errors, so let's add an `EventArgs` class for the required information:

```
    public class SpeakerIdentificationErrorEventArgs : EventArgs {
        public string ErrorMessage { get; private set; }

        public SpeakerIdentificationErrorEventArgs(string errorMessage)
        {
            ErrorMessage = errorMessage;
        }
    }
```

Again, the property should be self-explanatory.

In the `SpeakerIdentification` class, add two events, and one private member at the top of the class:

```
    public event EventHandler <SpeakerIdentificationStatusUpdateEventArgs>
        OnSpeakerIdentificationStatusUpdated;
    public event EventHandler <SpeakerIdentificationErrorEventArgs>
        OnSpeakerIdentificationError;

    private ISpeakerIdentificationServiceClient
  _speakerIdentificationClient;
```

The events will be triggered if we have any status updates, a successful identification, or errors. The `ISpeakerIdentificationServiceClient` object is the access point to the Speaker Recognition API. Inject this object through the constructor.

To make it easier to raise events, add two helper functions, one for each event. Call these `RaiseOnIdentificationStatusUpdated` and `RaiseOnIdentificationError`. They should accept the corresponding `EventArgs` object as parameters and trigger the corresponding event.

Adding speaker profiles

To be able to identify any speakers, we need to add profiles. Each profile can be seen as a unique person, which we can identify later.

At the time of writing, each subscription allows for 1,000 speaker profiles to be created. This also includes profiles created for verification, which we will look at later.

To facilitate creating profiles, we need to add some elements to our `AdministrationView` and `AdministrationViewModel` properties, so open these files.

In the View, add a new button for adding speaker profiles. Also add a list box, which will show all our profiles. How you lay out the UI is up to you.

The ViewModel will need a new `ICommand` property for the button. It will also need a `ObservableObject` property for our profile list; make sure it is of type `Guid`. We will also need to be able to select a profile, so add a `Guid` property for the selected profile.

Additionally, we need to add a new member to the ViewModel:

```
private SpeakerIdentification _speakerIdentification;
```

This is the reference to the class we created earlier. Create this object in the constructor, passing on an `ISpeakerIdentificationServiceClient` object, which you inject via the ViewModel's constructor. In the constructor, you should also subscribe to the events we created:

```
_speakerIdentification.OnSpeakerIdentificationError +=
OnSpeakerIdentificationError;
_speakerIdentification.OnSpeakerIdentificationStatusUpdated +=
OnSpeakerIdentificationStatusUpdated;
```

Basically, we want both event handles to update the status text with the message they carry:

```
Application.Current.Dispatcher.Invoke(() =>
{
    StatusText = e.Message;
});
```

The preceding code is for `OnSpeakerIdentificationStatusUpdated`. The same should be used for `OnSpeakerIdentificationError`, but set `StatusText` to be `e.ErrorMessage` instead.

In the function created for our `ICommand` property, we do the following to create a new profile:

```
private async void AddSpeaker(object obj)
{
    Guid speakerId = await
_speakerIdentification.CreateSpeakerProfile();
```

We make a call to our `_speakerIdentification` object's `CreateSpeakerProfile` function. This function will return a `Guid`, which is the unique ID of that speaker. In our example, we do not do anything further with this. In a real-life application, I would recommend mapping this ID to a name in some way. As you will see later on, identifying people through GUIDs is for machines, not people:

```
    GetSpeakerProfiles();
}
```

We finish the function by calling a `GetSpeakerProfile` function, which we will create next. This will fetch a list of all the profiles created, so that we can use these moving on:

```
private async void GetSpeakerProfiles()
{
    List<Guid> profiles = await
_speakerIdentification.ListSpeakerProfiles();

    if (profiles == null) return;
```

In our `GetSpeakerProfiles` function, we call `ListSpeakerProfiles` on our `_speakerIdentification` object. This will, as we will later see, fetch a list of GUIDs, containing the profile IDs. If this list is null, there is no point in moving on:

```
    foreach(Guid profile in profiles)
    {
        SpeakerProfiles.Add(profile);
    }
}
```

If the list does contain anything, we add these IDs to our `SpeakerProfiles`, the `ObservableCollection` property. This will show all our profiles in the UI.

This function should also be called from the `Initialize` function, so we populate the list when we start the application.

Back into the `SpeakerIdentification` class, create a new function called `CreateSpeakerProfile`. This should have return type `Task<Guid>` and be marked as `async`:

```
public async Task<Guid> CreateSpeakerProfile()
{
    try
    {
        CreateProfileResponse response = await
_speakerIdentificationClient.CreateProfileAsync("en-US");
```

We make a call to `CreateProfileAsync` on the API object. We need to specify the locale, which is used for the speaker profile. At the time of writing, `en-US` is the only valid option.

If the call is successful, we get a `CreateProfileResponse` object in response. This contains the ID of the newly created speaker profile:

```
if (response == null)
{
    RaiseOnIdentificationError(
        new SpeakerIdentificationErrorEventArgs
            ("Failed to create speaker profile."));
    return Guid.Empty;
}

return response.ProfileId;
}
```

If the `response` is null, we raise an error event. If it contains data, we return the `ProfileId` to the caller.

Add the corresponding `catch` clause to finish the function.

Create a new function called `ListSpeakerProfile`. This should return `Task<List<Guid>>` and be marked as `async`:

```
public async Task<List<Guid>> ListSpeakerProfiles()
{
    try
    {
        List<Guid> speakerProfiles = new List<Guid>();

        Profile[] profiles = await
_speakerIdentificationClient.GetProfilesAsync();
```

We create a list of type `Guid`, which is the list of speaker profiles we will return. Then we call the `GetProfilesAsync` method on our `_speakerIdentificationClient` object. This will get us an array of type `Profile`, which contains information on each profile. This is information such as creation time, enrollment status, last modified, and so on. We are interested in the IDs of each profile:

```
            if (profiles == null || profiles.Length == 0)
            {
                RaiseOnIdentificationError(new
    SpeakerIdentificationErrorEventArgs("No profiles exist"));
                return null;
            }

            foreach (Profile profile in profiles)
            {
                speakerProfiles.Add(profile.ProfileId);
            }

            return speakerProfiles;
        }
```

If we have any profiles returned, we loop through the array and add each `profileId` to the previously created list. This list is then returned to the caller, which in our case will be the ViewModel.

End the function with the corresponding `catch` clause. Make sure the code compiles and executes as expected before continuing. This means you should now be able to add speaker profiles to the service and get the created profiles displayed in the UI.

To delete a speaker profile, we will need to add a new function to `SpeakerIdentification`. Call this function `DeleteSpeakerProfile`, and let it accept a `Guid` as its parameter. This will be the ID of the given profile we want to delete. Mark the function as `async`. The function should look like the following:

```
public async void DeleteSpeakerProfile(Guid profileId)
{
    try
    {
        await _speakerIdentificationClient.DeleteProfileAsync(profileId);
    }
    catch (IdentificationException ex)
    {
        RaiseOnIdentificationError(new
SpeakerIdentificationErrorEventArgs($"Failed to
        delete speaker profile: {ex.Message}"));
    }
```

```
catch (Exception ex)
{
    RaiseOnIdentificationError(new
SpeakerIdentificationErrorEventArgs($"Failed to
    delete speaker profile: {ex.Message}"));
}
}
```

As you can see, the call to the `DeleteProfileAsync` method expects a `Guid` type, `profileId`. There is no return value, and as such, when we call this function, we need to call the `GetSpeakerProfile` method in our ViewModel.

To facilitate deletion of speaker profiles, add a new button to the UI, and a corresponding `ICommand` property in the ViewModel.

Enrolling a profile

With a speaker profile in place, we need to associate spoken audio with the profile. We do this through a process called **enrolling**. For speaker identification, enrolling is text-independent. This means that you can use whatever sentence you want for enrollment. Once the voice is recorded, a number of features will be extracted to form a unique voice-print.

When enrolling, the audio file you are using must be at least 5 seconds, and 5 minutes at most. Best practice states that you should accumulate at least 30 seconds of speech. This is 30 seconds *after* silence has been removed, so several audio files may be required. This recommendation can be avoided by specifying an extra parameter, as we will see in a bit.

How you choose to upload the audio file is up to you. In the smart-house application, we will use a microphone to record live audio. To do so, we will need to add a new NuGet package, called **NAudio**. This is an audio library for .NET, which simplifies audio work.

We will also need a class to deal with recording, which is out of scope for this book. As such, I recommend you copy the file `Recording.cs`, which can be found in the sample project, in the `Model` folder.

In the `AdministrationViewModel` ViewModel, add a private member for the newly copied class. Create the class and subscribe to the events defined in the `Initialize` function:

```
_recorder = new Recording();
_recorder.OnAudioStreamAvailable += OnRecordingAudioStreamAvailable;
_recorder.OnRecordingError += OnRecordingError;
```

We have an event for errors and one for available audio stream. Let `OnRecordingError` print the `ErrorMessage` to the status text field.

In `OnAudioStreamAvailable`, add the following:

```
Application.Current.Dispatcher.Invoke(() =>
{
     _speakerIdentification.CreateSpeakerEnrollment(e.AudioStream,
SelectedSpeakerProfile);
     });
```

Here we call `CreateSpeakerEnrollment` on the `_speakerIdentification` object. We will cover this function in a bit. The parameters we pass on are the `AudioStream`, from the recording, as well as the ID of the selected profile.

To be able to get audio files for enrollment, we need to start and stop the recording. This can be done by simply adding two new buttons, one for start and one for stop. They will then need to execute one of the following:

```
_recorder.StartRecording();
_recorder.StopRecording();
```

Back in the `SpeakerIdentification.cs` file, we create the new function, `CreateSpeakerEnrollment`. This should accept `Stream` and `Guid` as parameters, and be marked as `async`:

```
    public async void CreateSpeakerEnrollment(Stream audioStream, Guid
profileId) {
        try {
            OperationLocation location = await
_speakerIdentificationClient.EnrollAsync(audioStream, profileId);
```

In this function, we call the `EnrollAsync` function on the `_speakerIdentificationClient`. This function requires both the `audioStream` and `profileId` as parameters. An optional third parameter is a `bool` type variable, deciding whether or not you would like to use the recommended speech length or not. The default is `false`, meaning that you use the recommended setting of at least 30 seconds of speech.

If the call is successful, we get an `OperationLocation` object back. This holds a URL, which we can query for the enrollment status, which is precisely what we will do:

```
        if (location == null) {
            RaiseOnIdentificationError(new
SpeakerIdentificationErrorEventArgs("Failed to start enrollment
process."));
            return;
```

```
        }

        GetEnrollmentOperationStatus(location);
    }
```

First we make sure that we have the `location` data. Without it, there is no point in moving on. If we do have the `location` data, we call a function, `GetEnrollmentOperationStatus`, specifying the `location` as the parameter.

Add the corresponding `catch` clause to finish the function.

The `GetEnrollmentOperationStatus` method accepts the `OperationLocation` as a parameter. When we enter the function, we move into a `while` loop, which will run until the operation completes. We call `CheckEnrollmentStatusAsync`, specifying the `location` as the parameter. If this call is successful, it will return an `EnrollmentOperation` object, which contains data such as status, enrollment speech time, and an estimation of the time of enrollment left:

```
    private async void GetEnrollmentOperationStatus(OperationLocation
    location) {
        try {
            while(true) {
                EnrollmentOperation result = await
    _speakerIdentificationClient.CheckEnrollmentStatusAsync(location);
```

When we have retrieved the result, we check to see if the status is running or not. If it is not, the operation has either failed, succeeded, or not started. In any case, we do not want to check any further, so we send an update with the status and break out of the loop:

```
                if(result.Status != Status.Running)
                {
                    RaiseOnIdentificationStatusUpdated(new
    SpeakerIdentificationStatusUpdateEventArgs(result.Status.ToString(),
                        $"Enrollment finished. Enrollment status:
    {result.ProcessingResult.EnrollmentStatus.ToString()}"));
                    break;
                }

                RaiseOnIdentificationStatusUpdated(new
    SpeakerIdentificationStatusUpdateEventArgs(result.Status.ToString(),
                    "Enrolling..."));
                await Task.Delay(1000);
            }
        }
```

If the status is still running, we update the status and wait for 1 second before trying again.

With enrollment completed, there may be times where we need to reset the enrollment for a given profile. We can do so by creating a new function, in `SpeakerIdentification`. Name it `ResetEnrollments`, and let it accept a `Guid` as a parameter. This should be the profile ID of the speaker profile to reset. Execute the following inside a `try` clause:

```
await _speakerIdentificationClient
.ResetEnrollmentsAsync(profileId);
```

This will delete all audio files associated with the given profile, and also reset the enrollment status. To call this function, add a new button to the UI and a corresponding `ICommand` property in the ViewModel.

If you compile and run the application, you may have a result similar to the following screenshot:

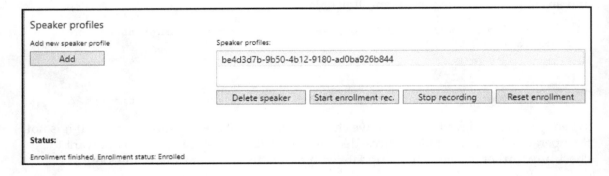

Identifying the speaker

The last step is to identify the speaker, which we will do in the `HomeView` and corresponding `HomeViewModel`. We do not need to modify the UI much, but we do need to add two buttons, to start and stop the recording. Alternatively, if you are not using a microphone, you can get away with one button for browsing to an audio file. Either way, add corresponding `ICommand` properties in the ViewModel.

We also need to add private members for the `Recording` class, and `SpeakerIdentification` class. Both should be created in the constructor, where we should inject `ISpeakerIdentificationServiceClient` as well.

In the `Initialize` function, subscribe to the required events:

```
    _speakerIdentification.OnSpeakerIdentificationError +=
OnSpeakerIdentificationError;
    _speakerIdentification.OnSpeakerIdentificationStatusUpdated +=
OnSpeakerIdentificationStatusReceived;

    _recording.OnAudioStreamAvailable += OnSpeakerRecordingAvailable;
    _recording.OnRecordingError += OnSpeakerRecordingError;
```

For both of the error event handlers, `OnSpeakerRecordingError` and `OnSpeakerIdentificationError`, we do not wish to print the error message here. For simplicity, we just output it to the debug console window.

The `OnSpeakerRecordingAvailable` event will be triggered when we have recorded some audio. This is the event handler that will trigger an attempt to identify the person speaking.

The first thing we need to do is to get a list of speaker profile IDs. We do so by calling `ListSpeakerProfiles`, which we looked at earlier:

```
    private async void OnSpeakerRecordingAvailable(object sender,
RecordingAudioAvailableEventArgs e)
    {
        try
        {
            List<Guid> profiles = await
_speakerIdentification.ListSpeakerProfiles();
```

With the list of speaker profiles, we call the `IdentifySpeaker` method on the `_speakerIdentification` object. We pass on the recorded audio stream and the profile list, as an array, as parameters to the function:

```
            _speakerIdentification.IdentifySpeaker(e.AudioStream,
profiles.ToArray());
        }
```

Finish the event handler by adding the corresponding `catch` clause.

Back in the `SpeakerIdentification.cs` file, we add the new function,
`IdentifySpeaker`:

```
    public async void IdentifySpeaker(Stream audioStream, Guid[]
speakerIds)
    {
        try
        {
            OperationLocation location = await
_speakerIdentificationClient.IdentifyAsync(audioStream, speakerIds);
```

The function should be marked as `async` and accept a `Stream` and an array of `Guid` as
parameters. To identify a speaker, we make a call to the `IdentifyAsync` function on the
`_speakerIdentificationClient` object. This requires an audio file, in the form of a
`Stream`, as well as an array of profile IDs. An optional third parameter is a `bool`, to indicate
whether or not you want to deviate from the recommended speech length.

If the call succeeds, we get an `OperationLocation` object back. This contains a URL, which
we can use to retrieve the status of the current identification process:

```
        if (location == null)
        {
            RaiseOnIdentificationError(new
SpeakerIdentificationErrorEventArgs ("Failed to identify speaker."));
            return;
        }
        GetIdentificationOperationStatus(location);
    }
```

If the resulting data contains nothing, we do not want to bother doing anything else. If it
does contain data, we pass it on as a parameter to the
`GetIdentifiactionOperationStatus` method:

```
    private async void GetIdentificationOperationStatus (OperationLocation
location)
    {
        try
        {
            while (true)
            {
                IdentificationOperation result = await
_speakerIdentificationClient.CheckIdentificationStatusAsync(location);
```

This function is quite similar to `GetEnrollmentOperationStatus`. We go into a `while` loop, which will run until the operation completes. We call `CheckIdentificationStatusAsync`, passing on the `location` as parameter, getting an `IdentificationOperation` as a result. This will contain data, such as status, the identified profiles ID, and the confidence of a correct result.

If the operation is not running, we raise the event with the status message and the `ProcessingResult`. If the operation is still running, we update the status and wait for one second before trying again:

```
if (result.Status != Status.Running)
{
        RaiseOnIdentificationStatusUpdated(new
SpeakerIdentificationStatusUpdateEventArgs(result.Status.ToString(),
$"Enrollment finished with message:{result.Message}.") { IdentifiedProfile
= result.ProcessingResult });
        break;
}

        RaiseOnIdentificationStatusUpdated(new
SpeakerIdentificationStatusUpdateEventArgs(result.Status.ToString(),
"Identifying..."));

        await Task.Delay(1000);
    }
}
```

Add the corresponding `catch` clause before heading back to the `HomeViewModel`.

The last piece in the puzzle is to create `OnSpeakerIdentificationStatusReceived`. Add the following inside it:

```
Application.Current.Dispatcher.Invoke(() =>
{
    if (e.IdentifiedProfile == null) return;

    SystemResponse = $"Hi
there,{e.IdentifiedProfile.IdentifiedProfileId}";
});
```

We check to see whether or not we have an identified profile. If we do not, we leave the function. If we have an identified profile, we give a response to the screen, stating who it is.

As with the administrative side of the application, this is a place where it would be convenient to have a name-to-profile ID mapping. As you can see from the following resulting screenshot, recognizing one `GUID` among many is not that easy:

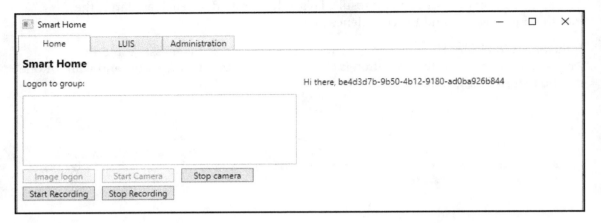

Verifying a person through speech

The process of verifying if a person is who they claim to be is quite similar to the identification process. To show how it is done, we will create a new example project, as we do not need this functionality in our smart-house Application.

Add the `Microsoft.ProjectOxford.SpeakerRecognition` and `NAudio` NuGet packages to the project. We will need the `Recording` class, which we used earlier, so copy this from the smart-house application's `Model` folder.

Open the `MainView.xaml` file. We need a few elements in the UI for the example to work. Add a `Button` element to add speaker profiles. Add two `Listbox` elements. One will hold available verification phrases, while the other will list our speaker profiles.

Add `Button` elements for deleting a profile, starting and stopping enrollment recording, resetting enrollment, and starting/stopping verification recording.

In the ViewModel, you will need to add two `ObservableCollection` properties: one of type `string`, the other of type `Guid`. One will contain the available verification phrases, while the other will contain the list of speaker profiles. You will also need a property for the selected speaker profile, and we also want a string property to show the status.

The ViewModel will also need seven ICommand properties, one for each of our buttons.

Create a new class in the Model folder, and call this SpeakerVerification. Add two new classes beneath this one, in the same file.

This first one is the event arguments that we pass on when we raise a status update event. The Verification property will, if set, hold the verification result, which we will see later:

```
public class SpeakerVerificationStatusUpdateEventArgs : EventArgs
{
    public string Status { get; private set; }
    public string Message { get; private set; }
    public Verification VerifiedProfile { get; set; }

    public SpeakerVerificationStatusUpdateEventArgs(string status, string message)
    {
        Status = status;
        Message = message;
    }
}
```

The next class is a generic event argument used when we raise an error event. In SpeakerVerification itself, add the following events:

```
public class SpeakerVerificationErrorEventArgs : EventArgs
{
    public string ErrorMessage { get; private set; }

    public SpeakerVerificationErrorEventArgs(string errorMessage)
    {
        ErrorMessage = errorMessage;
    }
}
```

For our convenience, add helper functions to raise these. Call them RaiseOnVerificationStatusUpdated and RaiseOnVerificationError. Raise the correct event in each of them:

```
public event EventHandler <SpeakerVerificationStatusUpdateEventArgs>
OnSpeakerVerificationStatusUpdated;

public event EventHandler<SpeakerVerificationErrorEventArgs>
OnSpeakerVerificationError;
```

We also need to add a private member, `ISpeakerVerificationServiceClient`. This will be in charge of calling the API. We inject this through the constructor.

Add the following functions to the class:

- `CreateSpeakerProfile`: No parameters, `async` function, return type `Task<Guid>`.
- `ListSpeakerProfile`: No parameters, `async` function, return type `Task<List<Guid>>`.
- `DeleteSpeakerProfile`: `Guid` as the required parameter, `async` function, no returned values.
- `ResetEnrollments`: `Guid` as the required parameter, `async` function, no returned values.

The contents of these functions can be copied from the corresponding functions in the smart-house application, as they are exactly the same. The only difference is that you need to change the API call from `_speakerIdentificationClient` to `_speakerVerificationClient`. Also, raising the events will require the newly created event arguments.

Next we need a function to list verification phrases. These are phrases that are supported to use for verification. When enrolling a profile, you are required to say one of the sentences in this list.

Create a function named `GetVerificationPhrase`. Have it return `Task<List<string>>`, and mark it as `async`:

```
public async Task<List<string>> GetVerificationPhrase()
{
    try
    {
        List<string> phrases = new List<string>();

        VerificationPhrase[] results = await
_speakerVerificationClient.GetPhrasesAsync("en-US");
```

We make a call to `GetPhrasesAsync`, specifying the language we want the phrases to be in. At the time of writing, English is the only possible choice.

If this call is successful, we will get an array of `VerificationPhrases` in return. Each element in this array contains a string with the phrase:

```
foreach(VerificationPhrase phrase in results) {
    phrases.Add(phrase.Phrase);
}
return phrases;
}
```

We loop through the array and add the phrases to our list, which we will return to the caller.

So, we have created a profile, and we have the list of possible verification phrases. Now we need to do the enrollment. To enroll, the service requires at least three enrollments from each speaker. That means you choose a phrase and enroll it at least three times.

When you do the enrollment, it is highly recommended to use the same recording device as you will use for verification.

Create a new function, called `CreateSpeakerEnrollment`. This should require a `Stream` and a `Guid`. The first parameter is the audio to use for enrollment. The latter is the ID of the profile we are enrolling. The function should be marked as `async`, and have no return value:

```
public async void CreateSpeakerEnrollment(Stream audioStream, Guid
profileId) {
    try {
        Enrollment enrollmentStatus = await
_speakerVerificationClient.EnrollAsync(audioStream, profileId);
```

When we call `EnrollAsync`, we pass on the `audioStream` and `profileId` parameters. If the call is successful, we get an `Enrollment` object back. This contains the current status of enrollment and specifies the number of enrollments you need to add before completing the process.

If the `enrollmentStatus` is null, we exit the function and notify any subscribers. If we do have status data, we raise the event to notify that there is a status update, specifying the current status:

```
if (enrollmentStatus == null) {
    RaiseOnVerificationError(new
SpeakerVerificationErrorEventArgs("Failed to start enrollment process."));
    return;
}

RaiseOnVerificationStatusUpdate(new
```

```
    SpeakerVerificationStatusUpdateEventArgs("Succeeded", $"Enrollment
    status:{enrollmentStatus.EnrollmentStatus}"));
        }
```

Add the corresponding `catch` clause to finish up the function.

The last function we need in this class is a function for verification. To verify a speaker, you need to send in an audio file. This file must be at least 1 second, and at most 15 seconds long. You will need to record the same phrase that you used for enrollment.

Call the `VerifySpeaker` function and make it require a `Stream` and `Guid`. The stream is the audio file we will use for verification. The `Guid` is the ID of the profile we wish to verify. The function should be `async`, and have no return type:

```
    public async void VerifySpeaker(Stream audioStream, Guid
speakerProfile) {
        try {
            Verification verification = await
_speakerVerificationClient.VerifyAsync(audioStream, speakerProfile);
```

We make a call to `VerifyAsync` from `_speakerVerificationClient`. The required parameters are `audioStream` and `speakerProfile`.

A successful API call will result in a `Verification` object in response. This will contain the verification results, as well as the confidence of the results being correct:

```
        if (verification == null) {
            RaiseOnVerificationError(new
SpeakerVerificationErrorEventArgs("Failed to verify speaker."));
            return;
        }

            RaiseOnVerificationStatusUpdate(new
SpeakerVerificationStatusUpdateEventArgs("Verified", "Verified speaker") {
VerifiedProfile = verification });
        }
```

If we do have a verification result, we raise the status update event. Add the corresponding `catch` clause to complete the function.

Back in the ViewModel, we need to wire up commands and event handlers. This is done in a similar manner as for speaker identification, and as such we will not cover the code in detail.

With the code compiling and running, the result may look similar to the following screenshot:

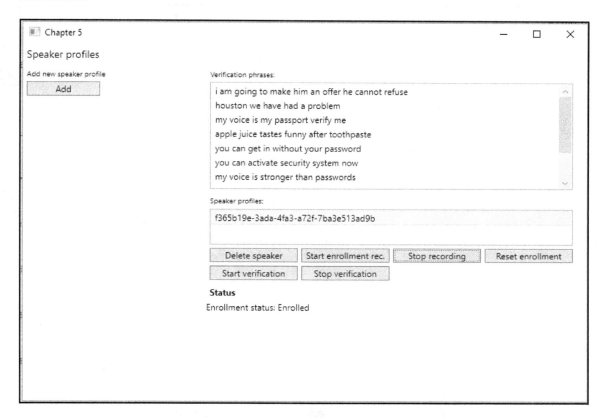

Here we can see that we have created a speaker profile. We have also completed the enrollment, and are ready to verify the speaker.

Verifying the speaker profile may result in the following:

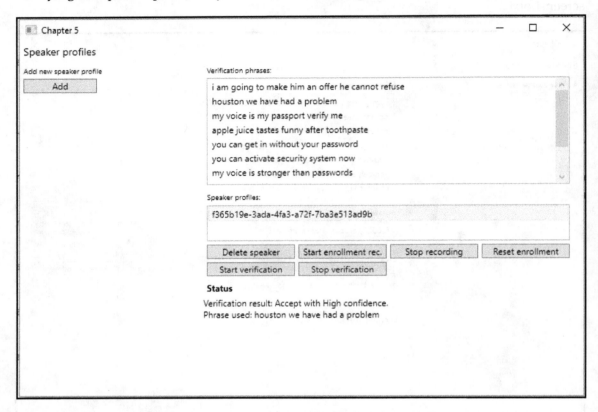

As you can see, the verification was accepted with high confidence.

If we try to verify using a different phrase, or let someone else try to verify as a particular speaker profile, we may end up with the following result:

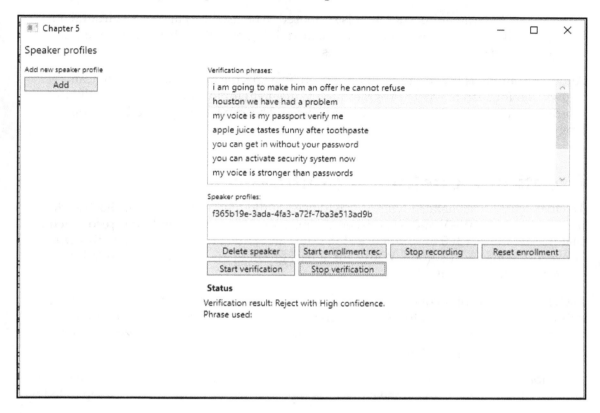

Here we can see that the verification has been rejected.

Customizing speech recognition

At the time of writing, the **Custom Recognition Intelligent Service** (**CRIS**) is still at the private beta stage. As such, we will not spend a lot of time on this, other than going through some key concepts.

When using speech-recognition systems, there are several components working together. Two of the more important components are acoustic and language models. The first one labels short fragments of audio into sound units. The second helps the system decide words, based on the likelihood of a given word appearing in certain sequences.

Although Microsoft has done a great job creating comprehensive acoustic and language models, there may still be times when you need to customize these models.

Imagine you have an application that is supposed to be used in a factory environment. Using speech recognition will require acoustic training of that environment, so that the recognition can separate usual factory noises.

Another example is if your application is used by a specific group of people. Say an application for search, where programming is the main topic. You would typically use words such as *object-oriented*, *dot net*, or *debugging*. This can be recognized by customizing language models.

Creating a custom acoustic model

To create custom acoustic models, you will need audio files and transcripts. Each audio file must be stored as WAV and be between 100 ms and 1 minute in length. It is recommended that there is at least 100 ms of silence at the start and end of the file. Typically, this will be between 500 ms and 1 second. With a lot of background noise, it is recommended to have silences in between content.

Each file should contain one sentence or utterance. Files should be uniquely named, and an entire set of files can be up to 2 GB. This translates to about 17 to 34 hours of audio, depending on the sampling rate. All files in one set should be placed in a zipped folder, which then can be uploaded.

Accompanying the audio files is a single file with the transcript. This should name the file and have the sentence next to the name. The filename and sentence should be separated by a tab.

Uploading the audio files and transcript will make CRIS process this. When this process is done, you will get a report stating the sentences that have failed or succeeded. If anything fails, you will get the reason for the failure.

When the dataset is uploaded you can create the acoustic model. This will be associated with the dataset you select. When the model is created, you can start the process to train it. Once the training is completed, you can deploy the model.

Creating a custom language model

Creating custom language models will also require a dataset. This set is a single plain-text file, containing sentences or utterances unique to your model. Each new line marks a new utterance. The maximum file size is 2 GB.

Uploading the file will make CRIS process it. Once the processing is done, you will get a report, which will print any errors, with the reason of failure.

With the processing done, you can create a custom language model. Each model will be associated with a given dataset of your selection. Once created, you can train the model, and when the training completes, you can deploy it.

Deploying the application

To deploy and use the custom models, you will need to create a deployment. You will name and describe the application. You can select acoustic models and language models. Be aware that you can only select one of each per deployed application.

Once created, the deployment will start. This process can take up to 30 minutes to complete, so be patient. When the deployment completes, you can get the required information by clicking on the application name. You will be given URLs you can use, as well as subscription keys to use.

To use the custom models with the Bing Speech API, you can overload `CreateDataClientWithIntent` and `CreateMicrophoneClient`. The overloads you will want to use specify both the primary and secondary API keys. You need to use the ones supplied by CRIS. Additionally, you need to specify the supplied URL as the last parameter.

Once this is done, you are able to use customized recognition models.

Summary

Throughout this chapter, we have focused on speech. We started by looking at how we can convert spoken audio to text and text to spoken audio. Using this, we modified our LUIS implementation so that we could speak commands and have conversations with the smart-house Application. From there, we moved on to see how we can identify a person speaking using the Speaker Recognition API. Using the same API, we also learned how to verify that a person is who they claim to be. Finally, we looked briefly at the core functionality of the Custom Recognition Intelligent Service.

In the following chapter, we will move back to textual APIs, where we will learn how to explore and analyze text in different ways.

6
Understanding Text

The previous chapter covered the Speech APIs. Throughout this chapter, we will look closer at more Language APIs. We will learn how to use spellcheck features. Moving on, we will see how to use web language models to generate and find the next word and sequences. We will then discover how to detect languages, key phrases, and sentiment in text. Finally, we will look briefly into linguistic analysis. Doing so will teach us how to explore the structure of text, discovering nouns, verbs, and more.

By the end of this chapter, we will have covered the following topics:

- Checking spelling and recognizing slang and informal language, common names, homonyms, and brands
- Breaking words, such as hashtags and URLs, into several words
- Finding the likelihood of a sequence of words appearing together, or a sequence appearing after a given word
- Detecting language, key phrases, and sentiment in text
- Executing linguistic analysis of text

Setting up a common core

Before we get into the details, we want to set ourselves up for success. At the time of writing, none of the Language APIs we will be covering have NuGet client packages. As such, we will need to call directly to the REST endpoints. Because of this, we will do some work beforehand, to make sure we get away with writing less code.

New project

We will not be adding the APIs to our smart house application. Go on and create a new project, using the MVVM template created in `Chapter 1`, *Getting Started with Microsoft Cognitive Services*:

1. Go into the NuGet package manager and install `Newtonsoft.Json`. This will help us deserialize API responses and serialize request bodies.
2. Right-click on **References**.
3. In the **Assemblies** tab, select **System.Web** and **System.Runtime.Serialization**.
4. Click **OK**.
5. In the `MainView.xaml` file, add a `TabControl` element. All our additional views will be added as `TabItems` in the MainView.

Web requests

All the APIs follow the same patterns. They call on their respective endpoints using either `POST` or `GET` requests. Further on, they pass on parameters as query strings, and some as a request body. Since they have these similarities, we can create one class that will handle all API requests.

In the `Model` folder, add a new class and call it `WebRequest`.

We need a few private variables:

```
private const string JsonContentTypeHeader = "application/json";

private static readonly JsonSerializerSettings _settings = new
JsonSerializerSettings
    {
        DateFormatHandling = DateFormatHandling.IsoDateFormat,
        NullValueHandling = NullValueHandling.Ignore,
        ContractResolver = new CamelCasePropertyNamesContractResolver()
    };

private HttpClient _httpClient;
private string _endpoint;
```

The constant, `JsonContentTypeHeader`, defines the content type we want to use for all API calls. `_settings` is a `JsonSerializerSettings` object, which specifies how we want JSON data to be (de)serialized.

The _httpClient is the object that will be used to make our API requests. The last member, _endpoint, will hold the API endpoint.

Our constructor will accept two parameters: one string for the URI, and one string for the API key:

```
public WebRequest(string uri, string apiKey)
{
    _endpoint = uri;
    _httpClient = new HttpClient();
    _httpClient.DefaultRequestHeaders.Add("Ocp-Apim-Subscription-Key",
apiKey);
}
```

We assign the uri to the corresponding member. Next, we create a new object of type HttpClient, and add one request header. This is the header containing the given apiKey.

The class will contain one function, MakeRequest. This should have the return type Task<TResponse>, meaning a type we specify when calling the function. It should accept three parameters: a HttpMethod, a query string, and a TRequest, meaning a request body we specify in the call. The function should be asynchronous:

```
public async Task <TResponse> MakeRequest <TRequest, TResponse>
(HttpMethod method, string queryString, TRequest requestBody =
default(TRequest))
```

The preceding lines show the complete function signature. Notice how we do not need to specify a request body, as there are some cases where it may be empty. We will cover what TRequest and TResponse may be, in a bit.

We enter a try clause:

```
try {
    string url = $"{_endpoint}{queryString}";
    var request = new HttpRequestMessage(method, url);

    if (requestBody != null)
        request.Content = new StringContent
(JsonConvert.SerializeObject(requestBody, _settings), Encoding.UTF8,
JsonContentTypeHeader);

    HttpResponseMessage response = await
_httpClient.SendAsync(request);
```

First, we create a `url`, consisting of our `_endpoint` and the `queryString`. Using this and the specified `method`, we create a `HttpRequestMessage` object.

If we have a `requestBody`, we add `Content` to the `request` object by serializing the `requestBody`.

With the request in order, we make an asynchronous call to `SendAsync` on the `_httpClient` object. This will call the API endpoint, returning a `HttpResponseMessage` containing the response.

If the `response` is successful, we want to get the `Content` as a string. This is done as follows:

1. Make an asynchronous call to `ReadAsStringAsync`. This will return a string.
2. Deserialize the string as a `TResponse` object.
3. Return the deserialized object to the caller.

In case there is no data in `responseContent`, we return a default `TResponse`. This will contain default values for all properties:

```
if (response.IsSuccessStatusCode)
{
    string responseContent = null;
    if (response.Content != null)
        responseContent = await response.Content.ReadAsStringAsync();
    if (!string.IsNullOrWhiteSpace(responseContent))
        return
JsonConvert.DeserializeObject<TResponse>(responseContent,_settings);

    return default(TResponse);
}
```

If the API response contains any error code, we try to get the error message as a string (`errorObjectString`). In a typical application, you would want to deserialize this and propagate it to the user. However, as this is a simple example application, we choose to output it to the `Debug` console window:

```
else
{
    if (response.Content != null &&
response.Content.Headers.ContentType.MediaType.Contains
(JsonContentTypeHeader))
    {
        var errorObjectString = await
response.Content.ReadAsStringAsync();
```

```
        Debug.WriteLine(errorObjectString);
    }
}
```

Make sure you add the corresponding `catch` clause. Output any exceptions to the `Debug` console window. Also, make sure you return a default `TResponse` if any exceptions occur.

Data contracts

As we need to (de)serialize JSON data as a part of requests and responses to the APIs, we need to create data contracts. These will act as the `TResponse` and `TRequest` objects, used in the `WebRequest` class.

Add a new folder, called **Contracts**, to the project. A typical data contract may look like the following:

```
[DataContract]
public class TextErrors {
    [DataMember]
    public string id { get; set; }

    [DataMember]
    public string message { get; set; }
}
```

This correlates to errors in the Text Analytics API. As you can see, it has two string properties, for `id` and `message`. Both may appear in a API response.

When discussing each API, we will see all request and response parameters in either table form or JSON format. We will not look at how each of these translates into a data contract, but it will take a similar form to that previously shown. It is then up to you to create the contracts needed.

The most important thing to note is that the property names must be identical to the corresponding JSON property.

Make sure the code compiles and that you can run the application before continuing.

Correcting spelling errors

The Bing Spell Check API leverages the power of machine learning and statistical machine translation to train and evolve a highly contextual algorithm for spell-checking. Doing so allows us to utilize this to perform spell-checking using context.

A typical spell-checker will follow dictionary-based rule sets. As you can imagine, this will need continuous updates and expansions.

Using the Bing Spell Check API, we can recognize and correct slang and informal language. It can recognize common naming errors and correct word-breaking issues. It can detect and correct words that sound the same, but differ in meaning and spelling (homophones). It can also detect and correct brands and popular expressions.

Create a new View in the `View` folder. Call the file `SpellCheckView.xaml`. Add a `TextBox` element for the input query. We will also need two `TextBox` elements for pre- and post-context. Add a `TextBox` element to show the result, and a `Button` element to execute the spell check.

Add a new ViewModel in the folder named `ViewModel`. Call the file `SpellCheckViewModel.cs`. Make the class public, and let it inherit from the `ObservableObject` class. Add the following private member:

```
private WebRequest _webRequest;
```

This is the `WebRequest` class we created earlier.

We need properties corresponding to our View. This means we need four `string` properties and one `ICommand` property.

 If you have not already done so, register for a free API key at `https://portal.azure.com`.

The constructor should look like this:

```
public SpellCheckViewModel()
{
    _webRequest = new WebRequest
("https://api.cognitive.microsoft.com/bing/v5.0/spellcheck/?",
"API_KEY_HERE");
    ExecuteOperationCommand = new DelegateCommand(
    ExecuteOperation, CanExecuteOperation);
}
```

We create a new object of type `WebRequest`, specifying the Bing Spell Check API endpoint, and the API key. We also create a new `DelegateCommand`, for our `ExecuteOperationCommand`, `ICommand`, property.

The `CanExecuteOperation` property should return `true` if our input query is filled in, and `false` otherwise.

To execute a call to the API, we do the following:

```
private async void ExecuteOperation(object obj)
{
    var queryString = HttpUtility.ParseQueryString(string.Empty);

    queryString["text"] = InputQuery;
    queryString["mkt"] = "en-us";
    //queryString["mode"] = "proof";

    if (!string.IsNullOrEmpty(PreContext))
queryString["preContextText"] = PreContext;

    if(!string.IsNullOrEmpty(PostContext))
    queryString["postContextText"] = PostContext;
```

First, we create a `queryString`, using `HttpUtility`. This will format the string, so it can be used in a URI.

As we will be calling the API using a `GET` method, we need to specify all parameters in the string. The required parameters are `text` and `mkt`, which are the input query and language, respectively. If we have entered `PreContext` and/or `PostContext`, we add these parameters as well. We will get into the different parameters in a bit.

To make the request, we need to make the following call:

```
    SpellCheckResponse response = await _webRequest.MakeRequest
<object, SpellCheckResponse>(HttpMethod.Get, queryString.ToString());
    ParseResults(response);
}
```

We call `MakeRequest` on the `_webRequest` object. As we are making a `GET` request, we do not need any request body, and we pass on `object` as `TRequest`. We expect a `SpellCheckResponse` contract in return. This will contain the resulting data, and we will look at the parameters in a bit.

When we have a response, we pass that on to a function, to parse it:

```
private void ParseResults(SpellCheckResponse response)
{
    if(response == null || response.flaggedTokens == null ||
response.flaggedTokens.Count == 0)
    {
        Result = "No suggestions found";
        return;
    }

    StringBuilder sb = new StringBuilder();
    sb.Append("Spell checking results:nn");
```

If we do not have any response, we exit the function. Otherwise, we create a StringBuilder to format the results:

```
foreach (FlaggedTokens tokens in response.flaggedTokens)
{
    if (!string.IsNullOrEmpty(tokens.token))
        sb.AppendFormat("Token is: {0}n", tokens.token);

    if(tokens.suggestions != null || tokens.suggestions.Count != 0)
    {
        foreach (Suggestions suggestion in tokens.suggestions)
        {
            sb.AppendFormat("Suggestion: {0} - with score: {1}n",
suggestion.suggestion, suggestion.score);
        }
        sb.Append("n");
    }
}
Result = sb.ToString();
```

If we have any corrected spellings, we loop through those. We add all suggestions to the StringBuilder, making sure we add the likelihood of the suggestion being correct. At the end, we make sure we output the result to the UI.

The following table describes all the parameters we can add to the API call:

Parameter	Description
text	The text we want to check for spelling and grammar errors.
mode	Current mode of spell check, it can be as follows: • **Proof**: Spelling corrections for long queries, typically as used in MS Word • **Spell**: Used for search engine corrections. Can be used for queries up to nine words (tokens)
preContextText	String that gives context to the text. *Petal* is valid, but if you specify bike in this parameter, it will be corrected to *Pedal*.
postContextText	String that gives context to the text. *Read* is valid, but if you specify carpet in this parameter, it may be corrected to *Red*.
mkt	For proof mode, language must be specified. Can currently be en-us, es-es, or pt-br. For Spell mode, all language codes are supported.

A successful response will be a JSON response, containing the following:

```
{
    "_type": "SpellCheck",
    "flaggedTokens": [
    {
        "offset": 5,
        "token": "Gatas",
        "type": "UnknownToken",
        "suggestions": [
        {
            "suggestion": "Gates",
            "score": 1
        }]
    }]
}
```

The offset is where the word appears in the text and token is the word that contains the error, while type describes the type of error. suggestions contains an array with the suggested correction and the probability of it being correct.

When the View and ViewModel have been correctly initialized, as seen in previous chapters, we should be able to compile and run the example.

An example output of running a spell check may give the following result:

Natural Language Processing using the Web Language Model

Using the **Web Language Model** (**Web LM**) API, we are able to do natural language processing. The language models are trained on web-scale, using data collected by Bing.

This API offers four key features:

- Joint probability of a sequence of words
- Conditional probability of one word following a sequence of words
- Most likely words to follow a given sequence
- Word breaking of strings without any spaces

To get started, add a new file, called WebLmView.xaml, to the View folder. In this view, we want to have two TextBox elements, one for our input query and one for the result View. In addition, we want four Button elements. Each of these will trigger one of the API features.

Next, we need to add a new ViewModel. Add a new file, called WebLmViewModel.cs, to the ViewModel folder. Add two string properties, corresponding to the input and output in the View. We also need to add four ICommand objects, which will be triggered when the buttons are pressed.

To be able to call the API, we add a private member of type WebRequest. Also, make sure the ViewModel inherits the ObservableObject.

 If you have not already done so, register for an API key at https://portal.azure.com.

Our constructor makes sure we create the ICommand objects, as well as the WebRequest object:

```
public WebLmViewModel()
{
    _webRequest = new
WebRequest("https://api.projectoxford.ai/text/weblm/v1.0/",
"API_KEY_HERE");
    BreakWordsCommand = new DelegateCommand(BreakWords,
CanExecuteOperation);
    CondProbCommand = new DelegateCommand(CondProb,
CanExecuteOperation);
    JointProbCommand = new DelegateCommand(JointProb,
CanExecuteOperation);
    GenerateNextWordsCommand = new DelegateCommand(GenerateNextWords,
CanExecuteOperation);
}
```

When we create the `WebRequest` object, we specify the API endpoint and our API key. The `CanExecuteOperation` should return `true` if the input is entered, and `false` otherwise.

Breaking a word into several words

If we have an application analyzing websites or texts, it may be convenient to break up words. With the increasing use of social media, we have hashtags, which may be hard to read as they come. Using the Web LM API, we can break these words into several words.

 Punctuation and exotic characters can be difficult to break, so try to limit input strings to lower case, alpha-numeric characters.

To utilize this feature, we need to make a `POST` call to the API. However, we do not need to pass on a request body, as all parameters are specified in the URL:

```
private async void BreakWords(object obj)
{
    var queryString = HttpUtility.ParseQueryString(string.Empty);

    queryString["model"] = "body";
    queryString["text"] = InputQuery;
    //queryString["order"] = "5";
    //queryString["maxNumOfCandidatesReturned"] = "5";

    WebLmWordBreakResponse response = await
_webRequest.MakeRequest<object, WebLmWordBreakResponse>(HttpMethod.Post,
$"breakIntoWords?{queryString.ToString()}");
```

We create a `queryString` from an empty base. Moving on, we enter the required parameters. The first of these is `model`. This is the model to use for breaking, and it is a string that can be a `title`, `anchor`, `query`, or `body`. The next required parameter is `text`. Any spaces in the text will be maintained in the result.

Optionally, we can enter the `order` of N-gram. The default value is 5, and the supported range is from 1-5. In addition, we can enter the number of candidates to be returned. The default is 5, which is okay for us.

With the query string in place, we call `MakeRequest`. As we do not pass on a request body, we leave `TRequest` to `object`. We expect a `WebLmWordBreakResponse` as the result. Notice that we specify `breakIntoWords` before the `queryString`. This is so the query string is formatted correctly:

```
if(response == null && response.candidates?.Length != 0)
{
    Result = "Could not break into words";
    return;
}

StringBuilder sb = new StringBuilder();

foreach (WebLmCandidates candidate in response.candidates)
{
    sb.AppendFormat("Candidate: {0}, with probability:
{1}n", candidate.words, candidate.probability);
}

Result = sb.ToString();
```

If we have a successful response, we loop through all the `candidates`. We make sure to output each candidate word, with the probability of the word being correct.

A successful call can result in the following JSON result:

```
{
    "candidates" :[
    {
        "words" : "test for word break",
        "probability" :   -13.911
    }]
}
```

We have an array of `candidates`, where each candidate contains `words` and the `probability` of correctness.

A successful API call can give the following output:

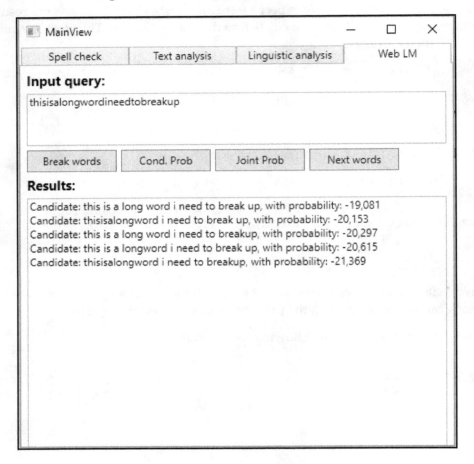

Generating the next word in a sequence of words

To improve writing usability for the end user, we can add next-word generation. By utilizing this feature, we can get the word that is most likely to follow a sequence, and suggest this for our user.

Executing this operation is a POST call, without a request body. As with word breaking, we pass on any parameter in the query string:

```
private async void GenerateNextWords(object obj) {
    var queryString = HttpUtility.ParseQueryString(string.Empty);

    queryString["model"] = "body";
    queryString["words"] = InputQuery;
    //queryString["order"] = "5";
    //queryString["maxNumOfCandidatesReturned"] = "5";

    WebLmNextWordResults response = await _webRequest.MakeRequest
<object, WebLmNextWordResults>(HttpMethod.Post,
$"generateNextWords?{queryString.ToString()}");
```

As you can see, the parameters needed for this call are similar to the word-breaking call. The two differences are that we add generateNextWords as the REST endpoint in the query string, and that we expect a WebLmNextWordResults as the result:

```
    if (response == null && response.candidates?.Length == 0) {
        Result = "Could not generate next words";
        return;
    }

    StringBuilder sb = new StringBuilder();
    foreach (WebLmNextWordCandidates candidate in response.candidates)
{
        sb.AppendFormat("Candidate: {0}, with probability: {1}n",
candidate.word, candidate.probability);
    }

    Result = sb.ToString();
```

If the result contains any candidates, we loop through them. Each candidate will contain a word, and the probability that this word is the next in a sequence. We make sure to display this in the UI.

A successful request can generate the following JSON result:

```
    {
        "candidates": [{ "word" : "range", "probability" :  -1.396 }]
    }
```

This translates into an array of `candidates`, where each candidate contains a `word`, and the `probability` that this is the next word.

Successfully completing this call may give the following result:

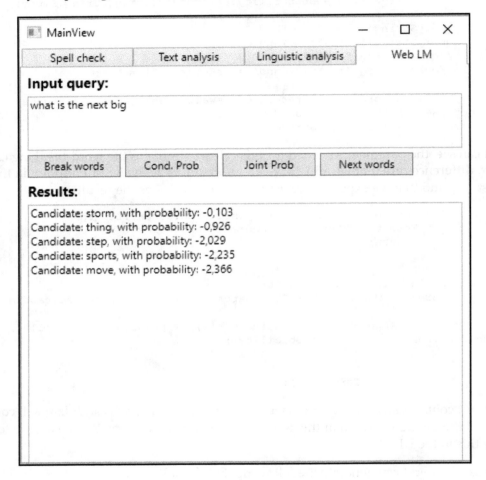

Learning if a word is likely to follow a sequence of words

Using the conditional probability feature, we can find the conditional probability of a given word following a sequence of words.

Like the previous two features, this is a POST call:

```
private async void CondProb(object obj)
{
    var queryString = HttpUtility.ParseQueryString(string.Empty);

    queryString["model"] = "body";
    //queryString["order"] = "5";

    var input = InputQuery.Split(';');

    WebLmConditionalProbRequest request = new
WebLmConditionalProbRequest
    {
        queries = new WebLmCondProbQueries[] {new WebLmCondProbQueries
{word = input[1], words = input[0]}}
    };
```

We create a new queryString, adding the model to use for calculations. The values can be title, anchor, body, or query. Optionally, we can pass on the N-gram order, which may be in the range of 1-5. The default is 5.

To make the UI a bit simpler for this example, we pass on a sequence and the given word in a special format. The input should be formatted as follows:

```
"my name; is"
```

This will allow us to split the string into two, allowing us to specify the sequence of words and the word itself. These should be added in a WebLmCondProbQueries object, in the WebLmConditionalProbRequest request contract:

```
WebLmCondProbResponse response = await _webRequest.MakeRequest
<WebLmConditionalProbRequest, WebLmCondProbResponse>(HttpMethod.Post,
$"calculateConditionalProbability?{queryString.ToString()}",request);
```

We call `MakeRequest`, specifying that the request body is of type `WebLmConditionalProbRequest` and that we expect a `WebLmCondResponse` in return. We precede the query string with `calculatedConditionalProbability` to ensure we contact the correct REST endpoint:

```
if (response == null && response.results?.Length == 0) {
    Result = "Could not calculate the conditional probability";
    return;
}

StringBuilder sb = new StringBuilder();

foreach (WebLmCondProbResult candidate in response.results) {
    sb.AppendFormat("Probability of '{0}' being the next word in '{1}'
is {2}n", candidate.word, candidate.words, candidate.probability);
}

Result = sb.ToString();
```

If the response is successful, and contains `results`, we loop through it. We output the given `word`, the sequence of `words`, and the `probability` that the `word` is the next in a sequence.

A successful result should result in a JSON similar to the following:

```
{
    "results":[ {
        "words": "hello world wide",
        "word": "web",
        "probability" :  -1.541 }]
}
```

This is an array of `results`. Each item contains the sequence of `words`, the `word` we are checking, and the `probability` of it being the next word.

With a successful call, we may get the following result:

Learning if certain words are likely to appear together

By using the **joint probability** feature, we can determine whether or not certain words will appear together.

We create a `queryString`, adding the `model` and, optionally, the N-gram `order` as parameters. Next, we create our `WebLmJointProbRequest` contract object. This should contain an array of strings, used as the query. As you can see, we take a quick way to get more samples, by using a comma separator:

```
private async void JointProb(object obj)
{
    var queryString = HttpUtility.ParseQueryString(string.Empty);
```

```
queryString["model"] = "body";
//queryString["order"] = "5";

WebLmJointProbRequest request = new WebLmJointProbRequest
{
    queries = InputQuery.Split(',')
};
```

With the request body and query string created, we call `MakeRequest`. We specify that the request body is of type `WebLmJointProbRequest` and expect a response of type `WebLmJointProbResponse`. Preceding the query string is the REST endpoint for this operation, `calculateJointProbability`:

```
WebLmJointProbResponse response = await _webRequest.MakeRequest
<WebLmJointProbRequest, WebLmJointProbResponse>(HttpMethod.Post,
$"calculateJointProbability?{queryString.ToString()}", request);
```

If the call is successful and contains any `results`, we loop through them. We output the given sequence of `words` and the joint `probability` that they appear together:

```
if (response == null && response.results?.Length == 0) {
    Result = "Could not calculate the joint probability";
    return;
}

StringBuilder sb = new StringBuilder();

foreach (WebLmJointProbResults candidate in response.results) {
    sb.AppendFormat("Probability of '{0}' to appear together is {1}n",
candidate.words, candidate.probability);
}

Result = sb.ToString();
```

A successful result should give the result as a JSON, like this:

```
{
    "results": [{
        "words" : "this",
        "probability " :  -3.541
    }]
}
```

This contains an array of `results`. Each result will contain the sequence of `words`, and the `probability` that they will appear together.

Giving this, a test run can present us with the following result:

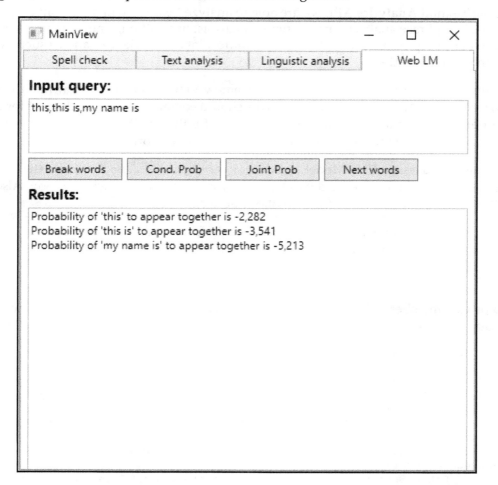

Extracting information through textual analysis

Using the **Textual Analytics API,** we are able to analyze text. We will cover language detection, key-phrase analysis, and sentiment analysis. In addition, a new feature is the ability to detect topics. This does, however, require a lot of sample text, and as such, we will not go into details on this.

For all our text analysis tasks, we will be using a new View. Add a new View into the `View` folder, called `TextAnalysisView.xaml`. This should contain a `TextBox` element for the input query. It should also have a `TextBox` element for the result. We will need three `Button` elements, one for each detection analysis we will perform.

We will also need a new ViewModel, so add `TextAnalysisViewModel.cs` to the `ViewModel` folder. In this we need two `string` properties, one for each `TextBox`. Also add three `ICommand` properties, one for each of our buttons.

 If you have not already done so, register for an API key at `https:// portal.azure.com`.

Add a private member, called `_webRequest`, of type `WebRequest`. With that in place, we can create our constructor:

```
public TextAnalysisViewModel()
{
    _webRequest = new
WebRequest("https://westus.api.cognitive.microsoft.com/text/analytics/v2.0/
","API_KEY_HERE");
    DetectLanguageCommand = new DelegateCommand(DetectLanguage,
CanExecuteOperation);
    DetectKeyPhrasesCommand = new DelegateCommand(DetectKeyPhrases,
CanExecuteOperation);
    DetectSentimentCommand = new DelegateCommand(DetectSentiment,
CanExecuteOperation);
}
```

The constructor creates a new `WebRequest` object, specifying the API endpoint and API key. We then go on to create the `DelegateCommand` objects for our `ICommand` properties. The `CanExecuteOperation` function should return `true` if we have entered the input query, and `false` otherwise.

Detecting language

The API can detect which language is used in text, from over 120 different languages.

This is a POST call, so we need to send in a request body. A request body should consist of documents. This is basically an array containing a unique id for each text. It also needs to contain the text itself:

```
private async void DetectLanguage(object obj)
{
    var queryString = HttpUtility.ParseQueryString("languages");
    TextRequests request = new TextRequests
    {
        documents = new List<TextDocumentRequest>
        {
            new TextDocumentRequest {id="FirstId", text=InputQuery}
        }
    };

    TextResponse response = await _webRequest.MakeRequest<TextRequests,
TextResponse>(HttpMethod.Post, queryString.ToString(), request);
```

We create a queryString, specifying the REST endpoint we want to reach. Then we go on to create a TextRequest contract, which contains documents. As we only want to check one piece of text, we add one TextDocumentRequest contract, specifying an id and the text.

When the request is created, we call MakeRequest. We expect the response to be of type TextResponse, and the request body to be of type TextRequests. We pass along POST as the call method, the queryString, and the request body.

If the response is successful, we loop through the detectedLanguages. We add the languages to a StringBuilder, also outputting the probability of that language being correct. This is then displayed in the UI:

```
if(response.documents == null || response.documents.Count == 0)
{
    Result = "No languages was detected.";
    return;
}

StringBuilder sb = new StringBuilder();

foreach (TextLanguageDocuments document in response.documents)
{
    foreach (TextDetectedLanguages detectedLanguage in
```

```
document.detectedLanguages)
        {
            sb.AppendFormat("Detected language: {0} with score {1}n",
detectedLanguage.name, detectedLanguage.score);
        }
    }

    Result = sb.ToString();
```

A successful response will contain the following JSON:

```
{
    "documents": [
    {
        "id": "string",
        "detectedLanguages": [
        {
            "name": "string",
            "iso6391Name": "string",
            "score": 0.0
        }]
    }],
    "errors": [
    {
        "id": "string",
        "message": "string"
    }]
}
```

This contains an array of `documents` – as many as provided in the request. Each document will be marked with a unique `id` and contain an array of `detectedLanguages`. These languages will have `name`, `iso6391Name`, and the probability (`score`) of being correct.

If any errors occur for any document, we will get an array of `errors`. Each error will contain the `id` of the document where the error occurred, and the `message` as a string.

A successful call may present the following result:

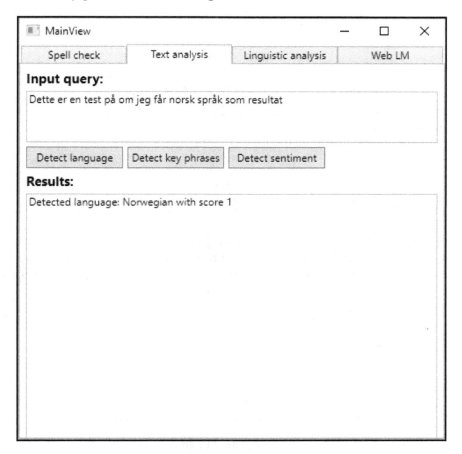

Extracting key phrases from text

Extracting key phrases from text may be useful if we want our application to know key talking points. Using this, we can learn what people are discussing in articles, discussions, or similar.

This call also uses the POST method, requiring a request body. As with language detection, we need to specify documents. Each document will need a unique ID, the text, and also the language used. At the time of writing, English, German, Spanish, and Japanese are the only languages supported.

To extract key phrases, we do the following:

```
private async void DetectKeyPhrases(object obj)
{
    var queryString = HttpUtility.ParseQueryString("keyPhrases");
    TextRequests request = new TextRequests
    {
        documents = new List<TextDocumentRequest>
        {
            new TextDocumentRequest { id = "FirstId", text =
InputQuery, language = "en" }
        }
    };

    TextKeyPhrasesResponse response = await
_webRequest.MakeRequest<TextRequests,
TextKeyPhrasesResponse>(HttpMethod.Post, queryString.ToString(), request);
```

As you can see, it is quite similar to detecting languages. We create a `queryString`, using `keyPhrases` as the REST endpoint. We create a request object of type `TextRequests`. We add the documents list, creating one new `TextDocumentRequest`. Again, we need the `id` and `text`, but we have also added a `language` tag:

```
if (response.documents == null || response.documents?.Count == 0)
{
    Result = "No key phrases found.";
    return;
}

StringBuilder sb = new StringBuilder();
foreach (TextKeyPhrasesDocuments document in response.documents)
{
    sb.Append("Key phrases found:n");
    foreach (string phrase in document.keyPhrases)
    {
        sb.AppendFormat("{0}n", phrase);
    }
}

Result = sb.ToString();
```

If the response contains any key phrases, we loop through them and output them to the UI. A successful response will provide the following JSON:

```
{
    "documents": [{
        "keyPhrases": [
```

```
        "string" ],
        "id": "string"
    }],
    "errors": [
    {
        "id": "string",
        "message": "string"
    } ]
}
```

Here we have an array of `documents`. Each document has a unique `id`, corresponding to the ID in the request. Each document also contains an array of strings, with `keyPhrases`.

As with language detection, any errors will be returned as well.

Learning if a text is positive or negative

Using sentiment analysis, we can detect whether or not a text is positive. If you have a merchandise website where users can submit feedback, this feature can automatically analyze if the feedback is generally positive or negative.

The sentiments scores are returned as a number between 0 and 1, where the higher number indicates positive sentiment.

As with the previous two analyses, this is a POST call, requiring a request body. Again, we need to specify documents, and each document requires a unique ID, the text, and the language:

```
private async void DetectSentiment(object obj)
{
    var queryString = HttpUtility.ParseQueryString("sentiment");
    TextRequests request = new TextRequests
    {
        documents = new List<TextDocumentRequest>
        {
            new TextDocumentRequest { id = "FirstId", text =
InputQuery, language = "en" }
        }
    };

    TextSentimentResponse response = await _webRequest.MakeRequest
<TextRequests, TextSentimentResponse>(HttpMethod.Post,
queryString.ToString(), request);
```

We create a `queryString`, pointing to `sentiment` as the REST endpoint. The data contract is `TextRequests`, containing `documents`. The document we pass on has a unique `id`, the `text`, and the `language`:

A call to `MakeRequest` will require a request body of type `TextSentimentRequests`, and we expect the result to be of type `TextSentimentResponse`.

If the response contains any `documents`, we loop through them. For each document, we check the `score`, and output whether or not the text is positive or negative. This is then shown in the UI:

```
if(response.documents == null || response.documents?.Count == 0)
{
    Result = "No sentiments detected";
    return;
}

StringBuilder sb = new StringBuilder();

foreach (TextSentimentDocuments document in response.documents)
{
    sb.AppendFormat("Document ID: {0}n", document.id);

    if (document.score >= 0.5)
        sb.AppendFormat("Sentiment is positive, with a score of{0}n",
document.score);
    else
        sb.AppendFormat("Sentiment is negative with a score of {0}n",
document.score);
}

Result = sb.ToString();
```

A successful response will result in the following JSON:

```
{
    "documents": [
    {
        "score": 0.0,
        "id": "string"
    }],
    "errors": [
    {
        "id": "string",
        "message": "string"
    }]
}
```

This is an array of documents. Each document will have a corresponding id as the request, and the sentiment score. If any errors have occurred, it will be entered as with language and key-phrase detection.

A successful test can look like the following:

Exploring text using linguistic analysis

Using the **Linguistic Analysis API,** we can explore the structure of text. We can access part-of-speech tagging and parsing, which allows us to tap into important concepts and actions. By using this API, we can understand the structure of a text. This can help us if we are mining customer feedback, interpreting user commands, or consuming web text.

As linguistic analysis is an advanced topic, we will not dive into all its details. Instead, we will go through a quick introduction to key concepts, and then see how we can do the analysis itself. We will not spend time on parsing the resulting data for the UI, so we will simply print the JSON result.

 For more information on linguistic analysis and natural language analysis, please refer to the Wikipedia article at `https://en.wikipedia.org/wiki/ Natural_language_processing`.

Introduction to linguistic analysis

At the time of writing, there are currently three available tools in the API. These are as follows:

- Sentences separation and tokenization
- Part-of-speech tagging
- Constituency parsing

The *sentences separation and tokenization* is the first step to take. This will break text into sentences, which may sound simple. However, a sentence may end in different stop characters. A period may mean the end of a sentence, but it may also mark an abbreviation.

When we have separate sentences from a text, we can tokenize it. In its simplest form, this means to split all sentences based on white spaces (for the English language). Punctuation will typically also be split into unique tokens, but if it is a part of an abbreviation, it will be a part of the abbreviation token. So, the word `Mrs.` will be one token, while `The end.` will be three tokens.

The next step is to identify part-of-speech for all words. This means we identify categories such as nouns and verbs. Different words may fall into different categories, based on the context.

Words in a text will be marked with a part-of-speech tag. This may be NN for nouns or VB for verbs. A complete list of part-of-speech tags can be found in Appendix B, *Additional Information on Linguistic Analysis*.

The final step is to parse constituency. This means identifying phrases in text, which allows us to find phrases in text and see the modifiers surrounding the phrase.

In these terms, a phrase is a group of words, where each word plays a specific role. In a sentence, a group of words can be moved or replaced, while the sentence should still remain fluent and grammatical.

We tag phrases, such as ADJP for an adjective phrase, or NP for a noun phrase. A complete list of all phrase types can be found in Appendix B, *Additional Information on Linguistic Analysis*.

At the time of writing, all analyses follow the specification of Penn Treebank (https://catalog.ldc.upenn.edu/docs/LDC95T7/cl93.html).

Analyzing text from a linguistic viewpoint

Following that brief introduction, we can now add linguistic analysis to our application. Add a new View to the View folder, and call the file LinguisticView.xaml. We will need to add a ListBox element to contain the analyzers we want to select from. We should also add TextBox elements for our input query and result View. Finally, we will need a Button element to execute the analysis.

Next, we add the ViewModel. Create a new file, called LinguisticViewModel.cs, and add it to the ViewModel folder. This will need an ObservableCollection property of type Analyzer to hold our analyzers. The Analyzer type is a data contract, which will become apparent in a bit. It will also need a List property of type Analyzer to hold the selected analyzers as well. Finally, we need two string properties for our input query and result View, as well as an ICommand property for our button.

We need to add a private member of type `WebRequest` to be able to execute our API calls. Our constructor should look like the following:

```
public LinguisticViewModel()
{
    _webRequest = new
WebRequest("https://api.projectoxford.ai/linguistics/v1.0/",
"API_KEY_HERE");
    ExecuteOperationCommand = new DelegateCommand(
    ExecuteOperation, CanExecuteOperation);

    GetAnalyzers();
}
```

We create a new `WebRequest` object, specifying the correct endpoint and API key. Then we create a new `DelegateCommand` for our `ICommand` property, `ExecuteOperationCommand`. As before, `CanExecuteOperation` should return `true` if our input query has been entered, and `false` otherwise.

When we create this ViewModel, we need to get the list of analyzers. This will be done in `GetAnalyzers`:

```
private async void GetAnalyzers()
{
    var queryString = HttpUtility.ParseQueryString("analyzers");

    Analyzer[] response = await _webRequest.MakeRequest<object,
Analyzer[]>(HttpMethod.Get,queryString.ToString());
```

To get analyzers, we need to make a `GET` call to the API. We create a `queryString`, which specifies `analyzers` as the REST endpoint. No more parameters are needed. When calling `MakeRequest`, we do not need any request bodies, so we leave `TRequest` as `object`. We expect the result to be an array of type `Analyzer`.

If we get a successful response, we loop through the array. We will add each element to our `Analyzer` property, which will display them in the UI:

```
    if (response == null || response.Length == 0) return;

    foreach (Analyzer analyzer in response) {
        Analyzers.Add(analyzer);
    }
```

A successful response will return an array of the analyzers available. The parameters for each analyzer are described in the following table:

Parameter	Description
id	A string naming the ID of the analyzer. Typically, this is in GUID format.
languages	Each language can support one or more languages. These will be available in this parameter.
kind	Describes the type of analysis provided.
specification	Each analyzer operates under a given specification, named in this parameter.
implementation	The name of the implementation of the given analyzer.

When we run an analysis, we can use multiple analyzers at the same time, so create a `SelectionChanged` event handler in the code behind the View. Let this add selected items to the `List` property in the ViewModel.

With the list of analyzers, we can now execute an analysis:

```
private async void ExecuteOperation(object obj)
{
    var queryString = HttpUtility.ParseQueryString("analyze");

    LinguisticRequest request = new LinguisticRequest
    {
        language = "en", analyzerIds = SelectedAnalyzers.Select(x =>
x.id).ToArray(), text = InputQuery
    };

    AnalyzerResults[] results = await
_webRequest.MakeRequest<LinguisticRequest,
AnalyzerResults[]>(HttpMethod.Post, queryString.ToString(), request);
```

This is a POST call. We start off by creating a queryString, pointing to our analyze REST endpoint. We need to add a request body, a data contract of type LinguisticRequest. This should contain the current language, an array with the IDs of all the analyzers we want to use, and the text to analyze.

Making a call to MakeRequest assumes we pass on a LinguisticRequest request type. It expects an array of AnalyzerResults as the response:

```
if(results == null || results.Length == 0) {
    Result = "Could not analyze text.";
    return;
}
StringBuilder sb = new StringBuilder();

foreach (AnalyzerResults analyzedResult in results) {
    sb.AppendFormat("{0}n", analyzedResult.result.ToString());
}

Result = sb.ToString();
```

If the result contains data, we loop through it and display the analysis result in the UI.

A successful result will result in a JSON response, as follows:

```
[ {
    "analyzerId" : "4fa79af1-f22c-408d-98bb-b7d7aeef7f04",
    "result" : ["NNP",",","NNP","VBP","PRP","NN","."]
} ]
```

We will have one item per analyzer. As you can see in the result field, this analyzer is the constituency parsing type, which is also known as phrase structure parsing. It displays all the phrase types detected.

A test run, with all analyzers selected, can provide us with a result shown in the following screenshot:

Summary

Throughout this chapter, we have focused on the Language APIs. We started by creating the parts needed to execute API calls to the different services. Following this, we looked at the Bing Spell Check API. Next, we learned how to use web language models to break words and calculate the probability of word sequences. We moved into more analytical APIs, where we learned how to detect languages, key phrases, and sentiment. We completed the chapter by taking a brief look at linguistic analysis.

The next chapter will take us from Language APIs into Knowledge APIs. In this chapter, we will learn how to recognize and identify entities based on context. In addition, we will learn how to use the Recommendations API.

7
Extending Knowledge Based on Context

"By leveraging Azure Machine Learning and the Recommendations API, we have launched a new Personalized Commerce Experience for retailers that grows shopper conversion and engagement on any channel."

- Frank Kouretas, Chief Product Officer at Orckestra

With the previous chapter, we covered the remaining Language APIs. In this chapter, we will look into the first two Knowledge APIs: the Entity Linking API and the Recommendations API. We will start by learning how to link entities in text. Using the Entity Linking API, we can identify different entities in text, based on the context. Moving on, we will look into the Recommendations API. This is well-suited for e-commerce applications, where you can recommend different items based on different criteria.

With this chapter completed, we will have covered the following topics:

- Recognizing and identifying separate entities in text, based on context
- Recommending items based on items frequently bought together
- Recommending items based on which items other customers who bought this item bought
- Recommending items based on a customer's previous activities

Linking entities based on context

Using the Entity Linking API, we can link entities in text based on the context. Doing so means that we can separate the meaning of a word, based on the usage in the given text. A word, such as *times*, may mean the newspaper *The New York Times*. The same word can also be used in a place name, `Times Square`. The context decides which of the two entities *times* represents. The API detects entities within given text, and relates all entities to a Wikipedia entry.

We are going to add entity-linking capabilities to our smart-house application. For now, we will just add a text field input, but in later chapters we will see how it can be utilized.

In Visual Studio, add the `Microsoft.ProjectOxford.EntityLinking` NuGet package to the project. This contains the client library required to use the API.

Add a new file, the `EntityLinking.cs` file, to the `Model` folder. Beneath the class, `EntityLinking`, add a new class called `EntityLinkingErrorEventArgs`. This will allow us to raise events if errors occur, and notify the caller.

Let it look like the following:

```
public class EntityLinkingErrorEventArgs {
    public string ErrorMessage { get; private set; }
    public EntityLinkingErrorEventArgs(string errorMessage) {
        ErrorMessage = errorMessage;
    }
}
```

Back into the `EntityLinking` class, we define our error event, and a private member for the Entity Linking client. In addition, we want to add a helper function to raise the event, called `RaiseOnEntityLinkingError`. This should accept the previously accepted event arguments created:

```
public event EventHandler<EntityLinkingErrorEventArgs>
EntityLinkingError;

private EntityLinkingServiceClient _entityLinkingServiceClient;
```

We create the `EntityLinkingServiceClient` object in our constructor:

```
    public EntityLinking(string apiKey)
    {
        _entityLinkingServiceClient = new
EntityLinkingServiceClient(apiKey, "ROOT_URI");
    }
```

When creating `EntityLinking`, we pass on the API key as a parameter. This is used when creating the service client. We also need to specify the root URI, as we have seen with some of the previous APIs.

 If you have not already done so, you can sign up for the Entity Linking API at `https://portal.azure.com`.

We need one function in this class, `LinkEntities`. This should accept two `strings` and one `int` as parameters. It should have the return type `Task<EntityLink[]>` and be marked as `async`:

```
    public async Task<EntityLink[]> LinkEntities(string inputText, string
selection = "", int offset = 0)
    {
        try {
            EntityLink[] linkingResponse = await
_entityLinkingServiceClient.LinkAsync(inputText, selection, offset);

            return linkingResponse;
        }
```

The only required parameter to the `LinkAsync` function on `_entityLinkingServiceClient` is `inputText`. This is the text in which the service will try to separate entities. If the last two parameters are not specified, the service will look for all the entities it can find.

If we enter a word into `selection`, the service will link entities with that name. If we enter this, we also need to add `offset`. This is the position of the first character of the word, where it is first found in the text.

Make sure to add the corresponding `catch` clause. Raise the error event if any exceptions are caught, using the exception message as a parameter in the event arguments.

Next we need to add a View, so create a new file, called `EntityLinkingView.xaml`, in the `View` folder.

We want to add four `TextBox` elements. Two of these should be bigger, as they are the input text and result text. Two should be smaller, as these will be for the entity selection and offset inputs. In addition, we will need a `Button` element, to link entities.

With the View in place, we can add a ViewModel. Add `EntityLinkingViewModel.cs` to the `ViewModel` folder. We need to add a private member of type `EntityLinking`. We will also need to add properties corresponding to our View. Add three `string` properties, corresponding to input text, result text, and entity selection. Add one `int` property, for our offset. Last, but not least, we need an `ICommand` property for our `Button`:

```
public EntityLinkingViewModel()
{
    LinkEntitiesCommand = new DelegateCommand(LinkEntities,
CanLinkEntities);

    _entityLinking = new EntityLinking("API_KEY_HERE");
    _entityLinking.EntityLinkingError += OnEntityLinkingError;
}
```

The constructor creates the `ICommand` property as a `DelegateCommand` object. `CanLinkEntities` should return true if we have input text, and false otherwise.

Further on, the constructor creates our `EntityLinking` object, specifying the API key. We also subscribe to the error event. `OnEntityLinkingError` should output the error message in the UI, if the API call fails.

The `LinkEntities` function will be responsible for calling the API and outputting the result:

```
private async void LinkEntities(object obj)
{
    EntityLink[] linkedEntities = await _entityLinking.LinkEntities
(InputText, Selection, Offset);

    if(linkedEntities == null || linkedEntities.Length == 0) {
        ResultText = "No linked entities found";
        return;
    }
```

We call `LinkEntities` on `_entityLinking`. The parameters are `InputText`, the entity `Selection`, and `Offset`, as mentioned previously. A successful result will return an array of type `EntityLink`. Each item in this array will contain the name, Wikipedia ID, and the probability of this entity being correctly identified.

It will also contain an array of matches. In this array, each item contains a given text, with the given entity in it. It will also contain an array of entries, where each item signifies a place in the text, identified by the first character's position.

Knowing this, we can format and print out the result:

```
StringBuilder sb = new StringBuilder();

sb.AppendFormat("Entities found: {0}nn", linkedEntities.Length);

foreach (EntityLink entity in linkedEntities)
{
    sb.AppendFormat("Entity '{0}'ntScore {1}ntWikipedia ID
'{2}'ntMatches in text: {3}nn", entity.Name, entity.Score,
entity.WikipediaID, entity.Matches.Count);

    foreach (var match in entity.Matches)
    {
        sb.AppendFormat("Text match: '{0}'n", match.Text);

        sb.Append("Found at position: ");
        foreach (var entry in match.Entries)
        {
            sb.AppendFormat("{0}t", entry.Offset);
        }

        sb.Append("nn");
    }
}

ResultText = sb.ToString();
```

Make sure the code compiles, and run it. A test run may give the following result:

In this test run, no given entity selections are specified; we get all entities recognized in the text.

If, in this context, we specify `Webb` as an entity, we will be presented with the following result:

Providing personalized recommendations

If you run an e-commerce site, a feature that is nice to have is recommendations. Using the Recommendation API, you can easily add this. Utilizing **Microsoft Azure Machine Learning,** the API can be trained to recognize items that should be recommended.

There are three common scenarios for recommendations:

- **Frequently Bought Together (FBT)**: FBT is the scenario where items that are often bought together with other items are recommended. An example of this is if you buy a mouse; the API will then recommend a keyboard.
- **Item to Item Recommendations (I2I)**: I2I is the scenario where certain items are often viewed after other items. Typically, this will be in the form of *people who visited this item also visited this other item*.
- **Customer to Item Recommendations (U2I)**: U2I is the scenario where you utilize a customer's previous actions to recommend items. If you sell movies, you can recommend other movies based on a customer's previous movie choices.

The general steps to use the Recommendations API are as follows:

1. Create a model.
2. Import the catalog data (the items in your e-commerce site).
3. Import usage data.
4. Build a recommendation model.
5. Consume recommendations.

While you can do all tasks programmatically, Microsoft has created a web interface for the first four steps. At the time of writing, this is still in beta; however, it does the job.

 If you have not already done so, sign up for an API key at
`https://portal.azure.com`.

Creating a model

To get started with creating a model, go to
`https://recommendations-portal.azurewebsites.net/`. Log on using the API key created:

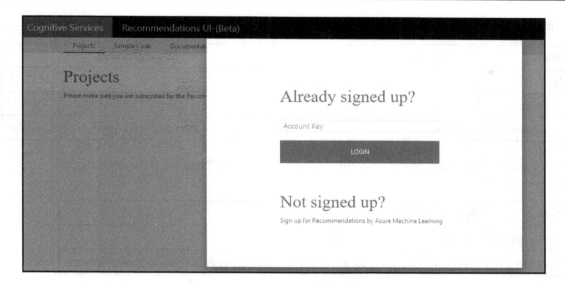

We need to add a project. One project will serve as one recommendation scenario.

We start by adding a project for a FBT scenario:

Importing catalog data

With the project created, we can add catalog data. This is where you would typically add items from your database. It needs to be uploaded in a file format, with a specific format.

The following table describes data that is required for each item in your catalog:

Name	Description
Item ID	A unique identifier for a given item
Item name	The name of the item
Item category	The category for the item, such as hardware, software, book genres, and similar

In addition, there are a few data fields that are optional. These are described in the following table:

Name	Description
Description	A description of the item
Feature list	A comma-separated feature list, that can enhance recommendations

A file with all the data included may have items that look like the following:

```
C9F00168, Kiruna Flip Cover, Accessories, Description of item,
compatibility = lumia, hardware type = mobile
```

It is typically better to add features, as this improves the recommendations. Any new item, which has little usage, is unlikely to be recommended if no features exist.

Features should be categorical. This means that a feature can be a price range. A price alone would not serve as a good feature.

You can add up to 20 features per item. When a catalog, with features for items, is uploaded, you need to do a rank build. This will rank each feature, where features of higher ranking typically will be better to use.

The code example for this chapter contains a sample catalog. We will use this for the following example. Alternatively, you can download some data from Microsoft, at `http://aka.ms/RecoSampleData`. We want to use the data from `MsStoreData.zip`.

With the files downloaded, we can upload the catalog to our project:

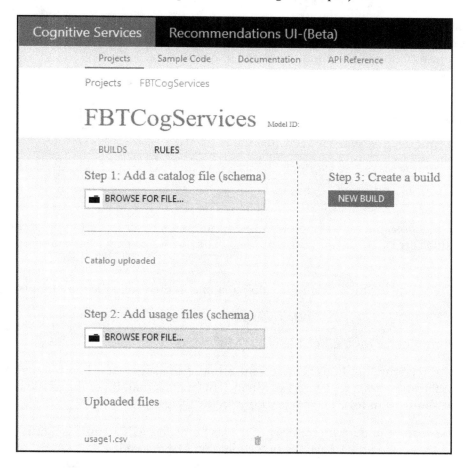

Click the **BROWSE FOR FILE** field. Browse to the sample files you downloaded and choose the `catalog.csv` file. This will upload the catalog and process it. As you can see in the preceding screenshot, it will tell you when the catalog is uploaded and processed, by displaying the **Catalog uploaded** status.

 The maximum number of items in a catalog is 100,000. Any given catalog files cannot be larger than 200 MB. If your file is larger, and you still have more items, you can upload several files.

Importing usage data

The next step we need to make is to import usage data. This is a file describing all transactions from your customers in the past. The file contains rows, with transactions, where each transaction is a comma-separated line with data.

The required data is as follows:

Name	Description
User ID	A unique identifier for each customer
Item ID	A unique identifier for items, which correlates to the catalog
Time	The time of the transaction

In addition, it is possible to have a field called **Event**. This describes the type of transaction. Allowed values are `Click`, `RecommendationClick`, `AddShopCart`, `RemoveShopCart` and `Purchase`.

Given the preceding example from the catalog, a line in the usage file may look as follows:

```
00030000D16C4237, C9F00168, 2015/08/04 T 11:02:37, Purchase
```

The maximum file size for a usage file is 200 MB.

The quality of recommendations relies on the amount of usage data. Typically, you should have about 20 transactions registered per item. This means that, if you have 100 items in the catalog, you should aim for 2,000 transactions in the usage file.

Note that the current maximum number of transactions the API accepts is 5 million. If new transactions are added above this, the oldest data will be deleted.

Again, you can find an example usage file at `http://aka.ms/RecoSampleData`. In our project, we need to click on the **BROWSE FOR FILE** field in **Step 2: Add usage files**. Find the file called `usage1.csv` and upload it. Once the file is uploaded and processed, it will be visible under **Uploaded files**, as seen in the preceding screenshot.

Building a model

With the catalog and usage data in place, it is time to create a build. Do so by clicking the **NEW BUILD** button, as seen in the preceding screenshot. This will result in the following dialog:

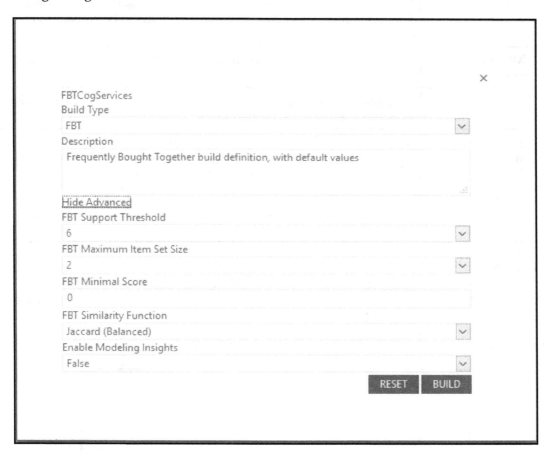

Make sure you select FBT as the build type. Add a suitable description, but note that the description cannot be longer than 512 characters.

A FBT build is a conservative recommender. This means that it counts the number of times two or three products are purchased together (co-occurring). The result is then sorted based on a similarity function.

The advanced parameters you can input can be default. The following table describes each parameter:

Parameter	Description
FBT Support Threshold	A number between 3 - 50 to describe how conservative the model is. This is the number of co-occurrences of items to be considered for modeling.
FBT Maximum Item Set Size	A number (either 2 or 3) to bind the number of items in a frequent set.
FBT Minimal Score	A number describing the minimum score a frequent set should have to be returned in a recommendation.
FBT Similarity Function	Defines the similarity function to be used for recommendation. Can be Lift (which favors serendipity), Co-occurrences (which favors predictability), or Jaccard (combining the two).
Enable Modeling Insights	Defines whether offline evaluation should be turned on or not. If true, a subset of the usage data will not be used for training, but reserved for testing instead.

With the parameters set, you need to click on the **BUILD** button as seen in the preceding screenshot. This will start the process of building and training the model. Note that this process can take anywhere from a few minutes to several hours, depending on the size of your usage data.

When the process completes, the status will be updated to look as follows:

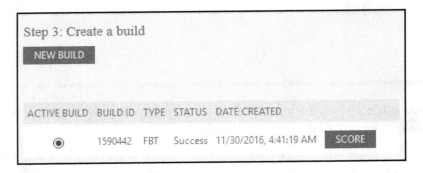

By clicking on the **SCORE** button, you will be taken to a page where you can test the API:

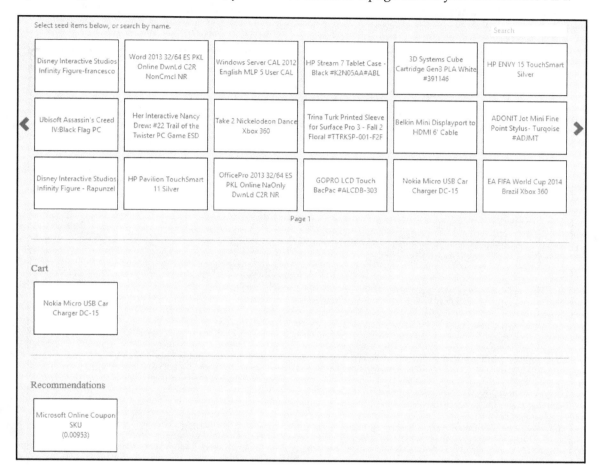

By selecting different items in the top window, you will get recommendations for that item. This is a nice way to verify your data, before putting it into action.

With the FBT model in place, we want to add an additional one. This is so we can use I2I and U2I recommendations.

Go through the same process we have just been through, using the same data as the FBT model. Select **Recommendation** as the build type. This should present you with the following screen:

Recommendation as the build type works for both I2I and U2I scenarios. The first one will predict items that are likely to be of interest for customers, given single or multiple items as input. The latter will give recommendations of items that are likely to be of interest, based on the history of the given user.

The advanced parameters can be left as default, and each of them is described in the following table:

Parameter	Description
Number of model iterations	A number from 10 - 50, that decides the number of iterations for the model. A higher number will give better recommendation accuracy, but will take longer to compute.
Number of model dimension	A number from 10 - 40, describing the number of features your model will try to find in the data. A greater number will allow for better fine-tuning of the resulting recommendations, but may prevent the model from finding a correlation between items.
Item cut-off lower bound	A number from 0 - 30 defining the minimum number of usages each item should have to be considered in the model.
Item cut-off upper bound	A number from 0 - 30 defining the maximum number of usages each item should have to be considered in the model.
User cut-off lower Bound	A number from 0 - 10 defining the minimum number of transactions a user must have performed to be considered in the model.
User cut-off upper bound	A number from 0 - 10 defining the maximum number of transactions a user must have performed to be considered in the model.
Enable modeling insights	Defines whether offline evaluation should be turned on or not. If true, a subset of the usage data will not be used for training, but reserved for testing instead.
Enable U2I	Set to true to enable U2I recommendations.

With all the parameters set, click on the **BUILD** button to build and train the model. Given the same amount of data as the FBT model, this should take a bit longer to execute. This will also be affected by the number of model iterations defined.

Once the process has finished, you will again have the possibility to test your model by clicking on the **SCORE** button.

For each model, you can create several builds. As default, the last one created will be marked as the active build. This will be used when getting recommendations.

Consuming recommendations

To use the recommendation models we just created, we will create a new example application. Create this using the MVVM template we created previously.

At the time of writing, there is no client package for the Recommendations API. This means we need to rely on web requests, as we saw in Chapter 6, *Understanding Text*. To speed up the development time, copy the WebRequest.cs file from the example code in Chapter 6, *Understanding Text*. Paste this file into the Model folder, and make sure to update the namespace.

 Remember to add references to System.Web and System.Runtime.Serialization.

As there is no need for much UI, we are going to add everything in the MainView.xaml file. We are going to need two ComboBox elements. These will list our recommendation models and catalog items. We also need a Button element to get the recommendations, and a TextBox element to show the resulting recommendations.

The corresponding ViewModel, MainViewModel.cs, will need properties to correspond to the UI elements. Add an ObservableCollection, of type RecommendationModel, which will hold our models. We will look at the type in a bit. We need a property of type RecommendationModel, holding the selected model. Add an ObservableCollection property of type Product, with a corresponding Product property for the available and selected properties. We will also need a string property for the results, and an ICommand property for our button.

Add a private member, of type WebRequest, so we can call the API.

Add a new file, called Product, in the Model folder. To use the items from our catalog, we will load the catalog file into the application, creating a Product for each item. Let Product look as follows:

```
public class Product {
    public string Id { get; set; }
    public string Name { get; set; }
    public string Category { get; set; }
```

```
public Product(string id, string name, string category) {
    Id = id;
    Name = name;
    Category = category;
}
}
```

We need the `Id` of an item, the `Name`, and the `Category`.

The constructor should create a `WebRequest` object:

```
public MainViewModel()
{
    _webRequest = new WebRequest
("https://westus.api.cognitive.microsoft.com/recommendations/v4.0/models/",
"API_KEY_HERE");
    RecommendCommand = new DelegateCommand(RecommendBook,
CanRecommendBook);

    Initialize();
}
```

When we create the `WebRequest` object, we specify the recommendation endpoint and our API key. `RecommendCommand` is the `ICommand` object, as a `DelegateCommand`. We need to specify the action to be executed, and the conditions under which we are allowed to execute the command. We should be allowed to execute the command if we have selected a recommendation model and a product.

Initialize will make sure we fetch our recommendation models and products:

```
private async void Initialize() {
    await GetModels();
    GetProducts();
}
```

The `GetModels` method will make a call to the API.

```
private async Task GetModels()
{
    RecommandationModels models = await _webRequest.MakeRequest
<object, RecommandationModels>(HttpMethod.Get, string.Empty);
```

This call is a `GET` request, so we specify this in `MakeRequest`. We do not need to add any query strings or request body, so we will leave these parameters empty. A successful call should result in a JSON response, that we deserialize into a `RecommendationModels` object. This is a data contract, so add a file called `Models.cs` in a folder called `Contracts`.

A successful result will give the following output:

```json
{
    "models": [
    {
        "id": "string",
        "name": "string",
        "description": "string",
        "createdDateTime": "string",
        "activeBuildId": 0,
        "catalogDisplayName": "string"
    }]
}
```

We have an array of `models`. Each item in this array has an `id`, a `name`, a `description`, `createdDateTime`, `activeBuildId`, and `catalogDisplayName`. Make sure the class `RecommendationModels` contains this data.

If the call succeeded, we add the models to the `ObservableCollection` of available models:

```
foreach (RecommandationModel model in models.models) {
    AvailableModels.Add(model);
}
SelectedModel = AvailableModels.FirstOrDefault();
}
```

When all items are added, we set the `SelectedModel` to the first available option.

To add the items from our catalog, we need to read from the catalog file. In the example code provided with the book, this file is added to the project and copied to the output directory. The `GetProducts` method will look as follows:

```
private void GetProducts() {
    try {
        var reader = new StreamReader (File.OpenRead("catalog.csv"));

        while(!reader.EndOfStream) {
            string line = reader.ReadLine();
            var productInfo = line.Split(',');
```

```
                    AvailableProducts.Add(new Product(productInfo[0],
productInfo[1], productInfo[2]));
                }

                SelectedProduct = AvailableProducts.FirstOrDefault();
            }
            catch(Exception ex) {
                Debug.WriteLine(ex.Message);
            }
        }
```

This is a basic file operation, reading in each line from the catalog. For each item, we get the required information, creating a `Product` per item. This is then added to the `AvailableProducts` in the `ObservableCollection` property, and the `SelectedProduct` is the first available.

Now that we have our recommendation models and our products, we can execute recommendations:

```
        private async void RecommendProduct(object obj)
        {
            var queryString = HttpUtility.ParseQueryString(string.Empty);
            queryString["itemIds"] = SelectedProduct.Id;
            queryString["numberOfResults"] = "10";
            queryString["minimalScore"] = "0";
            // queryString["includeMetadata"] = "";
            // queryString["buildId"] = "";

            Recommendations recommendations = await _webRequest.MakeRequest
    <object, Recommendations>(HttpMethod.Get,
    $"{SelectedModel.id}/recommend/item? {queryString.ToString()}");
```

The call to get recommendations is a `GET` request. We start by creating a `queryString`. This requires us to add `itemIds`, `numberOfResults`, and `minimalScore`.

The `itemIds` parameter can be either the ID of a selected product. The `numberOfResults` parameter depends on how many recommendations you would like to get returned. The `minimalScore` parameter will only be honored if this is an FBT recommendation.

We can, optionally, add `includedMetadata` and `buildId` as parameters. The first one is created for future use, so it will not affect anything at the time of writing. `buildId` is the number of a given build, in case you would like to use a build other than the active build.

We call the `MakeRequest` method on the `_webRequest` object. This is a `GET` request, and we need to specify the ID of the `SelectedModel` in the query string. We also need to add a bit to the query string, so we reach the correct endpoint. A successful response will result in JSON output, which will look as follows:

```
{
    "recommendedItems": [ {
        "items": [ {
            "id": "string",
            "name": "string",
            "metadata": "string"
        }],
        "rating": 0.0,
        "reasoning": [
            "string" ]
    }]
}
```

The result consists of an array of `recommendedItems`. Each item will have a `rating`, a string array of `reasoning`, and an array of `items`. The rating gives an indication of how likely a customer is to want the given item. Each `reasoning` provides us with a textual representation of the recommendation. Each item in the `items` array will correspond to an item in our catalog, containing the `id`, `name`, and `metadata`.

This result should be deserialized into a data contract of type `Recommandations`, so make sure you add this in the `Contracts` folder.

For FBT and I2I recommendations, we can use the same `GET` request. The difference is the `itemIds` parameter in the query string. For FBT recommendations, this can only be one single item. For I2I, it can be a comma-separated list of several items.

When we have made a successful call, we want to display this in the UI:

```
if(recommendations.recommendedItems.Length == 0) {
    Recommendations = "No recommendations found";
    return;
}

StringBuilder sb = new StringBuilder();
sb.Append("Recommended items:nn");
```

First, we check to see if we have any recommendations. If we do not have any, we will not move on. If we do have any items, we create a `StringBuilder` to format our output:

```
foreach(Recommendeditem recommendedItem in
recommendations.recommendedItems)  {
    sb.AppendFormat("Score: {0}n", recommendedItem.rating);

    foreach(string reason in recommendedItem.reasoning) {
        sb.AppendFormat("Reason: {0}n", reason);
    }

    foreach(Item item in recommendedItem.items)  {
        sb.AppendFormat("Item ID: {0}nItem Name: {1}n", item.id,
item.name);
    }

    sb.Append("n");
}
Recommendations = sb.ToString();
}
```

We loop through all the `recommendedItems`. We output the `rating`, and every `reasoning` for each item (typically, you will only get one reason per item). Moving on, we loop through all `items`, and output the `id` and `name`. This will be printed in the UI.

A successful test run may give the following result:

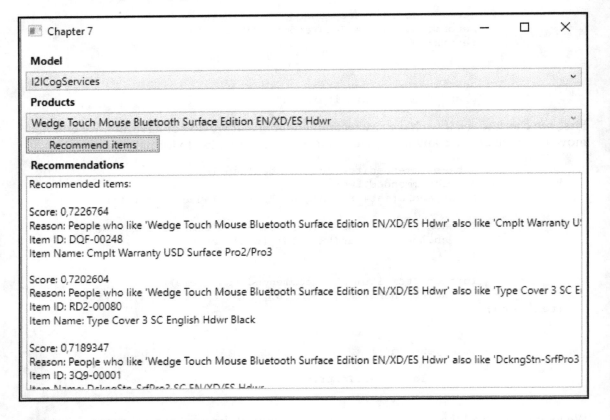

There are a few special cases to note:

- If the item list contains a single item, that does not exist in the catalog, an empty result is returned
- If the item list contains some items that are not in the catalog, these are removed from the query
- If the item list contains only cold items (items that have no usage data connected to them), the most popular recommendation is returned
- If the item list contains some cold items, recommendations are returned for the other items

Recommending items based on prior activities

To make recommendations based on user activity, we need a list of users. As this would be too cumbersome to create for an example, we will only look at what is required to make this recommendation.

The endpoint for this usage is a bit different, as it is another GET call. In code, it would look as follows:

```
$"{SelectedModel.id}/recommend/user?{queryString.ToString()}"
```

Parameters in the query string are as follows:

Parameter	Description
userId (required)	A unique identifier of a given user.
numberOfResults (required)	The number of recommendations returned.
itemsIds (optional)	A list or single id of the selected item(s).
includeMetadata (optional)	If true, include an item's metadata.
buildId (optional)	A number identifying the build we want to use. If none is specified, the active build is used.

A successful call will result in the same JSON output as the other recommendation models. Recommended items will, of course, be based on users' past activities.

Note that, to be able to use this, U2I must be set to true when creating a model build.

Summary

Throughout this chapter, we have taken our first look at the Knowledge APIs. We started by linking entities using the Entity Linking API. Doing so allows us to recognize entities based on context and link all entities of the same type in a text. Moving on, we dived into the Recommendations API. We learned how to set up recommendation models using existing catalog and usage data. Using these models, we learned how to utilize these in a simple example application.

In the next chapter, we will continue with Knowledge APIs. We will learn how to structure natural language queries and evaluate query expressions. In addition, we will learn how to add autocompletion to natural language queries.

8
Querying Structured Data in a Natural Way

In the previous chapter, we learned how we could use the current context to extend our knowledge on a certain topic. Throughout this chapter, we will continue with the Knowledge APIs. More specifically, we will learn how to explore relationships between academic papers and journals. We will see how we can interpret natural language queries, and get query expressions. Using these expressions, we will learn how to find academic entities. The next part will focus more on how to set up this kind of service on your own. At the end, we will look into the QnA Maker, to see how we can create FAQ services from existing content.

When we have completed this chapter, we will have covered the following topics:

- Interpreting natural language user queries using the Academic API
- Assisting the user with queries, using autocomplete features
- Using said queries to retrieve academic entities
- Calculating the distribution of academic entities from the queries
- Hosting the Knowledge Exploration Service with your own schema
- Creating a FAQ service from existing content using the QnA Maker

Tapping into academic content using the Academic API

Microsoft Academic Graph (**MAG**) is a knowledge base for web-scale, heterogeneous entity graphs. Entities model scholarly activities, containing information such as field of study, author(s), institution, and more.

Data contained in MAG is indexed from the Bing web index. As this is continuously indexed, the data is always up to date.

Using the Academic API, we can tap into this knowledge base. Combining search suggestions, research paper graph search results, and histogram distributions, the API enables a knowledge-driven and interactive dialog.

When a user searches for research papers, the API can provide query completion. It may suggest queries based on the input. With a complete query, we can evaluate a query expression. This will retrieve a set of matching paper entities from the knowledge base.

Setting up an example project

To be able to test the Academic API, we want to create a new example project. Create this from the MVVM template created in Chapter 1, *Getting Started with Microsoft Cognitive Services*.

The Academic API does not have any client packages available. This means we need to call the API ourselves. Copy the WebRequest.cs file from the Model folder in the Smart-House application and into the Model folder of the newly created project. Make sure to correct the namespace.

To be able to compile this, we will need to add references to System.Web and System.Runtime.Serializable. We will also be working with JSON, so go ahead and add the Newtonsoft.Json package through NuGet Package Manager.

As this will be the only API tested in this sample project, we can add UI elements in the MainView.xaml file. Open this file now.

Our View should have a `TextBox` element for our input query. It should have a `ComboBox` element to list suggested query expressions. We need three `Button` elements, one for `Interpret`, one for `Evaluate`, and one for `Histogram`, all functions we will be executing. Last, but not least, we need a `TextBox` element to display our results.

In the `MainViewModel.cs` file, we will need to add corresponding properties. Add three `string` properties, one for the input query, one for the results, and one for the selected query expression. Add an `ObservableCollection` property, of the type `string`, for our available query expressions. We also need three `ICommand` properties, one for each of our buttons.

Add a private member for our `WebRequest` object. Make the constructor look like the following:

```
public MainViewModel()
{
    _webRequest = new
WebRequest("https://api.projectoxford.ai/academic/v1.0/",
    "API_KEY_HERE");

    InterpretCommand = new DelegateCommand(Interpret, CanInterpret);
    EvaluateCommand = new DelegateCommand(Evaluate,
CanExecuteCommands);
    CalculateHistogramCommand = new DelegateCommand
(CalculateHistogram,
    CanExecuteCommands);
}
```

 If you have not already done so, sign up for an API key at `https://portal.azure.com`.

The `CanInterpret` parameter should return true if we have entered any text into the query text box. The `CanExecuteCommands` parameter should return true if we have selected a query expression. We will cover `Interpret`, `Evaluate`, and the `CalculateHistogram` parameters in the coming pages.

Make sure the application compiles and runs before continuing.

Interpreting natural language queries

The query expressions the API expects to evaluate a query are not in a natural language format. To ensure that users can make queries in a natural way, we need to interpret their input.

When calling the Interpret feature of the API, it accepts a query string. This will be returned, formatted to reflect the user intent, using academic grammar. In addition, this feature can be called as the user is writing, to provide an interactive experience.

The request is a GET request:

```
private async void Interpret(object obj)
{
    var queryString = HttpUtility.ParseQueryString(string.Empty);

    queryString["query"] = InputQuery;
    queryString["complete"] = "1";
    //queryString["count"] = "10";
    //queryString["offset"] = "0";
    //queryString["timeout"] = "1000";
    //queryString["model"] = "latest";
```

We start the call by creating a `queryString` variable. The parameters we can input are specified in the following table:

Parameter	Description
query (required)	The query from the user.
complete (optional)	If this is set to 1, the service will return suggestions, using the query as a prefix. 0 means no autocomplete.
count (optional)	The maximum number of interpretations to return.
offset (optional)	The index of the first interpretation. Useful to use if a lot of results are expected and you add pagination.
timeout (optional)	Timeout specified in milliseconds. Only results found before this limit will be returned.
model (optional)	The name of the model you want to query. Defaults to the latest.

We call the API to get interpretations:

```
InterpretResponse response = await _webRequest.MakeRequest<object,
InterpretResponse>(HttpMethod.Get,
$"interpret?{queryString.ToString()}");

if (response == null || response.interpretations.Length == 0)
    return;
```

As this is a `GET` request, we do not need to specify any request bodies. We do, however, expect a result to be serialized into an `InterpretResponse` object. This is a data contract, containing properties from the result.

A successful call to the API will result in a JSON response, which looks as follows:

```
{
    "query": "papers by jaime", "interpretations": [
    {
        "prob": 2.429e-006,
        "parse": "<rule id="#GetPapers"> papers by <attr
name="academic#AA.AuN">
        jaime teevan </attr></rule>",
        "rules": [
        {
            "name": "#GetPapers",
            "output": {
                "type": "query",
                "value": "Composite(AA.AuN=='jaime teevan')"
            }
        }]
    }]
}
```

The result contains the original `query`. It also contains an array with `interpretations`. Each item in this array consists of the data shown in the following table:

Data field	Description
prob	Probability of the current interpretation being correct. The scale goes from 0 to 1, where 1 is the highest.
parse	This is an XML string showing interpretations for each part of the string.
rules	An array with one or more rules defined. There will always be one rule for the Academic API.
rules[x].name	Name of the current rule.

`rules[x].output`	Output of the current rule.
`rules[x].output.type`	The type of the rule output. This will always be "query" for the Academic API.
`rules[x].output.value`	The output value for the rule. This will be a query expression string.

Create the `InterpretResponse` data contract based on the preceding JSON output.

We are interested in the last data field, `rules[x].output.value`. This is the query expression string, which we will use to evaluate queries.

When the API call has succeeded, we want to update the `ObservableCollection` class of the available query expressions:

```
    ObservableCollection<string> tempList = new
ObservableCollection<string>();

    foreach (Interpretation interpretation in response.interpretations)
    {
        foreach (Rule rule in interpretation.rules) {
            tempList.Add(rule.output.value);
        }
    }

    AvailableQueryExpressions = tempList;
    QueryExpression = AvailableQueryExpressions.FirstOrDefault();
```

We loop through all `interpretations`, adding the `outputvalue` from a rule, to our `AvailableQueryExpressions`.

Finally, we set the selected `QueryExpression` to be the first available. This is just for our own convenience.

A successful test run can generate the following results:

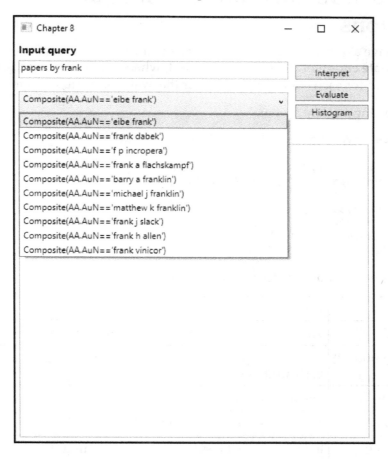

An unsuccessful call will produce an error response code. The response codes that can be generated are as follows:

Response code	Description
400	Bad argument, request parameter is missing
401	Invalid subscription key
403	The call volume quota has been exceeded
404	The requested resources are not found
500	Internal server error

Finding academic entities from query expressions

Now that we have a query expression available, we can retrieve a set of academic entities using the **Evaluate** endpoint. This is a GET request, where we need to specify the attributes we want returned for each entity. We will cover the available attributes later.

We start by creating a query string:

```
private async void Evaluate(object obj)
{
    string queryString = $"expr={QueryExpression} &
    attributes=Id,Ti,Y,D,CC,AA.AuN";

    //queryString += "&model=latest";
    //queryString += "&count=10";
    //queryString += "&offset=0";5
    //queryString += "&orderby=name:asc";
```

The parameters we can add are described in the following table:

Parameter	Description
expr (required)	The query expression found in the Interpret call.
attributes (optional)	A comma-separated list of attributes to be included in the response. Each attribute is case sensitive.
model (optional)	The model you wish to use for a query. Defaults to *latest*.
count (optional)	The number of entities to return.
offset (optional)	Index of the first result to return; can be useful for pagination purposes.
orderby (optional)	Specifies the order to sort the entities.

Note that, while the attributes parameter is optional, you should specify which attributes you want. If none are specified, only the entity ID is returned.

We call the API:

```
EvaluateResponse response = await _webRequest.MakeRequest<object,
EvaluateResponse>(HttpMethod.Get, $"evaluate?{queryString}");

if (response == null || response.entities.Length == 0)
    return;
```

As this is a `GET` request, we do not need any request bodies. With a successful call, we expect an `EvaluateResponse` object in return. This is a data contract, which will be deserialized from the JSON response.

A successful response will give a JSON response like the following (depending on the attributes specified):

```
{
    "expr": "Composite(AA.AuN=='jaime teevan')",
    "entities": [
    {
        "prob": 2.266e-007,
        "Ti": "personalizing search via automated analysis of interests
and
        activities",
        "Y": 2005,
        "CC": 372,
        "AA": [
        {
            "AuN": "jaime teevan",
            "AuId": 1968481722
        },
        {
            "AuN": "susan t dumais",
            "AuId": 676500258
        },
        {
            "AuN": "eric horvitz",
            "AuId": 1470530979
        }]
    }]
}
```

The response contains the query expression we used. It also contains an array of entities. Each item in this array will contain the probability of it being correct. It will also contain all attributes we specified, either in the form of string or numeric values. It can also be in the form of objects, which we will need to have data contracts for.

For our request, we specified some attributes. These were entity ID, title, year of publication and date, citation count, and author name. Knowing that, we can do the following to output the result:

```
StringBuilder sb = new StringBuilder();
sb.AppendFormat("Expression {0} returned {1} entities\n\n",
response.expr,
    response.entities.Length);
```

```
    foreach (Entity entity in response.entities)
    {
        sb.AppendFormat("Paper title: {0}\n\tDate: {1}\n", entity.Ti,
entity.D);

        sb.Append("Authors:\n");
        foreach (AA author in entity.AA)
        {
            sb.AppendFormat("\t{0}\n", author.AuN);
        }

        sb.Append("\n");
    }
    Results = sb.ToString();
```

A successful call can give the following output:

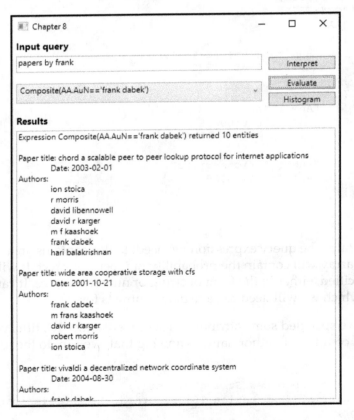

Any error responses will produce response codes, as described previously.

Calculating the distribution of attributes from academic entities

Another feature of the Academic API is the possibility to calculate the distribution of attribute values for a set of paper entities. This can be done by calling the `calchistogram` API endpoint.

This is a GET request, so we start by creating a query string:

```
string queryString = $"expr={QueryExpression}&attributes=Y,F.FN";

//queryString += "&model=latest";
//queryString += "&count=10";
//queryString += "&offset=0";
```

The parameters we can specify are the same as with `Evaluate`, except we do not have the `orderby` parameter. For this call, we want to get the year of publication (`Y`) and the field of study name (`F.FN`).

We make the call to the API, not specifying any request bodies:

```
HistogramResponse response = await _webRequest.MakeRequest<object,
HistogramResponse>(HttpMethod.Get, $"calchistogram?{queryString}");

if (response == null || response.histograms.Length == 0)
    return;
```

If the call succeeds, we expect a `HistogramResponse` object in return. This is a data contract, which should contain the data from the JSON response.

A successful request should give the following JSON response (depending on the requested attributes):

```
{
    "expr": "And(Composite(AA.AuN=='jaime teevan'),Y>2012)",
    "num_entities": 37,
    "histograms": [
    {
        "attribute": "Y",
        "distinct_values": 3,
        "total_count": 37,
        "histogram": [
        {
            "value": 2014,
            "prob": 1.275e-07,
            "count": 15
```

```
            },
            {
                "value": 2013,
                "prob": 1.184e-07,
                "count": 12
            },
            {
                "value": 2015,
                "prob": 8.279e-08,
                "count": 10
            }]
        },
        {
            "attribute": "F.FN",
            "distinct_values": 34,
            "total_count": 53,
            "histogram": [
            {
                "value": "crowdsourcing",
                "prob": 7.218e-08,
            "count": 9
        },
        {
            "value": "information retrieval",
            "prob": 4.082e-08,
            "count": 4
        },
        {
            "value": "personalization",
            "prob": 2.384e-08,
            "count": 3
        },
        {
            "value": "mobile search",
            "prob": 2.119e-08,
            "count": 2
        }]
    }]
}
```

The response contains the original query expression we used. It will give us a count on the number of matching entities. An array of histograms is also present. This will contain an item for each of the attributes we requested. The data for each item is described in the following table:

Data field	Description
attribute	The attribute name.
distinct_values	The number of distinct values matching entities for this attribute.
total_count	The total number of value instances among matching entities for this attribute.
histogram	An array with histogram data for this attribute.
histogram[x].value	The value for the current histogram.
histogram[x].prob	The probability of matching entities with this attribute value.
histogram[x].count	The number of matching entities with this value.

With a successful response, we loop through the data, presenting it in the UI:

```
StringBuilder sb = new StringBuilder();

sb.AppendFormat("Totalt number of matching entities: {0}\n",
response.num_entities);

foreach (Histogram histogram in response.histograms)
{
    sb.AppendFormat("Attribute: {0}\n", histogram.attribute);
    foreach (HistogramY histogramY in histogram.histogram)
    {
        sb.AppendFormat("\tValue '{0}' was found {1} times\n",
histogramY.value,
        histogramY.count);
    }

    sb.Append("\n");
}
Results = sb.ToString();
```

A successful call can give us the following result:

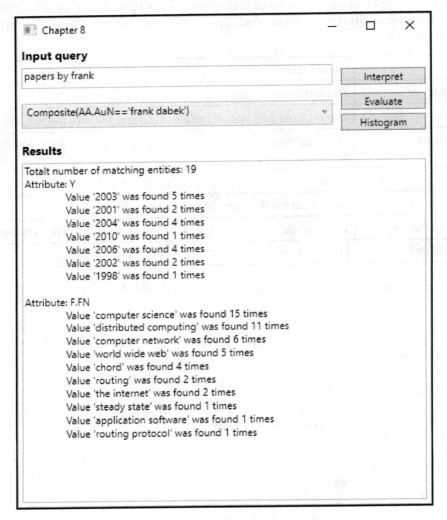

An unsuccessful API call will provide us with an error, containing a response code. These are the same as described for the `Interpret` feature.

Entity attributes

A rather important part of this API is the usage of attributes. You most definitely will want to get some data from the query, but not all.

We saw how to specify attributes in each request. The following table describes all available attributes. Please make sure that all attributes specified in a request are correct per casing:

Attribute	Description
Id	Entity ID
Ti	Paper title
Y	Paper year
D	Paper date
CC	Citation count
ECC	Estimated citation count
AA.AuN	Author name
AA.AuId	Author ID
AA.AfN	Author affiliation name
AA.AfId	Author affiliation ID
F.FN	Name of field of study
F.Fid	Field of study ID
J.JN	Journal name
J.JId	Journal ID
C.CN	Conference series name
C.Cid	Conference series ID
Rid	Reference ID
W	Words from paper title/abstract for full text search
E	Extended metadata

The extended metadata is described in the following table:

Attribute	Description
DN	Display name of the paper
D	Description
S	Sources (web sources of the paper, sorted by static rank)
S.Ty	Source type (HTML/Text/PDF/DOC/PPT/XLS/PS)
S.U	Source URL
VFN	Venue Full Name - Full name of journal or conference
VSN	Venue Short Name - Short name of the journal or conference
V	Journal volume
I	Journal issue
FP	First page of paper
LP	Last page of paper
DOI	Digital Object Identifier

Creating the backend using the Knowledge Exploration Service

The **Knowledge Exploration Service** (**KES**) is, in some ways, the backend for the Academic API. It allows us to build a compressed index from structured data, authoring grammar to interpret natural language.

To get started with KES, we need to install the service locally.

 To download the KES installer, go to
https://www.microsoft.com/en-us/download/details.aspx?id=51488.

With the installation comes some example data, which we will use.

The steps required to have a working service are as follows:

1. Define a schema.
2. Generate data.
3. Build the index.
4. Author grammar.
5. Compile grammar.
6. Host service.

Defining attributes

The schema file defines the attribute structure in our domain. When we previously discussed the Academic API, we saw a list of different entity attributes, which we could retrieve through the queries. This is defined in a schema.

If you open the file, `Academic.schema`, in the `Example` folder found where KES is installed, you will see the attributes defined. We have a title, year, and keyword, which are basic attribute types. In addition, we have a `Composite` attribute, for the author. This attribute contains more attributes, related to an author.

Each attribute will support all attribute operations. There may be cases where this is not desired. Explicitly defining the operations for a given attribute may reduce the index size. In the case of the author ID, we just want to be able to check if it is equal to something, which we can achieve by adding the following:

```
{"name":"Author.Id", "type":"Int32", "operations":["equals"]}
```

Adding data

With a schema defined, we can add some data. The example contains a file, called `Academic.data`, which holds all the example data. Open the file to study how the data can look.

Each line in the data file specifies the attribute values for an object. It can also contain a `logprob` value, which will indicate the return order of matching objects.

Building the index

With the attribute schema and data file in place, we can build the compressed binary index. This will hold all our data objects.

Using our example files, we can build the index by running the following command:

```
kes.exe build_index Academic.schema Academic.data Academic.index
```

A successful execution should produce the file `Academic.index`, which we will use when we are hosting the service.

When running the command, the application will continuously output the status, which can look like the following:

```
00:00:00 Input Schema: \Programs\KES\Example\Academic.schema
00:00:00 Input Data: \Programs\KES\Example\Academic.data
00:00:00 Output Index: \Programs\KES\Example\Academic.index
00:00:00 Loading synonym file: Keyword.syn
00:00:00 Loaded 3700 synonyms (9.4 ms)
00:00:00 Pass 1 started
00:00:00 Total number of entities: 1000
00:00:00 Sorting entities
00:00:00 Pass 1 finished (14.5 ms)
00:00:00 Pass 2 started
00:00:00 Pass 2 finished (13.3 ms)
00:00:00 Processed attribute Title (20.0 ms)
00:00:00 Processed attribute Year (0.3 ms)
00:00:00 Processed attribute Author.Id (0.5 ms)
00:00:00 Processed attribute Author.Name (10.7 ms)
00:00:00 Processed attribute Author.Affiliation (2.3 ms)
00:00:00 Processed attribute Keyword (20.6 ms)
00:00:00 Pass 3 started
00:00:00 Pass 3 finished (15.5 ms, 73 page faults)
00:00:00 Post-processing started
00:00:00 Optimized attribute Title (0.1 ms)
00:00:00 Optimized attribute Year (0.0 ms)
00:00:00 Optimized attribute Author.Id (0.0 ms)
00:00:00 Optimized attribute Author.Name (0.5 ms)
00:00:00 Optimized attribute Author.Affiliation (0.2 ms)
00:00:00 Optimized attribute Keyword (0.6 ms)
00:00:00 Global optimization
00:00:00 Post-processing finished (17.2 ms)
00:00:00 Finalizing index
00:00:00 Total time: 157.6 ms
00:00:00 Peak memory usage: 23 MB (commit) + 0 MB (data file) = 23 MB
```

Understanding natural language

After we have built an index, we can start creating our grammar file. This specifies what natural language the service can understand, and how they can translate into semantic query expressions. Open the academic.xml file to see an example of how a grammar file can look.

The grammar is based on a **W3C** standard for speech recognition, called **SRGS**. The top-level element is the grammar element. This requires an attribute, root, to specify the root rule, which is the starting point of the grammar.

To allow attribute references, we add the import element. This needs to be a child of the grammar element and should come before anything else. It contains two required attributes, the name of the schema file to import, and a name which elements can use for referencing the schema. Note that the schema file must be in the same folder as the grammar file.

Next in line is the rule element. This defines a structural unit, which specifies what query expressions the service can interpret. A rule element requires an id attribute. Optionally, you can add an example element, used to describe phrases that may be accepted by the rule element. In that case, this will be a child element of the rule.

A rule element also contains an item element. This groups a sequence of grammar constructs, and can be used to indicate repetitions of the sequence. Alternatively, it can be used to specify alternatives, together with one-of elements.

One-of elements specify expansions among one of the item elements. The item *by* may be defined as a one-of element, with *written by* and *authored* by as expansions.

Using the ruleref element allows us to create more complex expressions by using simpler rules. It simply references other rules by adding a URI attribute.

The attrref element references an index attribute, which allows us to match against attributes in the index. The attribute URI is required, which must specify the index schema and attribute name to reference. This must match a schema imported through the import element.

The tag element defines the path through the grammar. This element allows you to assign variables or execute functions to help the flow of the grammar.

Once the grammar file is completed, we can compile it into binary grammar. This is done by running the following command:

```
kes.exe build_grammar Academic.xml Academic.grammar
```

Running this command will produce output similar to the following:

```
Input XML: \Programs\KES\Example\Academic.xml
Output Grammar: \Programs\KES\Example\Academic.grammar
```

Local hosting and testing

With the index and grammar in place, we can go on to test the service locally. Locally testing the service allows for rapid prototyping, which allows us to define the scheme and grammar quickly.

When we are doing testing locally, KES only supports up to 10,000 objects, and 10 requests per second. It also terminates after a total of 1,000 requests have been executed. We will see how to bypass these restrictions in a bit.

To host KES locally, run the following command:

```
Kes.exe host_service Academic.grammar Academic.index -port 8080
```

This will start up the service, running on port 8080. To verify that it is working as intended, open your browser and go to http://localhost:8080.

Doing so should present you with the following screen:

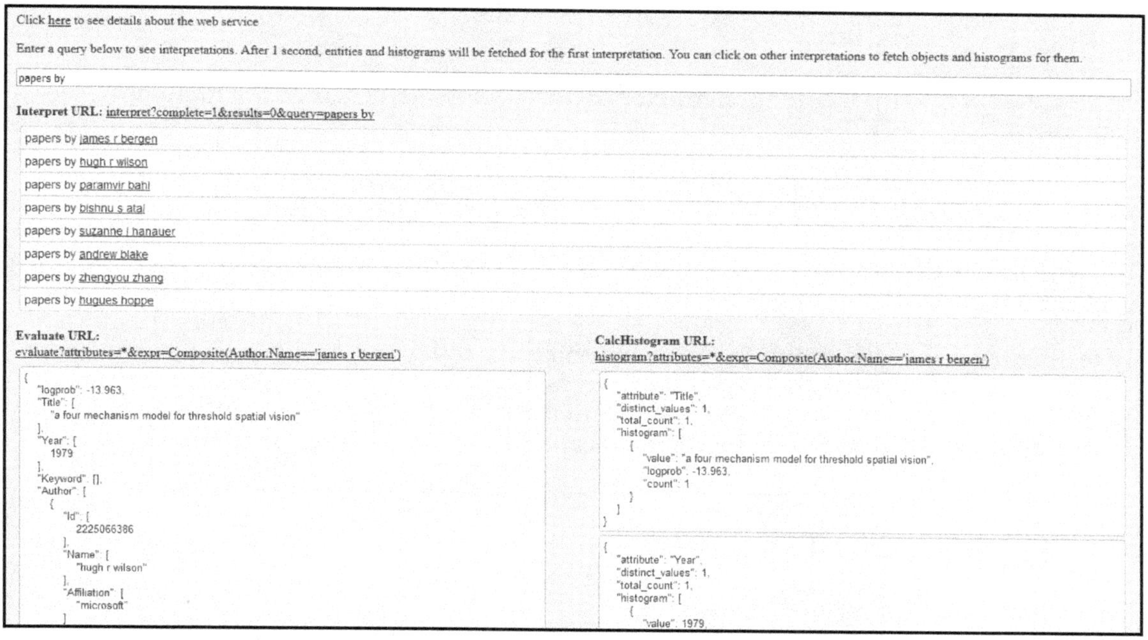

Running KES as a local service also allows us to use the Academic API for testing. We are going to do some modifications to our example application, created for the Academic API, to support this.

First, we are going to modify the `WebRequest.cs` file. We need to make sure we can change the endpoint, so add the following function to the class:

```
public void SetEndpoint(string uri) {
    _endpoint = uri;
}
```

Next, we need to add a new `TextBox` element to the `MainView.xaml` file. This will allow us to enter a URL. This needs a corresponding string property in the `MainViewModel.cs` file. When changing this property, we need to call `SetEndpoint` on the `_webRequest` object. This can look as follows:

```
private string _endpoint;
public string Endpoint {
    get { return _endpoint; }
    set {
        _endpoint = value;
```

```
                RaisePropertyChangedEvent("Endpoint");
                _webRequest?.SetEndpoint(value);
        }
    }
```

Finally, we need to update the constructor of our `ViewModel`. Change the first line to the following:

```
    Endpoint = "https://api.projectoxford.ai/academic/v1.0/";
    _webRequest = new WebRequest(Endpoint, "API_KEY_HERE");
```

This will let the default endpoint be the original API address, but allows us to use the application to test KES locally.

By testing the application with the local endpoint, the following result can be produced:

Note that `evaluate` and `calchistogram` will need to update attributes in the request of the test application for it to work with the local KES:

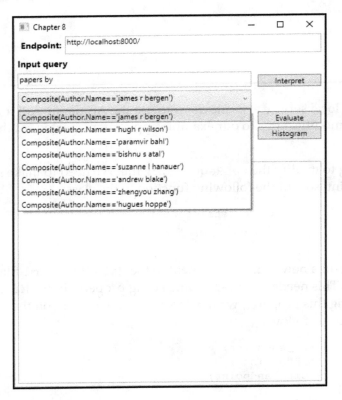

Going for scale

While it is nice to be able to create local prototypes, the limitations ensure that we need to deploy the service elsewhere for production. In this case, this means deploying KES to Microsoft Azure.

We will look into the steps required to deploy KES to Microsoft Azure.

Hooking into Microsoft Azure

The first step is to download the **Azure Publish Settings** file. This needs to be saved as `AzurePublishSettings.xml` and stored in the directory where `kes.exe` runs.

 You can find the Azure Publish Settings file at `https://manage.windowsazure.com/publishsettings/`.

There are two ways to build and host KES without restrictions. The first way is to boot up a **Windows Virtual Machine** in Azure. On this VM, you would follow the steps as we have done locally. This allows for rapid prototyping, but without any restrictions.

The second way is to run `kes.exe` locally, but adding `--remote` as a parameter. This will create a temporary Azure VM, build the index, and upload the index to a specified target blob storage. An example command could look as follows:

```
kes.exe build_index

http://<account>.blob.core.windows.net/<container>/Academic.schema
http://<account>.blob.core.windows.net/<container>/Academic.full.data
http://<account>.blob.core.windows.net/<container>/Academic.full.index
--remote Large
```

This process can take from 5-10 minutes, so ideally, prototyping should be done locally, or through an Azure VM.

Deploying the service

With the grammar and index in place and prototyping done, we can deploy the service to a Microsoft Azure Cloud Service.

To learn how to create a Microsoft Azure Cloud Service, head over to `https://azure.microsoft.com/en-us/documentation/articles/cloud-s ervices-how-to-create-deploy/`.

To deploy the service to a staging slot, run the following command:

```
kes.exe deploy_service

http://<account>.blob.core.windows.net/<container>/Academic.grammar
http://<account>.blob.core.windows.net/<container>/Academic.index
<serviceName> large --slot Staging
```

This will allow us to perform basic tests before deploying the service to a production slot. When the testing is done, we can deploy it to production by running the same command again, specifying `Production` as the last parameter.

When the service is deployed, we can test it by visiting `http://<serviceName>.cloudapp.net` in a browser.

Answering FAQs using QnA Maker

QnA Maker allows us to use existing **frequently asked questions (FAQ)** to create a bot that answers these questions. We can generate a knowledge base from existing FAQs, and train a model from it.

To get started, head over to `https://qnamaker.ai`. Log on or register, by clicking **Sign in**, in the top right corner. This will present you with the following screen:

If no services have been created yet, the list will be empty.

Creating a knowledge base from frequently asked questions

If no services have been created, we can create one by clicking on the **Create new service** tab. This will present us with the following screen:

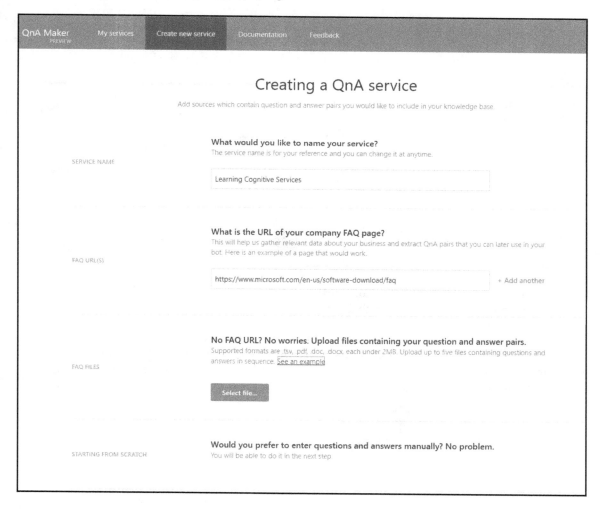

1. Enter a name for the service.
2. Enter the baseline FAQs to use. This can either be in the form of one or more URLs, or a file containing questions and answer pairs. For our example, we will be generating a knowledge base from the URL.

3. Let the rest of the settings be default.
4. Click **Create**.

If you do not have any FAQ to use, you can use the following from Microsoft:
`https://www.microsoft.com/en-us/software-download/faq`

Once the knowledge base has been created, you will be taken to a page with all the question and answer pairs. This is presented as shown in the following screenshot:

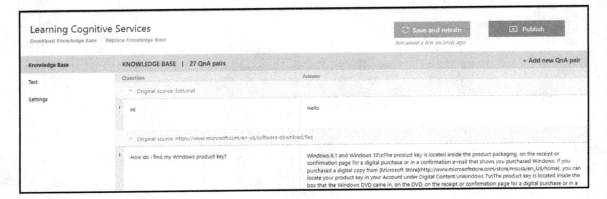

On this page, we can look through all question and answer pairs, from all our FAQ sources. We can also add new pairs, by clicking **Add new QnA pair**.

Selecting any given question will present us with a context menu, in the top right corner of the question. This context menu gives us the option to add alternative phrasings, or delete the pair altogether. This can be useful if a question can be asked in multiple ways. This looks like the following image:

Training the model

Every time we make changes to the knowledge base, it is wise to click **Save and retrain**. This will ensure our model is up to date, with the most current question and answer pairs.

Once we have retrained the model, we can test it. This can be done by going to the **Test** tab, on the left-hand side. This will present us with the following **Chat** window:

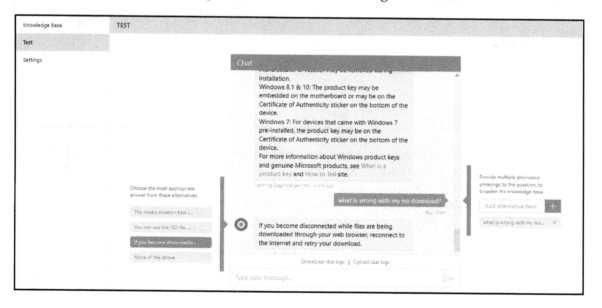

From this **Chat** dialog, we can test some or all of our questions, to verify that we get the correct answers. We can also improve the model by asking questions in different ways. In some cases, this will present us with the wrong answer.

If we have been presented with the wrong answer, we can change this by selecting the correct one. With any given question, the possible answers will be listed to the left of the **Chat** window, ordered by probability. Selecting the correct answer, and retraining the model will ensure a correct answer when asking the same question later.

Publishing the model

Once we are done with training it is time to publish the service. We can do so by clicking **Publish** in the top right corner. This will present us with the following screen:

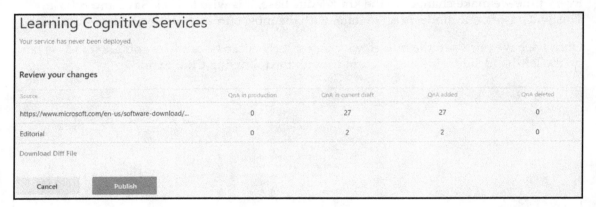

This tells us how many question and answer pairs we have added and/or deleted. It also tells us how many we already have in production, and if we have already published them. This can be very useful to ensure we are not deleting too much or causing disruption to the service. If we need to, we can download a file to clearly see the changes.

Once we are happy with the changes, we click **Publish**. Doing so will present us with a basic HTTP request we can try, as shown in the following screenshot:

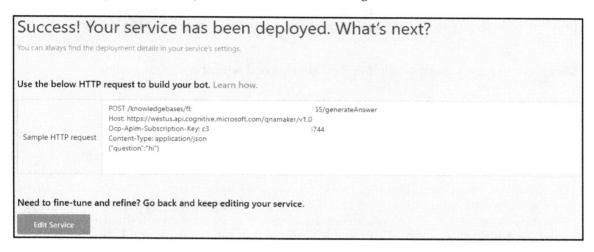

In the preceding screenshot, we can see the endpoint to use, the required application ID, the subscription key, and a sample question in the request body. All those parameters are required to get a successful response.

A successful call to the service will provide us with a JSON response as follows:

```
{ "Answer": "Sample response", "Score": "0" }
```

If we have an application using this, we can decide not to use the answer, if the score has fallen below a certain threshold.

Typically, we would be using bots of different kinds to use this service. We can, for example, add this to a Skype or slackbot, or simply integrate it with a chatbot on a customer support site.

Improving the model

When the model is published, and requests are made to the endpoint, these are logged. These can be useful to find errors in the answers. Going to the **Test** tab, with the **Chat** window, at the QnA Maker site, we can download chat logs. This can be done by clicking **Download chat logs**, right before the message window.

If we upload this file, by clicking **Upload chat logs**, we can replay all the questions asked. This allows us to see the answers given to all questions asked, and correct any errors. The chat will automatically find the number of questions asked. You can navigate between different questions with the navigation menu that appears, once a chat log has been uploaded.

Remember to retrain the model when you are finished with the improvements.

Summary

Throughout this chapter, we have learned about the Academic API and Knowledge Exploration Service. We looked at how to interpret natural language queries to get query expressions for evaluation. Through this evaluation, we have retrieved academic papers from the Microsoft Academic Graph knowledge base. From there, we have learned how to set up the Knowledge Exploration Service itself, going from schemas all the way to deploying it to a Microsoft Azure Cloud Service. In the end, we learned how to set up a simple QnA Maker service.

In the next chapter, we will move into the Search APIs, learning how to utilize the different search APIs offered by Bing.

9
Adding Specialized Searches

The previous chapter explored the relationship between academic papers and journals, learning how to search for academic papers. This chapter will move us into the last of the top-level APIs, Search. Through this chapter, we will learn how to search for web content. We will see how we can search for the latest news for certain key words or categories. Further on, we will search for images and videos, and learn how to automatically suggest search queries for the end-user.

When the chapter is complete, we will have learned the following:

- How to search for web pages and documents
- How to search for news articles
- How to search for images and videos
- How to add auto suggestions in applications
- Filtering search results based on safe search policies

Searching the web from the smart-house application

The Bing Web Search API provides us with a search experience similar to what we find at `http://bing.com/search`. It returns results relevant to any queries.

A response for any request to this API will contain web pages, images, videos, and news articles. In a typical scenario, this is the API you would use for any of these searches.

Note that, in a real-life scenario, all requests should be made from a server-side application, not from a client, like we are doing in the example.

 If you have not already done so, sign up for the Bing Web Search API at `https://portal.azure.com`. You can read more on the API at `https://azure.microsoft.com/en-us/services/cognitive-services/bing-web-search-api/`.

Preparing the application for web searches

Before diving into the required technicalities for web searches, we are going to prepare our smart-house application.

Add a new View in the `Views` folder, called `BingSearchView.xaml`. At the very least, this should contain two `Combobox` elements, one for the search type and one for the search filter. We need one `TextBox` element for our search query, as well as one `Button` element to execute the search. Finally, we need a `TextBox` element to display the search result.

To accompany the search types and search filter, we add a new file, called `BingSearchTypes.cs`, in the `Model` folder. Add the two following `enums`:

```
public enum BingSearchType {
    Web, News, NewsCategory
}

public enum SafeSearch {
    Strict, Moderate, Off
}
```

Adding this allows us to use both the Bing Web Search and Bing News Search APIs. The latter will be discussed later. The second `enum`, `SafeSearch`, will also be discussed in more detail later.

We need a new ViewModel. Add a new file, called `BingSearchViewModel.cs`, to the `ViewModels` folder. In this, we need to add two `string` properties, for our search query and the search results. We will also need one property of type `BingSearchType`, to represent the selected search type. Also needed is a property of type `SafeSearch`, to represent the selected safe-search filter. An `ICommand` property is needed for our button.

In addition, we need to be able to display the values from the previously created `SafeSearch` enums. This can be achieved by adding the following properties:

```
public IEnumerable<BingSearchType> AvailableSearchTypes  {
    get {
        return Enum.GetValues
(typeof(BingSearchType)).Cast<BingSearchType>();
    }
}

public IEnumerable<SafeSearch> SafeSearchFilter {
    get {
        return Enum.GetValues(typeof(SafeSearch)).Cast<SafeSearch>();
    }
}
```

We get all the values from each `enum`, and return that as an `IEnumerable`.

At the time of writing, none of the search APIs have any NuGet client packages, so we need to make the web requests ourselves. Copy the `WebRequest.cs` file we used in earlier chapters into the `Model` folder. Rename the file to `BingWebRequest.cs` and the class to `BingWebRequest`.

As all API calls are `GET` requests, we can simplify this class a bit. Remove the URL parameter from the constructor, and remove the `_endpoint` member completely. Doing so allows us to simplify the `MakeRequest` function, as follows:

```
public async Task<TResponse> MakeRequest<TResponse>(string url) {
    try {
        var request = new HttpRequestMessage(HttpMethod.Get, url);
        HttpResponseMessage response = await
_httpClient.SendAsync(request);

        if (response.IsSuccessStatusCode) {
            string responseContent = null;

            if (response.Content != null)
                responseContent = await
response.Content.ReadAsStringAsync();
            if (!string.IsNullOrWhiteSpace(responseContent))
                return JsonConvert.DeserializeObject<TResponse>
(responseContent, _settings);

            return default(TResponse);
        }
```

We do not need a request body, and have removed the `TRequest` and corresponding code. We have also hard-coded the HTTP method, and said that we will specify the complete URL endpoint when calling the function. The rest of the function should stay the same.

 Remember to add references to `System.Web` and `System.Runtime.Serialization`.

With that in place, we can move on. Make sure the code compiles and executes before continuing.

Searching the web

To be able to use Bing Web Search, we create a new class. Add a new file, called `BingSearch.cs`, to the `Models` folder.

We add a member of type `BingWebRequest`, which we create in the constructor:

```
private BingWebRequest _webRequest;

public BingSearch() {
    _webRequest = new BingWebRequest("API_KEY_HERE");
}
```

Create a new function called `SearchWeb`. This should accept two parameters, a string for the search query and a `SafeSearch` parameter. The function should be marked as `async` and return a `Task<WebSearchResponse>`. `WebSearchResponse` is a data contract we will learn more about in a bit:

```
public async Task<WebSearchResponse> SearchWeb(string query, SafeSearch
safeSearch)
{
    string endpoint = string.Format("{0}{1}&safeSearch={2} &count=5&mkt=en-
US",
    "https://api.cognitive.microsoft.com/bing/v5.0/search?q=", query,
safeSearch.ToString());
```

First, we construct our endpoint, which points us to the web search service. We make sure we specify the query, q, the `safeSearch` selection, and the market, `mkt`. The latter two will be discussed later in the chapter.

The only required parameter is the query string. This should not exceed a length of 1,500 characters. Other optional parameters are described in the following table:

Parameter	Description
responseFilter	**Comma-delimited** list of the result types to include in the response. If not specified, results will contain all types. Legal values include `Computation`, `Images`, `News`, `RelatedSearches`, `SpellSuggestions`, `TimeZone`, `Videos`, and `WebPages`.
setLang	Two-letter language code to specify the language for user interface strings.
textDecorations	Specifies whether or not the query term is highlighted in the results. Defaults to false.
textFormat	The type of formatting to apply to display strings. Can be either raw or HTML, with Raw being the default.

There are a few more parameters. They are, however, common to all searches, and will be discussed at the end of the chapter.

With the endpoint in place, we can move on:

```
try {
    WebSearchResponse response = await
_webRequest.MakeRequest<WebSearchResponse>(endpoint);

    return response;
}
catch (Exception ex) {
    Debug.WriteLine(ex.Message);
}

return null;
```

With the newly constructed endpoint, we call `MakeRequest` on the `_webRequest` object. We specify the API key and endpoint as parameters to this call, and we expect a `WebSearchResponse` object as a response.

`WebSearchResponse` is a data contract, which we get by deserializing the JSON response from the API service. The top-level object will contain objects with the different result types. Look in the code samples provided, in the file called `BingSearchResponse.cs`, for a complete data contract.

 For a complete list of response objects from Bing Web Search, visit
https://msdn.microsoft.com/en-us/library/dn760794.aspx#searchres
ponse.

Heading back to the `BingSearchViewModel.cs` file, we can add `BingSearch` as a member. Let the constructor look as follows:

```
public BingSearchViewModel() {
    _bingSearch = new BingSearch();
    SearchCommand = new DelegateCommand(Search, CanSearch);
}
```

The `CanSearch` parameter should return true if we have any text entered into the search query text field. `Search` should, for now, look as follows:

```
private async void Search(object obj) {
    switch (SelectedSearchType) {
        case BingSearchType.Web:
            var webResponse = await _bingSearch.SearchWeb(SearchQuery,
SelectedSafeSearchFilter);
            ParseWebSearchResponse(webResponse as WebSearchResponse);
            break;
        default:
            break;
    }
}
```

We call the `SearchWeb` function on the `_bingSearch` object, passing on the `SearchQuery` and `SelectedSafeSearchFilter` properties as parameters. With a successful response, we send the response to a new function, `ParseWebSearch`:

```
private void ParseWebSearchResponse(WebSearchResponse webSearchResponse) {
    StringBuilder sb = new StringBuilder();

    Webpages webPages = webSearchResponse.webPages;

    foreach (WebValue website in webPages.value)
    {
        sb.AppendFormat("{0}\n", website.name);
        sb.AppendFormat("URL: {0}\n", website.displayUrl);
```

```
        sb.AppendFormat("About: {0}\n\n", website.snippet);
    }

    SearchResults = sb.ToString();
}
```

When we interpret the results from a web search, we are interested in the resulting `webPages`. For each web page, we want to output the name, the display URL, and a descriptive snippet.

A successful test run with the web search should present us with the following result:

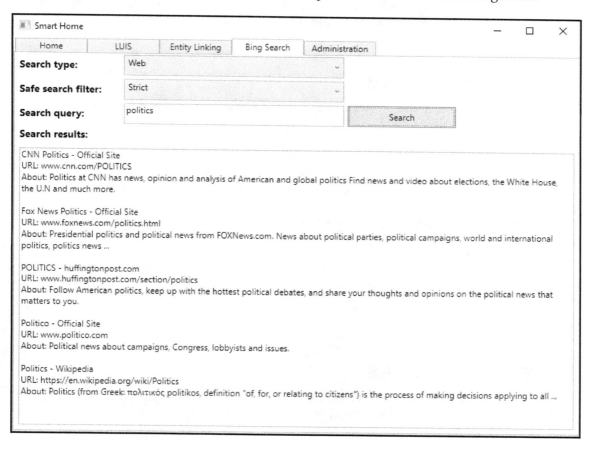

Result objects from a web search contain a `RankingResponse` object. This will identify how the results will typically be displayed on a search website, ordered in a mainline and sidebar. In a production system, you should always aim to display results in the order specified by `RankingResponse`.

This can be done in two ways. One is to use the specified ID field to rank all results. The other way is a bit more complex. It involves splitting the results based on answer types and result index.

Apart from the queries we have seen until now, we can also query for computations (for instance, 2 + 2), time-zone calculations, and related searches. These queries will result in JSON responses, a bit different from the regular web search.

Getting the news

Using the Bing News Search API, we can search for news in several ways. There are three endpoints we use for this API:

- `/news`: Get top news articles, based on category
- `/news/search`: Get news articles based on a search query
- `/news/trendingtopics`: Get top trending news topics

In our smart-house application, we will add the first two, while we will only cover the last one theoretically.

 If you have not already done so, sign up for the Bing News Search API at `https://portal.azure.com`.

News from queries

A lot of the groundwork for query-based news searches have already been done in the web search sample. To search for news based on given queries, we need to add a new function in the `BingSearch` class.

Open the `BingSearch.cs` file and add a new function called `SearchNews`. This should accept a `string` and a `SafeSearch` parameter. The function should be marked as `async`, and return a `Task<BingNewsResponse>` object:

```
public async Task<BingNewsResponse> SearchNews(string query, SafeSearch
safeSearch)
{
    string endpoint = string.Format("{0}{1}&safeSearch={2}&count=5&mkt=en-
US",
        "https://api.cognitive.microsoft.com/bing/v5.0/news/search?q=", query,
        safeSearch.ToString());
```

We construct an endpoint, consisting of the URL, the search query, and the `safeSearch` parameter. Notice how we specify the market, `mkt`, as well as limiting the `count` to 5. Both these parameters will be described later in the chapter.

The only required parameter is the query string, `q`. Apart from parameters described for web searches (`setLang`, `textDecorations`, and `textFormat`), we can also specify a parameter called `originalImg`. This is a Boolean value, which, if set to true, will provide a URL to the original image (for any image in the article). If that is set to false, which is the default, a URL for the thumbnail is provided.

With an endpoint in place, we can call the API:

```
    try {
        BingNewsResponse response = await
_webRequest.MakeRequest<BingNewsResponse>(endpoint);

        return response;
    }

    catch (Exception ex) {
        Debug.WriteLine(ex.Message);
    }

    return null;
```

We call `MakeRequest`, on the `_webRequest` object, passing on the endpoint as parameter.

A successful call will result in a JSON response, which we deserialize into a `BingNewsResponse` object. This object needs to be created as a data contract.

The `BingNewsResponse` object will contain an array of news articles. Each item in this array will contain the article name, URL, image, description, publishing date, and more.

 For full details of each item in the news article array, visit
https://msdn.microsoft.com/en-us/library/dn760793.aspx#newsartic
le.

With that in place, we can head back into the `BingSearchViewModel.cs` file and modify the `Search` function. We do so by adding a case for `BingSearchType.News`, inside the `switch` statement:

```
case BingSearchType.News:
    var newsResponse = await _bingSearch.SearchNews(SearchQuery,
SelectedSafeSearchFilter);
    ParseNewsResponse(newsResponse as BingNewsResponse);
    break;
```

A successful response will be parsed and displayed in the UI:

```
private void ParseNewsResponse(BingNewsResponse bingNewsResponse) {
    StringBuilder sb = new StringBuilder();

    foreach(Value news in bingNewsResponse.value) {
        sb.AppendFormat("{0}\n", news.name);
        sb.AppendFormat("Published: {0}\n", news.datePublished);
        sb.AppendFormat("{0}\n\n", news.description);
    }

    SearchResults = sb.ToString();
}
```

We are mostly interested in the news article name, the date it is published, and a description.

A good test run of this should present us with the following result:

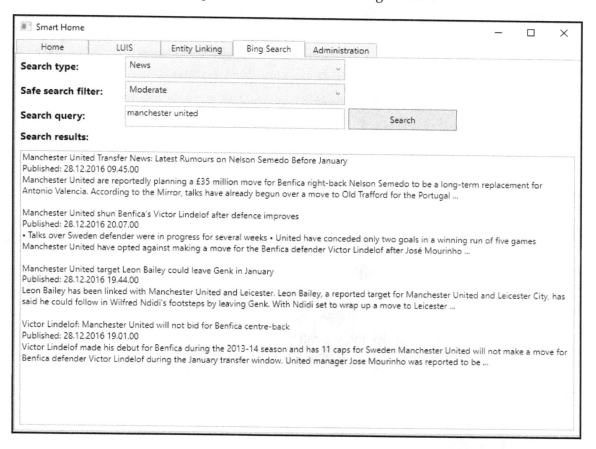

News from categories

When we want to get the top articles for certain categories, we go through a similar procedure to regular news queries. The difference lies in the endpoint we construct.

Let us create a new function, SearchNewsCategory, in the BingSearch class:

```
public async Task<BingNewsResponse> SearchNewsCategory(string query)
{
    string endpoint = string.Format("{0}{1}&mkt=en-US",
"https://api.cognitive.microsoft.com/bing/v5.0/news?category=", query);
```

Here we have a category parameter, with the topic we wish to search for. This is an optional parameter. If it is empty, we will get the top news article for all categories.

For this search, we can specify two different markets, en-GB and en-US. Each of these comes with a list of pre-defined categories that are currently supported:

 For a complete list of supported categories, visit https://msdn.microsoft.com/en-us/library/dn760793.aspx#categorie sbymarket.

```
try {
    BingNewsResponse response = await
_webRequest.MakeRequest<BingNewsResponse>(endpoint);

    return response;
}

catch (Exception ex) {
    Debug.WriteLine(ex.Message);
}

return null;
```

With the newly constructed endpoint, we call MakeRequest on the _webRequest object. This should result in the same response object as for regular news queries. In our ViewModel, we add a case for this search type, in the Search function. With the response, we utilize the already created ParseNewsResponse to get the data we want.

Trending news

The search for trending news is only available for the en-US and zh-CN markets. To execute this search, make a request to the following URL:https://api.cognitive.microsoft.com/bing/v5.0/news/trendingtopics

No parameters are required by this call, but you can add filters, such as the common filters we will discuss later. The only exception is the freshness filter, which will not work for this request.

A successful call to this endpoint will result in a `TrendingTopicAnswer` object, containing an array of trending topics. Each item in this array will contain the following data:

Data field	Description
`image`	A link to a related image
`isBreakingNews`	A Boolean indicating whether this topic is considered breaking news
`name`	The title of the topic
`query`	A query string that would return this topic
`webSearchUrl`	A URL to the Bing search results for this topic
`webSearchUrlPingSuffix`	A query string fragment to identify the `webSearchUrl`

Searching for images and videos

The Bing Image Search API and Bing Video Search API allow us to search directly for images or videos. These APIs should only be used if you just need image or video content. There is a possibility that calling these APIs will affect performance and relevance negatively, and as such, one should aim to use the Bing Web Search API.

 If you have not already done so, sign up for the Bing Image Search API and the Bing Video Search API at `https://portal.azure.com`.

Using a common user interface

As we do not need image or video search in our Smart House application, we will go on to create a new project. Create this project using the MVVM template created in `Chapter 1`, *Getting Started with Microsoft Cognitive Services*.

These APIs do not come with any client packages. As before, we should really make these calls from the server-side application, not the client application. In any case, we need to copy the `BingWebRequest.cs` file from the smart-house application to the `Model` folder. Make sure to change the namespace.

Remember to add references to `System.Web` and `System.Runtime.Serialization`.

We will need to install the `Newtonsoft.Json` NuGet package for our deserialization to work. Do so through the NuGet package manager.

As we will output some of the results as text, we can get away with one common user interface.

Open the `MainView.xaml` file. Add two `TextBox` elements, one for the search query and one for the result. We need a `ComboBox` element to select between search types. Finally, we need to add a `Button` element for our search command.

In the `MainViewModel.xaml` file, we need to add an `enum` with the search types. Add the following at the bottom of the file, beneath the class:

```
public enum SearchType {
    ImageSearch,
    VideoSearch,
}
```

We are only interested in image and video searches with queries. In addition to these search forms, both APIs can search for trending images/videos. The Bing Video Search API also allows us to get more detail on any given video we already have searched for.

In the `MainViewModel` class, we need to add two `string` properties corresponding to our `TextBox` elements. We will also need a property of type `SearchType`, to indicate the selected search type. To indicate what search types we have available, we add an `IEnumerable` property, as follows:

```
public IEnumerable<SearchType> SearchTypes {
    get {
        return Enum.GetValues(typeof(SearchType)).Cast<SearchType>();
    }
}
```

The last property we need to add to our ViewModel is the `ICommand` property, which will be bound to our `Button` element.

Now we need to create a new class, so create a new file, called `BingSearch.cs`, in the `Model` folder. This will be responsible for constructing the correct endpoints and executing both search types.

We will need to add a member of type `BingWebRequest`. This should be created in the constructor:

```
private BingWebRequest _webRequest;

public BingSearch() {
    _webRequest = new BingWebRequest("API_KEY_HERE");
}
```

That is all we need to do there for now.

Back in the ViewModel, we need to add a member of type `BingSearch`. With that in place, we can create our constructor:

```
public MainViewModel() {
    _bingSearch = new BingSearch();

    SearchCommand = new DelegateCommand(Search);

    SelectedSearchType = SearchTypes.FirstOrDefault();
}
```

With the ViewModel in place, we can do some searches.

Searching for images

For our example, we will only be executing the image search based on user queries. To allow this, we will need to add a function in the `BingSearch` class. Call the function `SearchImages`, and let it accept a string as parameter. The function should return `Task<ImageSearchResponse>` and be marked as `async`. `ImageSearchResponse` will, in this case, be a data contract object, with data deserialized from our response:

```
public async Task<ImageSearchResponse> SearchImages(string query)
{
    string endpoint = string.Format("{0}{1}",
    "https://api.cognitive.microsoft.com/bing/v5.0/images/search?q=",
    query);
```

We start by constructing our endpoint. In this case, we only specify the query parameter, `q`. This is a required parameter.

Apart from the common query parameters, which we will see later, we can also add the following parameters:

Parameter	Description
`cab`	Bottom coordinate of the region to crop, in a value from 0.0 to 1.0. Measured from the top-left corner.
`cal`	The left coordinate of the region to crop, in a value from 0.0 to 1.0.
`car`	The right coordinate of the region to crop, in a value from 0.0 to 1.0.
`cat`	The top coordinate of the region to crop, in a value from 0.0 to 1.0.
`ct`	The crop type to use. Currently the only legal value is 0 - Rectangular.

In addition, we can specify the following parameters as filters:

Filter name	Description
`aspect`	Filter images by aspect ratio. Legal values are `Square`, `Wide`, `Tall`, and `All`.
`color`	Filter images by specific colors.
`imageContent`	Filter images by image content. Legal values are `Face` and `Portrait`.
`imageType`	Filter images by image types. Legal values are `AnimatedGif`, `Clipart`, `Line`, `Photo`, and `Shopping`.
`license`	Filter images by license that applies to the image. Legal values are `Public`, `Share`, `ShareCommercially`, `Modify`, `ModifyCommercially`, and All.
`size`	Filter images by size. Legal values are `Small` (< 200x200 pixels), `Medium` (200x200 to 500x500 pixels), `Large` (>500x500 pixels), `Wallpaper`, and `All`.
`height`	Only get results with a specific height.
`width`	Only get results with a specific width.

With the endpoint in place, we can execute the request:

```
try {
    ImageSearchResponse response = await
_webRequest.MakeRequest<ImageSearchResponse>(endpoint);

    return response;
}
catch (Exception ex) {
    Debug.WriteLine(ex.Message);
}

return null;
```

We call `MakeRequest` on the `_webRequest` object, passing on the endpoint as a parameter. A successful call will result in an `ImageSearchResponse`, which is the deserialized data contract object, from the JSON response.

The resulting object will contain a lot of data. Among that data is an array, which contains information about images. Each item in that array contains data, such as image name, date published, URL, and image ID.

For a complete list of the data available in a response, visit
`https://msdn.microsoft.com/en-us/library/dn760791.aspx#images`.

Heading over to `MainViewModel.cs`, we can now create the `Search` function:

```
private async void Search(object obj) {
    SearchResult = string.Empty;

    switch(SelectedSearchType) {
        case SearchType.ImageSearch:
            var imageResponse = await
_bingSearch.SearchImages(SearchQuery);
            ParseImageResponse(imageResponse);
            break;
        default:
            break;
    }
}
```

With a successful response, we parse the `imageResponse`. Normally, this would mean displaying images in a list or similar, but we will but we will take the easier option by outputting textual information:

```
private void ParseImageResponse(ImageSearchResponse imageResponse)
{
    StringBuilder sb = new StringBuilder();
    sb.Append("Image search results:\n\n");
    sb.AppendFormat("# of results: {0}\n\n",
imageResponse.totalEstimatedMatches);

    foreach (Value image in imageResponse.value) {
        sb.AppendFormat("\tImage name: {0}\n\tImage size: {1}\n\tImage
host: {2}\n\tImage URL:
        {3}\t\n\n", image.name, image.contentSize,
image.hostPageDisplayUrl, image.contentUrl);
    }

    SearchResult = sb.ToString();
}
```

We print out the number of matches in the search. Then we loop through the image array, printing the name, size, host, and URL of each image.

A successful test run should present us with the following screen:

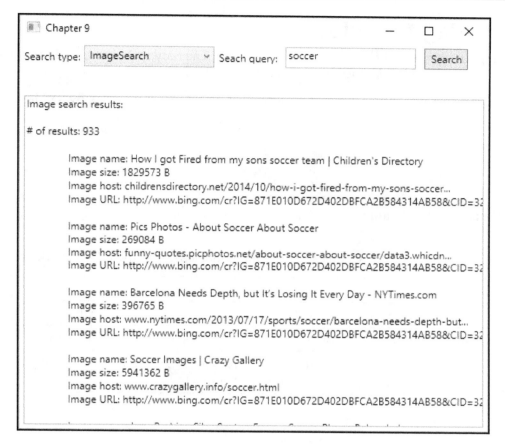

In addition to the query-based image search, we can also search for trending images. To do so, you would have to call the following endpoint:`https://api.cognitive.microsoft.com/bing/v5.0/images/trending`.

Currently this is only available for the following markets: `en-US`, `en-CA`, and `en-AU`. A successful call to this endpoint will result in an array of categories. Each item in this array will contain an array of trending images, as well as the title of the category.

Searching for videos

Searching for videos is about the same as for images. The only real difference is how we construct the endpoint, and the response we get.

We are going to add a new function in the `BingSearch` class, to accompany a video search:

```
public async Task<VideoSearchResponse> SearchVideos(string query)
{
        string endpoint = string.Format("{0}{1}",
"https://api.cognitive.microsoft.com/bing/v5.0/videos/search?q=", query);
```

As you can see, there is only one required parameter, the query string, q. We can also specify a few optional parameters, which are common to all the search APIs, and will be described later.

Aside from common filters, video can also filter results based on the following filters:

Filter	Description
pricing	Filter videos by price. Legal values are Free, Paid, and All.
resolution	Filter by resolution. Legal values are 480p, 720p, 1080p, and All.
videoLength	Filter videos by length. Legal values is Short (< 5 minutes), Medium (5 to 20 minutes), Long (> 20 minutes), and All.

With the endpoint in place, we call the API:

```
try {
    VideoSearchResponse response = await
_webRequest.MakeRequest<VideoSearchResponse>(endpoint);

    return response;
}

catch (Exception ex) {
    Debug.WriteLine(ex.Message);
}

return null;
```

We call `MakeRequest` on the `_webRequest` object, passing on the endpoint as a parameter. A successful call will result in a `VideoSearchResponse` object. This is a data contract, deserialized from the JSON response.

Among other data, it will contain an array of videos. Each item in this array contains video name, description, publisher, duration, URL, and more.

For a complete list of data available in the search response, visit
https://msdn.microsoft.com/en-US/library/dn760795.aspx#videos.

To be able to search for videos, we add a new case, in the `Search` function, in `MainViewModel`:

```
case SearchType.VideoSearch:
    var videoResponse = await _bingSearch.SearchVideos(SearchQuery);
    ParseVideoResponse(videoResponse);
    break;
```

We call the newly created `SearchVideos`, passing on the search query as a parameter. If the call succeeds, we go on to parse the video:

```
private void ParseVideoResponse(VideoSearchResponse videoResponse)
{
    StringBuilder sb = new StringBuilder();
    sb.Append("Video search results:\n\n");
    sb.AppendFormat("# of results: {0}\n\n",
    videoResponse.totalEstimatedMatches);

    foreach (VideoValue video in videoResponse.value) {
        sb.AppendFormat("\tVideo name: {0}\n\tVideo duration: {1}\n\tVideo
URL: {2}\t\n",
        video.name, video.duration, video.contentUrl);

        foreach(Publisher publisher in video.publisher) {
            sb.AppendFormat("\tPublisher: {0}\n", publisher.name);
        }

        sb.Append("\n");
    }
    SearchResult = sb.ToString();
}
```

As for images, we just show video information textually. In our example, we choose to show the video name, duration, URL, and all publishers of a video.

A successful video search should give the following result:

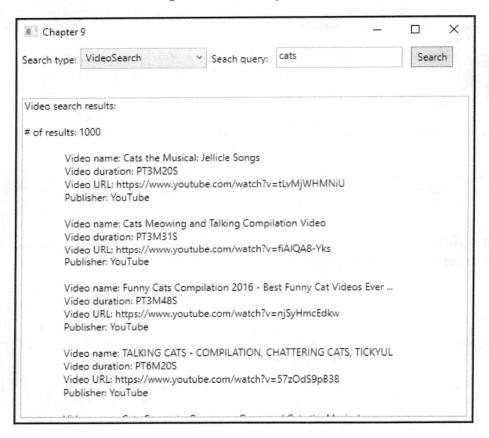

In addition to the query-based video search, we can also search for trending videos. To do so, you would have to call the following endpoint:`https://api.cognitive.microsoft.com/bing/v5.0/videos/trending`.

Currently, this is only available for the following markets: `en-US`, `en-CA` and `en-AU`. A successful call to this endpoint will result in an array of categories and tiles. Each item in the category array will contain a title and an array of subcategories. Each subcategory will contain an array of tiles and the title. Each item in a tile array will contain the video thumbnail and a query to use to get the specific video.

If we want to get more information about any video, we can query the following endpoint: `https://api.cognitive.microsoft.com/bing/v5.0/videos/details`.

This requires us to specify an `id`, to identify a video. We can also specify the `modulesRequested`. This is a comma-separated list of the details we want. Currently, the legal values are `All`, `RelatedVideos`, and `VideoResult`.

 For a complete list of data available in the response from a details query, visit `https://msdn.microsoft.com/en-US/library/dn760795.aspx#video`.

Helping the user with auto suggestions

Auto suggestions are a great way to enhance the user experience. The typical use case is where, whenever a user enters some text into a text field, a list of suggested words is displayed.

 If you have not already done so, sign up for the Bing Autosuggest API at `https://portal.azure.com`.

Adding Autosuggest to the user interface

As textboxes in WPF do not contain any auto-suggestion features, we need to add some on our own. We are going to use a third-party package, so install the `WPFTextBoxAutoComplete` package through the NuGet package manager, in our example project.

In the `MainView.xaml` file, add the following attribute to the starting `Window` tag:

```
xmlns:behaviors="clr-namespace: WPFTextBoxAutoComplete;
assembly=WPFTextBoxAutoComplete"
```

We will also need to make sure that the `TextBox` binding for our search query updates whenever the user enters data. This can be done by making sure the `Text` attribute looks as follows:

```
Text="{Binding SearchQuery, UpdateSourceTrigger=PropertyChanged}"
```

In the same `TextBox` element, add the following:

```
behaviors:AutoCompleteBehavior.AutoCompleteItemsSource = "{Binding
Suggestions}"
```

In the ViewModel, the `MainViewModel.cs` file, we need the corresponding property. This should be an `IEnumerable<string>` object. This will be updated with the result from the auto-suggest query we will perform in a bit.

Suggesting queries

To get auto-suggestions, we first add a new class. Add a new file, called `BingAutoSuggest.cs`, to the `Model` folder. The `BingAutoSuggest` class should have a member of type `BingWebRequest`, which should be created in the constructor.

Create a new function, called `Suggest`. This should accept a `string` as a parameter, returning a `Task<List<string>>` object. Mark the function as `async`.

We start by constructing an endpoint, where we specify the query string, q. This field is required. We also specify the market, `mkt`, although this is not required. We do not need any other parameters. Before we execute the API call, we create a list of suggestions, which we will return to the caller:

```
public async Task<List<string>> Suggest(string query) {
    string endpoint = string.Format("{0}{1}&mkt=en-US",
"https://api.cognitive.microsoft.com/bing/v5.0/suggestions/?q=", query);

    List<string> suggestionResult = new List<string>();
```

We make a call to `MakeRequest` on the `_webRequest` object, passing on the endpoint as parameter. If the call succeeds, we expect the JSON response to deserialize into a `BingAutoSuggestResponse` object. This object will contain an array of `suggestionGroups`, where each item contains an array of `SearchSuggestions`.

Each item of `SearchSuggestion` contains a URL, display text, a query string, and a search kind. We are interested in the display text, which we add to the `suggestionResult` list. This list is returned to the caller:

```
try {
    BingAutoSuggestResponse response = await
_webRequest.MakeRequest<BingAutoSuggestResponse>(endpoint);

    if (response == null || response.suggestionGroups.Length == 0)
        return suggestionResult;

    foreach(Suggestiongroup suggestionGroup in response.suggestionGroups) {

        foreach(Searchsuggestion suggestion in
suggestionGroup.searchSuggestions) {

            suggestionResult.Add(suggestion.displayText);
        }
    }
}

catch(Exception ex) {
    Debug.WriteLine(ex.Message);
}

return suggestionResult;
```

 For a complete description of response data, go to https://msdn.microsoft.com/en-us/library/mt711395.aspx#suggestions.

In the `MainViewModel.cs` file, we want to get suggestions as we type. We create a new function, as follows:

```
private async void GetAutosuggestions() {

    var results = await _autoSuggest.Suggest(SearchQuery);

    if (results == null || results.Count == 0) return;

    Suggestions = results;
}
```

This will call the newly created `Suggest` function, with the current value of the `SearchQuery`. If any results are returned, we assign this to the `SuggestionsIEnumerable` we created earlier. We make sure to call this function when we set the value in the `SearchQuery` property.

In the UI, this will have the first suggestion automatically populated in the search-query field. This is not ideal for users, but it will do for our test example.

Search commonalities

For all the APIs we have covered, there are a few similarities. We will cover those now.

Languages

It is highly recommended to specify which market you want results for. Searches will typically return results for the local market and language of the user, based on the current location. As you can imagine, this is not always what the user wants. By specifying the market, you can tailor the search results for the user.

How you choose to solve this technically is dependent on the requirements of your application. For a smart-house application, you would probably allow the user to set the market in the settings. For a web application created only for French users in France, you would probably not allow the user to change the market.

Specifying the market is done by adding a `mkt` parameter to the `GET` request. This should then specify the market code, for example, `en-US`, for English in the United States.

 While any API may support a specific market, some features may not support a given market.

A subset of the languages supported is English, Spanish, German, Dutch, French, Portuguese, Traditional Chinese, Italian, Russian, and Arabic.

In addition, we can specify a `cc` parameter to the `GET` request. This specifies a country; typically, the country the user is in. The parameter should be in the form of a two-letter country code, for instance, GB for United Kingdom.

A wide variety of countries can be specified, and the list is continuously subject to change.

Pagination

Some searches may yield a large number of results. In these cases, you may want to do pagination. This can be achieved by specifying `count` and `offset` parameters in the GET request.

If you want 10 results per page, you would start by setting count to 10, and offset to 0 for the first page. When the user navigates to the next page, you would keep `count` at 10, but increase `offset` to 10. For the next page, you would increase `offset` to 20, and so on.

The maximum number of results returned in each query (the count parameter) varies for each API. See the following table for the current maximum count per API:

API	Maximum search results	Default search results
Bing News Search	100	10
Bing Web Search	50	10
Bing Image Search	150	35
Bing Video Search	105	35

Filters

We have seen some filters for individual APIs. In addition to these, there are a couple of filters which can be applied to all searches.

Safe search

The safe search filter can be used to filter search results for adult content. This parameter is added in the request URL.

The `safeSearch` parameter can be one of the following values:

- **Off**: All result items will be returned.
- **Moderate**: Result items can contain adult text, but no adult images or videos will be included.
- **Strict**: No adult text, images, or videos are included in the result items.

Note that, if the IP address of the user indicates a location that requires the Strict safe search, this setting will be ignored. Bing will, in this case, default to the Strict policy.

If the parameter has not been set, it defaults to moderate.

Freshness

By adding the `freshness` parameter to a request, you can filter search results based on the age of result items. The values that can be specified are as follows:

- **Day**: Results from the last 24 hours.
- **Week**: Results from the last 7 days.
- **Month**: Results from the last 30 days.

Errors

Among all the APIs we have covered, there are a few possible response codes you may receive for each request. The following table describes all possible response codes:

Code	Description
200	Successful request.
400	One or more required query parameters are missing, or one of the parameters is invalid. More details are described in the `ErrorResponse` field.
401	The provided subscription key is invalid or missing.
403	Typically returned if the monthly quota is exceeded. Can also be used if the caller does not have permission to access the requested resource.
410	HTTP protocol has been used instead of HTTPS, which is the only supported protocol.
429	The quota per second has been exceeded.

Summary

Throughout this chapter, we have looked at the different Bing Search APIs. We started by looking at how we could use Bing Web Search to search for all kinds of content. Next, we found the latest news, based on query strings and categories. From there, we moved on to image and video searches. In addition to this, we looked at how to enhance the user experience, by adding auto suggestions, using the Bing Autosuggestion API.

In the next, and final, chapter, we will wrap things up. We will complete our Smart House application by connecting the pieces; we will also take a look at the road ahead.

10
Connecting the Pieces

The previous chapter focused on the last API umbrella, covering Bing Search APIs. Throughout this chapter, we will connect the pieces. Our smart-house application can currently utilize several APIs, but mostly individually. We will see how to connect LUIS, image analysis, Bing News Search, and Bing Speech APIs together. We will also look at the next steps that you can take after completing this book.

Completing this chapter will take us through the following topics:

- Making an application smarter, by connecting several APIs
- Real-life applications utilizing Microsoft Cognitive Services
- Next steps

Connecting the pieces

Until now, we have seen all the different APIs, mostly as individual APIs. The whole idea behind the smart-house application is to utilize several APIs at the same time.

Throughout this chapter, we will add a new intent in LUIS. This intent is for getting the latest news, optionally for different topics.

Further on, we want to actually search for news, using the Bing News API. We will do so by allowing the end user to speak a command, converting spoken audio to text, with the Bing Speech API.

When we have some news articles, we want to get the headline, publishing date, and description. In case there is a corresponding image to the article, we want to get a description of the image. We will do this by adding the Computer Vision API.

With all the news article information in place, we want to get that read back to us. We will do this by converting text to spoken audio.

Creating an intent

Let us start by adding our new intent. Head over to `https://www.luis.ai`, and log on with the credentials created in `Chapter 4`, *Letting Applications Understand Commands*. From the front page, go into your smart-house application.

Before we start creating the intent, we need to add a new entity. As we want the possibility to get updates on news within certain topics, we will add a `NewsCategory` entity, as shown in the following screenshot:

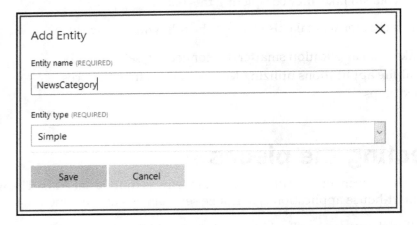

We do not need there to be any children, as this entity will work on its own.

Now we can add a new intent. Go to **Intents**, on the left-hand side and click **Add intent**. This will open the intent creation dialog. Enter a fitting name for the intent, such as **GetNews:**

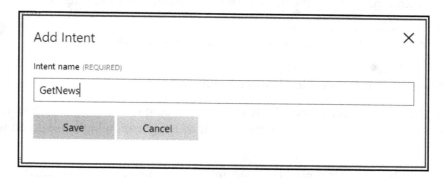

We also need to add an example command:

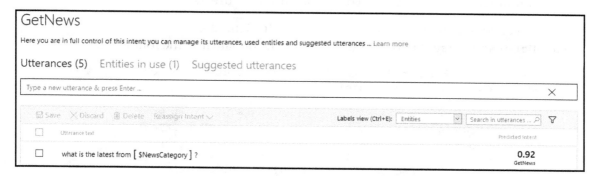

Add five or six more examples of how you would utter this intent. Make sure you train the model before continuing.

You can verify the model for testing by going to **Train & Test** in the left-hand side menu.

Updating the code

With the new intent, we can start to update the smart-house application.

Executing actions from intents

The first step we need to do is to add an enum variable containing the intents. Create a new file called LuisActions.cs, in the Model folder, and add the following content to it:

```
public enum LuisActions {
    None, GetRoomTemperature, SetRoomTemperature, GetNews
}
```

If you have any other intents defined, add them as well.

This enum will be used later, to see which action to execute when triggered. For instance, if we ask to get the latest sports news, GetNews will be triggered, which will go on to retrieve news.

To make things a bit easier for ourselves, we are going to use the existing LUIS example for the rest of the chapter. An alternative would be to add this to the HomeView, where we could continuously listen to spoken commands from the users.

Now we need to update the LuisViewModel.cs file. Find the OnLuisUtteranceResultUpdated function. Let us update it to the following:

```
private void OnLuisUtteranceResultUpdated(object sender,
LuisUtteranceResultEventArgs e)
{
    Application.Current.Dispatcher.Invoke(async () => {
        StringBuilder sb = new StringBuilder(ResultText);
        _requiresResponse = e.RequiresReply;

        sb.AppendFormat("Status: {0}\n", e.Status);
        sb.AppendFormat("Summary: {0}\n\n", e.Message);
```

At this time, we have not added anything new. We have removed the output of entities, as we do not need this anymore.

This is new. If we find that any actions have been triggered, we want to do something. We call a new function, TriggerActionExecution, passing on the name of the intent as a parameter:

```
if (!string.IsNullOrEmpty(e.IntentName))
    await TriggerActionExectution(e.IntentName, e.EntityName);
```

We will get back to this function shortly.

Complete `OnLuisUtteranceResultUpdated` by adding the following code:

```
        ResultText = sb.ToString();
    });
}
```

Again, you should see that there are no new features. We have, however, removed the last `else` clause. We do not want to have the application speak the summary to us anymore.

Create the new `TriggerActionExecution` function. Let it accept a `string` as the parameter, and have it return a `Task`. Mark the function as `async`:

```
private async Task TriggerActionExectution(string intentName) {
    LuisActions action;
    if (!Enum.TryParse(intentName, true, out action))
        return;
```

First we parse the `actionName` (intent name). If we have not defined the action, we will not do anything else.

With an action defined, we go into a `switch` statement to decide what to do. As we are only interested in the `GetNews` case, we break out from the other options:

```
    switch(action) {
        case LuisActions.GetRoomTemperature:
        case LuisActions.SetRoomTemperature:
        case LuisActions.None:
        default:
            break;
        case LuisActions.GetNews:
          break;
    }
}
```

Make sure that the code compiles before continuing.

Searching news on command

Next, we will need to modify the `Luis.cs` file. As we have defined an entity for the news topic, we want to ensure that we get this value from the LUIS response.

Add a new property to `LuisUtteranceResultEventArgs`:

```
public string EntityName { get; set; }
```

This will allow us to add the news topic value, if received.

We need to add this value. Locate `ProcessResult` in the `Luis` class. Modify the `if` check to look like the following:

```
if (!string.IsNullOrEmpty(result.TopScoringIntent.Name)) {
    var intentName = result.TopScoringIntent.Name;
    args.IntentName = intentName;
}

else {
    args.IntentName = string.Empty;
}

if(result.Entities.Count > 0) {
var entity = result.Entities.First().Value;

if(entity.Count > 0)  {
    var entityName = entity.First().Value;
    args.EntityName = entityName;
}
}
```

We make sure that the intent name, of the top scoring intent, is set, and pass it on as an argument to the event. We also check if there is any entities set, and if so, pass on the first one. In a real-life application, you would probably check other entities as well.

Back into the `LuisViewModel.cs` file, we can now account for this new property. Let the `TriggerActionExecution` method accept a second `string` parameter. When calling the function, we can add the following parameter:

```
await TriggerActionExectution(e.IntentName, e.EntityName);
```

To be able to search for news, we need to add a new member of the `BingSearch` type. This is the class we created in the previous chapter:

```
private BingSearch _bingSearch;
```

Create the object in the constructor.

Now we can create a new function, called `GetLatestsNews`. This should accept a `string` as the parameter, and return `Task`. Mark the function as `async`:

```
private async Task GetLatestNews(string queryString)
{
    BingNewsResponse news = await _bingSearch.SearchNews (queryString,
SafeSearch.Moderate);

    if (news.value == null || news.value.Length == 0)
        return;
```

When this function is called, we `SearchNews` on the newly created `_bingSearch` object. We pass on the `queryString`, which will be the action parameter, as the parameter. We also set the safe search to `Moderate`.

A successful API call will result in a `BingNewsResponse` object, which will contain an array of news articles. We are not going into more details on this class, as we covered it in `Chapter 9`, *Adding Specialized Searches*.

If no news is found, we simply return from the function. If we do find news, we do the following:

```
    await ParseNews (news.value[0]);
```

We call a function, `ParseNews`, which we will get back to in a bit. We pass on the first news article, which will be parsed. Ideally, we would go through all the results, but for our case, this is enough to illustrate the point.

The `ParseNews` method should be marked as `async`. It should have the return type `Task`, and accept a parameter of type `Value`:

```
private async Task ParseNews(Value newsArticle)  {
    string articleDescription = $"{newsArticle.name}, published
{newsArticle.datePublished}. Description:
    {newsArticle.description}. ";

    await _ttsClient.SpeakAsync(articleDescription,
CancellationToken.None);
}
```

We create a string containing the headline, the publishing date, and the news description. Using this, we call `SpeakAsync` on the `_ttsClient` to have the application read the information back to us.

With this function in place, we can execute the action. In `TriggerActionExecuted`, call `GetLatestsNews` from the `GetNews` case. Make sure to await the call.

With the application compiling, we can go for a test run:

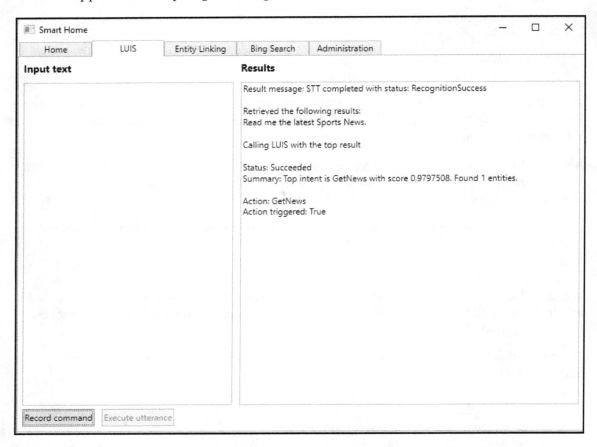

Naturally, the effects are not as good in an image as in real life. With a microphone and speakers or headset connected, we can ask for the latest news, using audio, and get the news read back to us with audio.

Describing news images

News articles often come with corresponding images as well. As an addition to what we already have, we can add image analysis.

The first step we need to do is to add a new NuGet package. Search for the `Microsoft.ProjectOxford.Vision` package, and install this using the NuGet package manager.

In the `LuisViewModel.cs` file, add the following new member:

```
private IVisionServiceClient _visionClient;
```

This can be created in the constructor:

```
_visionClient = new VisionServiceClient("FACE_API_KEY", "ROOT_URI");
```

This member will be our access point to the Computer Vision API.

We want to get a string describing the image in the `ParseNews` function. We can achieve this by adding a new function, called `GetImageDescription`. This should accept a `string` parameter, which will be the image URL. The function should have return type `Task<string>` and be marked as `async`:

```
private async Task<string> GetImageDescription(string contentUrl)
{
    try {
        AnalysisResult imageAnalysisResult = await
_visionClient.AnalyzeImageAsync(contentUrl, new List<VisualFeature>() {
VisualFeature.Description });
```

In this function, we call `AnalyzeImageAsync` on the `_visionClient`. We want the image description, so we specify this in a list of `VisualFeature`. If the call succeeds, we expect an object of type `AnalysisResult`. This should contain image descriptions, ordered by probability of correctness.

If we do not get any descriptions, we return `none`. If we do have any descriptions, we return the text of the first one:

```
    if (imageAnalysisResult == null ||
imageAnalysisResult.Description?.Captions?.Length == 0)
        return "none";
    return imageAnalysisResult.Description.Captions.First().Text;
}
```

If any exceptions occur, we print the exception message to the debug console. We also return none to the caller:

```
catch(Exception ex) {
    Debug.WriteLine(ex.Message);
    return "none";
}
}
```

In ParseNews, we can get the image description by adding the following at the top of the function:

```
string imageDescription = await GetImageDescription
(newsArticle.image.thumbnail.contentUrl);
```

With an image description, we can modify the articleDescription string to the following:

```
string articleDescription = $"{newsArticle.name}, published
        {newsArticle.datePublished}. Description:
        {newsArticle.description}. Corresponding image is
        {imageDescription}";
```

Running the application and asking for news will now also describe any images. That concludes our smart-house application.

Real-life applications using Microsoft Cognitive Services

There are some examples of applications that currently utilize Microsoft Cognitive Services. We will look at some of them here.

Uber

Most of you have probably already heard of Uber. For those that have not, here is a short summary.

Uber is an app that was created to match drivers with people looking for rides. People can open the app, and request a ride. Drivers (registered Uber drivers, that is) located nearby can then pick up the person requesting a ride. After a ride, the driver is payed through the app.

To ensure a more secure experience, a photo of the driver is sent to the passenger. This way, passengers can feel safe that the driver is who they say they are. This may cause problems, as drivers may not always look like their photo. They may have grown a beard, or shaved off a beard, or similar changes may have occurred.

To account for this, Uber decided to add a new feature. Each driver needs to sign in when they are using the app. Doing so will periodically request them to take a selfie. This image is then sent to the Face API for verification. If the verification fails, due to glare from glasses, or something similar, the driver is requested to remove such items.

According to Uber, they spent around 3 weeks implementing the Face API into their systems.

DutchCrafters

DutchCrafters is an American company that sells handmade furniture. They do have a physical store, but more importantly, they have an e-commerce website. This site contains more than 10,000 products, where each product can be customized.

They had a low conversion rate on their site, and as an attempt to improve this, they used manual recommendations. Manually adding recommended products on each product is rather time consuming. Looking into their options, they discovered the Recommendations API from Microsoft Cognitive Services.

They were already relying on REST APIs, and as such implementing the Recommendations API was quick. DutchCrafters have stated that they spent 5 days in total implementing the functionality needed.

As their site was already built with ASP.NET and running on IIS, they decided to move everything to the cloud. Doing so has improved their site, and with the addition of the Recommendations API, their foundation has improved.

At the time of writing, they are utilizing the *You might like this* feature, recommending 10 items per product. They are also looking into adding real-time recommendations, based on users' history, which we have seen is possible using the Recommendations API.

A direct result of implementing the Recommendations API is an improvement of the conversion rate. They have seen a three times increase in the conversion rate, with about 15% of the sales coming from recommended products.

CelebsLike.me

CelebsLike.me is a web application from Microsoft. It is primarily created to show off some of the features of Microsoft Cognitive Services.

The purpose of the application is to find your celebrity doppelganger. You can upload a photo, or use one found online, and the app will match faces found with similar celebrities.

The app takes advantage of the Bing Image Search API, the Computer Vision API, and the Face API. It recognizes celebrity faces in web images. When someone uploads a photo of themselves, facial features will be used to find matching celebrities.

Pivothead - wearable glasses

Pivothead is a company working with wearable technology. They have combined eyeglasses with high-quality cameras, providing still images and videos. These glasses allow people to capture vivid point-of-view content of what they see. Pivothead currently have customers in the consumer market, but also in the business market.

Over time, Pivothead had seen growing success, but could not seem to create a device to help visually impaired and/or blind people. They struggled with the technology, as machine learning itself can be quite complex. When they learned of Microsoft Cognitive Services, they were able to reach a breakthrough.

If a person is wearing the glasses, they can slide a finger along an earpiece. This will capture an image of what is in front of the person. The glasses utilize five APIs from Microsoft Cognitive Services. These are Computer Vision, Emotion, Face, Speech, and LUIS.

With the image of whatever is in front of a person, the image is analyzed. The person wearing the glasses will then get the image described through an earpiece. If a person is detected, the gender, how they look, what they are doing, their age, and their emotion is detected and described. If text is detected, it will be read back to the person.

According to Pivothead, they spent around 3 months developing prototypes of these glasses. They also stated that they could have done it in 3 weeks, had they been working with it full time.

Zero Keyboard

The app **Zero Keyboard** was created by a Finnish company called **Blucup**. The company had discovered a common problem for salespeople. They wanted a way for salespeople to capture customer data and generate leads while on the go.

They started developing an app for iOS, Android, and Windows Phone, to help solve this problem. The idea behind the app is to record customer information, which then is automatically stored in the **Customer Relationship Management (CRM)** system.

At the time of development, Microsoft Cognitive Services emerged, and Blucup decided to give it a go. Earlier, they had tried a few open source speech recognition software and image analysis software. None provided the quality and features needed.

Using the Computer Vision API, the app can take pictures of business cards or identification badges, and identify text. This data is directly uploaded to their CRM system. By using the Speech API, sales representatives can also record voice memos for each contact.

Blucup states that Microsoft Cognitive Services delivers very accurate data. In addition, they have been able to implement the needed APIs rapidly, as the APIs are a good match from a developer standpoint.

The common theme

As you can see from all these examples, Microsoft Cognitive Services provides good quality. It is also quick to implement, which is important when considering new APIs.

Another great thing about the APIs is that you do not need to be a data scientist to use them. Even though the technology powering the APIs is complex, we, as developers, do not need to think about it. We can focus on what we do best.

Where to go from here

By now you should know the basics of Microsoft Cognitive Services, enough to get started with building your own applications.

A natural way forward is to play around with the different APIs. The APIs are continuously improved and worked upon. It is worth going through the API documentation, to keep up with changes and to learn more. In addition, Microsoft keeps adding new APIs to the services. Through the writing process of this book, I have seen three new APIs added. Those might be interesting to look into.

Another possibility is to build upon the smart-house application that we have started on. We have put down some groundwork, but there are still a lot of opportunities. Perhaps you can work on improving what we have already got. Maybe you can see some opportunities to mix in other APIs, which we have covered.

Reading through this book might have given you some ideas of your own. A great way forward would be to implement them.

Like we have seen, there are many possible areas to use the APIs for. Only the imagination limits the usage.

Perhaps this book has triggered a deeper interest in machine learning. Everything we have seen so far is machine learning. Even though it is more complex than just using APIs, it might be worth exploring.

Summary

Through this chapter, we have completed our journey. We created a new intent for news retrieval. We learned how to deal with an action, triggered from this intent. Based on voice commands, we managed to fetch the latest news, for one topic, and have the smart-house application read it back to us. Next, we went on to see what kind of real-life applications are utilizing Microsoft Cognitive Services today. Finally, we concluded this chapter by looking at some natural next steps that you can take after completing this book.

LUIS Entities and Additional Information on Linguistic Analysis

In this appendix, we will be start with listing LUIS prebuilt entities and then going through part-of-speech tags, followed by the phrase types.

LUIS pre-built entities

The following list shows all the available entities that can be added to your application:

- DatetimeV2
- Datetime
- Number
- Ordinal
- Percentage
- Temperature
- Dimension
- Money

- Age
- Geography
- Encyclopedia
- URL
- Email
- Phone Number

 A complete and updated list of pre-built entities can be found at `https://docs.microsoft.com/en-us/azure/cognitive-services/LUIS/pre-builtentities.`

Part-of-speech tags

The following table describes all available **part-of-speech** tags:

Tag	Description	Example
$	Dollar	$
``	Opening quotation mark	` ``
' '	Closing quotation mark	' "
(	Opening parenthesis	([{
)	Closing parenthesis	)] }
,	Comma	,
--	Dash	--
.	Sentence terminator	. ! ?
:	Colon or ellipsis	: ; ...
CC	Conjunction, coordinating	and
CD	Numeral, cardinal	nine
DT	Determiner	the
EX	Existential there	there
FW	Foreign word	je ne sais quoi

IN	Preposition or subordinating conjunction	in
JJ	Adjective, numeral, or ordinal	ninth
JJR	Adjective, comparative	better
JJS	Adjective, superlative	cheapest
LS	List item marker	(a) (b) 1 2 A B A. B.
MD	Modal auxiliary	can
NN	Noun, common, singular or mass	potato
NNP	Noun, proper, singular	Chicago
NNPS	Noun, proper, plural	Springfields
NNS	Noun, common, plural	mice
PDT	Pre-determiner	half
POS	Genitive marker	' 's
PRP	Pronoun, personal	she
PRP$	Pronoun, possessive	hers
RB	Adverb	clinically
RBR	Adverb, comparative	further
RBS	Adverb, superlative	best
RP	Particle	on
SYM	Symbol	% &
TO	*to* as preposition or infinitive marker	to
UH	Interjection	uh hooray
VB	Verb, base form	assign
VBD	Verb, past tense	gave
VBG	Verb, present, participle or gerund	assigning
VBN	Verb, past participle	assigned
VBP	Verb, present tense, not third person singular	assign
VBZ	Verb, present tense, third person singular	assigns

WDT	WH-determiner	that
WP	WH-pronoun	whom
WP$	WH-pronoun, possessive	whose
WRB	Wh-adverb	however

Phrase types

A complete and updated list of phrase types can be found at
https://www.microsoft.com/cognitive-services/en-us/Linguistic-An
alysis-API/documentation/Constituency-Parsing.

The following table describes all available phrase types:

Label	Description	Example
ADJP	Adjective phrase	*so rude*
ADVP	Adverb phrase	*clear through*
CONJP	Conjunction phrase	*as well as*
FRAG	Fragment, used for incomplete or fragmentary inputs	*Highly recommended...*
INTJ	Interjection	*Hooray*
LST	List marker, including punctuation	*#4)*
NAC	Not a constituent, used to indicate scoping of a non-constituent phrase	*and for a good deal* in you get things and for a good deal
NP	Noun phrase	*a tasty potato pancake*
NX	Used within certain complex NPs to mark the head	
PP	Prepositional phrase	*in the pool*
PRN	Parenthetical	(so called)
PRT	Particle	*out* in "ripped out"

QP	Quantity phrase (that is, complex measure/amount) within a noun phrase	*around $75*
RRC	Reduced relative clause	*still unresolved* in "many issues still unresolved"
S	Sentence or clause	*This is a sentence.*
SBAR	Subordinate clause, often introduced by a subordinating conjunction	*as I left* in "I looked around as I left."
SBARQ	Direct question introduced by a WH-word or WH-phrase	*What was the point?*
SINV	Inverted declarative sentence	*At no time were they aware.* (Note how the normal subject *they* was moved to be placed after the verb *were*)
SQ	Inverted yes/no question, or main clause of a WH- question	*Did they get the car?*
UCP	Unlike coordinated phrase	*small and with bugs* (note how an adjective and a preposition phrase are conjoined with *and*)
VP	Verb phrase	*ran into the woods*
WHADJP	WH-adjective phrase	*how uncomfortable*
WHADVP	WH-adverb phrase	*when*
WHNP	WH-noun phrase	*which potato, how much soup*
WHPP	WH-prepositional phrase	*in which country*
X	Unknown, uncertain, or unbracketable.	first *the* in "the... the soup"

A complete and updated list of part-of-speech tags can be found at https://www.microsoft.com/cognitive-services/en-us/Linguistic-Analysis-API/documentation/POS-tagging.

B
License Information

The appendix contains several third-party libraries, which have different licenses. All libraries, along with applicable licenses, are covered in the next pages.

Video Frame Analyzer

Copyright (c) Microsoft. All rights reserved.

Licensed under the MIT license.

Microsoft Cognitive Services: `http://www.microsoft.com/cognitive`

Microsoft Cognitive Services GitHub: `https://github.com/Microsoft/Cognitive`

Copyright (c) Microsoft Corporation

All rights reserved.

MIT License:

Permission is hereby granted, free of charge, to any person obtaining a copy of this software and associated documentation files (the "Software"), to deal in the Software without restriction, including without limitation the rights to use, copy, modify, merge, publish, distribute, sublicense, and/or sell copies of the Software, and to permit persons to whom the Software is furnished to do so, subject to the following conditions:

The above copyright notice and this permission notice shall be included in all copies or substantial portions of the Software.

THE SOFTWARE IS PROVIDED ""AS IS"", WITHOUT WARRANTY OF ANY KIND, EXPRESS OR IMPLIED, INCLUDING BUT NOT LIMITED TO THE WARRANTIES OF MERCHANTABILITY, FITNESS FOR A PARTICULAR PURPOSE AND NONINFRINGEMENT. IN NO EVENT SHALL THE AUTHORS OR COPYRIGHT HOLDERS BE LIABLE FOR ANY CLAIM, DAMAGES OR OTHER LIABILITY, WHETHER IN AN ACTION OF CONTRACT, TORT OR OTHERWISE, ARISING FROM, OUT OF OR IN CONNECTION WITH THE SOFTWARE OR THE USE OR OTHER DEALINGS IN THE SOFTWARE.

OpenCvSharp3

 This license has also been called the **New BSD License** or **Modified BSD License**. See also the *2-clause BSD License*.

Redistribution and use in source and binary forms, with or without modification, are permitted provided that the following conditions are met:

1. Redistributions of source code must retain the above copyright notice, this list of conditions and the following disclaimer.
2. Redistributions in binary form must reproduce the above copyright notice, this list of conditions and the following disclaimer in the documentation and/or other materials provided with the distribution.
3. Neither the name of the copyright holder nor the names of its contributors may be used to endorse or promote products derived from this software without specific prior written permission.

THIS SOFTWARE IS PROVIDED BY THE COPYRIGHT HOLDERS AND CONTRIBUTORS "AS IS" AND ANY EXPRESS OR IMPLIED WARRANTIES, INCLUDING, BUT NOT LIMITED TO, THE IMPLIED WARRANTIES OF MERCHANTABILITY AND FITNESS FOR A PARTICULAR PURPOSE ARE DISCLAIMED. IN NO EVENT SHALL THE COPYRIGHT HOLDER OR CONTRIBUTORS BE LIABLE FOR ANY DIRECT, INDIRECT, INCIDENTAL, SPECIAL, EXEMPLARY, OR CONSEQUENTIAL DAMAGES (INCLUDING, BUT NOT LIMITED TO, PROCUREMENT OF SUBSTITUTE GOODS OR SERVICES; LOSS OF USE, DATA, OR PROFITS; OR BUSINESS INTERRUPTION) HOWEVER CAUSED AND ON ANY THEORY OF LIABILITY, WHETHER IN CONTRACT, STRICT LIABILITY, OR TORT (INCLUDING NEGLIGENCE OR OTHERWISE) ARISING IN ANY WAY OUT OF THE USE OF THIS SOFTWARE, EVEN IF ADVISED OF THE POSSIBILITY OF SUCH DAMAGE.

Newtonsoft.Json

The MIT License (MIT)

Copyright (c) 2007 James Newton-King

Permission is hereby granted, free of charge, to any person obtaining a copy of this software and associated documentation files (the "Software"), to deal in the Software without restriction, including without limitation the rights to use, copy, modify, merge, publish, distribute, sublicense, and/or sell copies of the Software, and to permit persons to whom the Software is furnished to do so, subject to the following conditions:

The above copyright notice and this permission notice shall be included in all copies or substantial portions of the Software.

THE SOFTWARE IS PROVIDED "AS IS", WITHOUT WARRANTY OF ANY KIND, EXPRESS OR IMPLIED, INCLUDING BUT NOT LIMITED TO THE WARRANTIES OF MERCHANTABILITY, FITNESS FOR A PARTICULAR PURPOSE AND NONINFRINGEMENT. IN NO EVENT SHALL THE AUTHORS OR COPYRIGHT HOLDERS BE LIABLE FOR ANY CLAIM, DAMAGES OR OTHER LIABILITY, WHETHER IN AN ACTION OF CONTRACT, TORT OR OTHERWISE, ARISING FROM, OUT OF OR IN CONNECTION WITH THE SOFTWARE OR THE USE OR OTHER DEALINGS IN THE SOFTWARE.

NAudio

Microsoft Public License (Ms-PL)

This license governs use of the accompanying software. If you use the software, you accept this license. If you do not accept the license, do not use the software.

Definitions

The terms **reproduce**, **reproduction**, **derivative works**, and **distribution** have the same meaning here as under U.S. copyright law.

A *contribution* is the original software, or any additions or changes to the software.

A *contributor* is any person that distributes its contribution under this license.

Licensed patents are a contributor's patent claims that read directly on its contribution.

Grant of Rights

(A) Copyright Grant- Subject to the terms of this license, including the license conditions and limitations in section 3, each contributor grants you a non-exclusive, worldwide, royalty-free copyright license to reproduce its contribution, prepare derivative works of its contribution, and distribute its contribution or any derivative works that you create.

(B) Patent Grant- Subject to the terms of this license, including the license conditions and limitations in section 3, each contributor grants you a non-exclusive, worldwide, royalty-free license under its licensed patents to make, have made, use, sell, offer for sale, import, and/or otherwise dispose of its contribution in the software or derivative works of the contribution in the software.

Conditions and Limitations

(A) **No Trademark License**: This license does not grant you rights to use any contributors' name, logo, or trademarks.

(B) If you bring a patent claim against any contributor over patents that you claim are infringed by the software, your patent license from such contributor to the software ends automatically.

(C) If you distribute any portion of the software, you must retain all copyright, patent, trademark, and attribution notices that are present in the software.

(D) If you distribute any portion of the software in source code form, you may do so only under this license by including a complete copy of this license with your distribution. If you distribute any portion of the software in compiled or object code form, you may only do so under a license that complies with this license.

(E) The software is licensed **as-is**. You bear the risk of using it. The contributors give no express warranties, guarantees or conditions. You may have additional consumer rights under your local laws which this license cannot change. To the extent permitted under your local laws, the contributors exclude the implied warranties of merchantability, fitness for a particular purpose and non-infringement.

Index

www.ingramcontent.com/pod-product-compliance
Lightning Source LLC
Chambersburg PA
CBHW080614060326
40690CB00021B/4690